Richard Cordley

A History of Lawrence, Kansas

From the first Settlement to the Close of the Rebellion

Richard Cordley

A History of Lawrence, Kansas
From the first Settlement to the Close of the Rebellion

ISBN/EAN: 9783337207243

Printed in Europe, USA, Canada, Australia, Japan

Cover: Foto ©ninafisch / pixelio.de

More available books at **www.hansebooks.com**

Truly Yours
Richard Cordley

A HISTORY

OF

LAWRENCE, KANSAS

FROM

THE FIRST SETTLEMENT

TO

THE CLOSE OF THE REBELLION

BY

RICHARD CORDLEY, D. D.

WHO CAME TO KANSAS IN 1857; PASTOR OF PLYMOUTH CONGREGATIONAL CHURCH
AT LAWRENCE FROM 1857 TO 1875 AND 1884 TO PRESENT TIME
AN EYE WITNESS OF THE QUANTRILL RAID

PUBLISHED BY E. F. CALDWELL
LAWRENCE, KANSAS

1895
LAWRENCE JOURNAL PRESS

Copyright 1895, by E. F. CALDWELL.
All rights reserved.

PREFACE.

About three years ago, it was suggested that the writer prepare a history of Lawrence covering the period of its early settlement. Without realizing what was involved in such an undertaking, he consented. Since coming to understand the difficulties in the way he has often been inclined to withdraw his consent. It soon became evident that no history can ever be written which will be satisfactory to those who took part in those early struggles. It was a time of intense excitement, and those who passed through those scenes retain vivid impressions of them. Any description will seem tame compared with the graphic picture they have in mind.

Then it is impossible to do justice to all the actors engaged. The movement that saved Kansas was of the people, rather than of the leaders. There were leaders, but they were leaders chiefly because they went before. They did not create the movement, nor the sentiment out of which it grew. The people moved towards Kansas of their own impulse. They did not go at the beck of any man. They followed certain men because they were going their way. If all the leaders had failed them they would have chosen others and gone on. They were moved by individual conviction and a common impulse. Men and women who have never been heard displayed a spirit of self sacrifice and heroism as worthy of remembrance as anything history records of the noted names. No history can do honor to all who deserve it.

PREFACE.

It is becoming quite common to under-rate the heroism that saved Kansas for freedom. The cold blooded historian goes mousing among old letters and he finds that these early, heroes were men and women, of like frailties with ourselves. But the glory of heroism is not that angels come down to mingle in the affairs of men, but that common men and women, when the occasion demands, can rise to such sublime heights of heroism and self sacrifice.

It becomes the people of Kansas to appreciate her own history and the men who laid the first foundations. It was the heroic age, and in the future it will take its place with Plymouth Rock and Lexington.

The writer acknowledges his indebtedness to those who have written before him. It would be impossible to name all the writers who have been of service to him. The following are among the number:

A. T. Andreas, History of the State of Kansas; especially his military history and county histories; Charles Robinson, The Kansas Conflict; Leverett W. Spring, Kansas; D. W. Wilder, Kansas Annals; Eli Thayer, The Kansas Crusade; J. H. Gihon, Governor Geary's Administration; United States Biographical Dictionary; J. N. Holloway, History of Kansas; W. A. Phillips, Conquest of Kansas; C. S. Gleed, Kansas Memorial; The publications of Kansas State Historical Society.

The writer gladly acknowledges his special obligation to Hon. F. G. Adams of the State Historical Society who has at all times given him free access to the remarkable collection of early newspapers which are on file in the rooms of that institution.

RICHARD CORDLEY.

CONTENTS.

                                                                                              PAGE

PREFACE.. iii

CHAPTER I.

The Kansas-Nebraska Bill.—The North Aroused.—The Emigrant Aid Company.—Eli Thayer, Amos A. Lawrence and Dr. Charles Robinson.—The First New England Emigrants Reach Mount Oread, Organize a Town Company and Lay Out the Town.—"What Shall We Call It?"—Pitching Tents and Building Cabins.—Pioneer Boarding House... 1

CHAPTER II.

Reinforcements.—The Disgust of the Kid-gloved Contingent.—First Sabbath Services.—The First Funeral.—Town Site Troubles.—"Shoot to Hit."—First Election for Delegate to Congress.—Judge Wakefield.—The First School.—Three Newspapers.—Winter in Tents and Cabins... 15

CHAPTER III.

Spring Election, March 30th, 1855.—Excitement in Missouri.—An Army of Voters Invade Lawrence.—Missouri Voters Elect a Kansas Legislature.—Slavery Triumphant and Exultant.—Free-State Men Despondent and Indignant.—What Shall We Do?—Dr. Robinson's Policy.—"Bogus Legislature" Repudiated...................... 28

CHAPTER IV.

The Conflict Begun.—The Dow Murder.—The Branson Rescue.—Sheriff Jones Appeals to the Governor.—The Governor Calls Out the Militia.—Missouri Responds to the Call.—The Wakarusa War.—The Army at Franklin.—Preparations for Defense............... 45

CHAPTER V.

Governor Shannon Alarmed.—Telegraphs the President for Regular Troops.—They Do Not Come.—The Governor Visits Lawrence.—Confers with the Free-State Men.—A Treaty of Peace.—The Militia Go Home.—A Love Feast at Lawrence.—The Murder of Barber.—Old John Brown.. 62

CHAPTER VI.

A Hard Winter.—Conflict Takes a New Form in the Spring.—The Courts Come to the Rescue.—Judge Lecompte's Charge.—The Grand Jury's Indictment.—High Treason.—The Sacking of Lawrence.—Burning of the Free-State Hotel and Printing Offices..... 80

CHAPTER VII.

The Summer of 1856.—Outrages Everywhere.—Lawrence Invested by Pro-Slavery "Forts".—The Capture of Franklin, Fort Saunders and Fort Titus.—Titus a Prisoner.—Governor Shannon Makes Another Treaty.—Governor Shannon Resigns,—Daniel Woodson Acting Governor... 104

CHAPTER VIII.

Retaliation.—Martial Law.—Militia Called Out.—Missouri Responds.—Tweny-eight Hundred March on Lawrence.—Governor John W. Geary Arrives.—Appears in Lawrence with Troops.—The Militia Sent Home.—" The Benign Influences of Peace."......... 123

CHAPTER IX.

The Bogus Legislature Again.—Governor Geary Comes into Collision with It.—He is Bitterly Assailed by Pro-Slavery Leaders.—Resigns in March.—Walker and Stanton.—Peace and Progress and Prosperity.—Lawrence and her Voluntary City Government.—Martial Law Once More.. 138

CHAPTER X.

Lecompton Constitutional Convention.—The Census and Apportionment.—Free-State Men Ignore It.—Election of Territorial Legislature.—Shall We Vote?—Free-State Men Carry the Election.—Oxford and the Cincinnati Directory.—Walker Throws Out the Fraudulent Returns.—Is Removed from Office 146

CHAPTER XI.

The Territorial Legislature Adjourns to Lawrence.—The Bogus Laws Sent Home.—The Lawrence Charter.—A City Government at Last.—Samuel Medary Governor...... 154

CHAPTER XII.

Lawrence in 1858.—The Ebb of the Tide.—Spring Immigration which Failed to Come.—The Underground Railroad.—Progress in Building; In Churches.—Temperance in Lawrence.—The Drouth of 1860.—The Last Territorial Legislature.—Kansas Admitted into the Union.—A Free State... 51

CHAPTER XIII.

The Beginning of the Civil War.—Exposed Condition of Kansas.—Her Interest in the Conflict.—The First Enlistments.—The Battle of Wilson's Creek.—The Contrabands.—Lawrence in Close Touch with the Soldiers... 175

CHAPTER XIV.

The Lawrence Raid.—Its Antecedents and Causes.—William C. Quantrill, Its Unique Character.—Other Raids.—Its Unparalleled Brutality.. 187

CHAPTER XV.

The Lawrence Raid.—The Approach.—The Charge and the Surprise.—The Surrender of the Hotel.—The Burning and the Killing Begin.—Four Hours of Slaughter.—Marvelous Escapes.—The Heroism of the Women.. 198

CHAPTER XVI.

The Lawrence Raid.—The Departure and Pursuit.—The Scene Left Behind.—The Burial of the Dead.—The Ruin and the Loss.—Sympathy and Help.—Rebuilding the Town..................... 233

CHAPTER XVII.

Another Summer.—Lawrence Restored.—Improvements.—The New Bridge.—Enalrgement.—New Alarm.—Price is Coming.—Preparations for Defense.—Martial Law.—Militia Ordered Out.—The Battles on the Blue.—A Night of Anxiety.—"Joy Cometh in the Morning."—The War is Over.—Peace at Last.................. 253

CHAPTER I.

THE KANSAS-NEBRASKA BILL.—THE NORTH AROUSED.—THE EMIGRANT AID COMPANY.—ELI THAYER, AMOS A. LAWRENCE AND DR. CHARLES ROBINSON.—THE FIRST NEW ENGLAND EMIGRANTS REACH MOUNT OREAD, ORGANIZE A TOWN COMPANY AND LAY OUT THE TOWN.—"WHAT SHALL WE CALL IT?"—PITCHING TENTS AND BUILDING CABINS.—PIONEER BOARDING HOUSE.

When the Kansas-Nebraska bill passed, May 25, 1854, there was a feeling of despondency all over the north. The discussion of the bill had been long and exciting, and the whole country had joined in it. It was discussed in every newspaper, in every gathering of citizens, in every school lyceum. It was everywhere felt that its passage opened Kansas to slavery, and that was thought to be equivalent to making Kansas a slave state. Kansas lay beyond Missouri, and Missouri was a slave state. The border counties of Missouri had a large slave population, and an intense pro-slavery sentiment. The south pressed the passage of the bill for the sole purpose of securing Kansas to slavery, and when the bill had passed she felt assured that her end was gained. In the natural order of things this conclusion would have been justified by the sequel. In the natural order of things the people of Missouri would have passed over into Kansas and shaped her institutions to suit themselves. Therefore the south was jubilant and the north despondent when the bill passed.

But after the first shock was over, people began to ask "What can be done now?" The question so long discussed had taken too strong a hold on the public mind to be dropped. Congress had thrown the territory open to slavery. Was there any other way of keeping it out? Mr. Eli Thayer, of

Worcester, Massachusetts, proposed to meet the question on the terms of the bill itself. The bill provided that the people of the territory should themselves determine whether it should be slave or free. "Let us settle Kansas with people who will make it free by their own voice and vote." William H. Seward had foreshadowed this policy in a speech in the United States Senate. "Come on, then, gentlemen of the slave states. Since there is no escaping your challenge, we accept it in the name of freedom. We will engage in competition for the virgin soil of Kansas, and God give the victory to the side which is stronger in numbers, as it is in right."

The contest, therefore, was transferred to the plains of Kansas. The north had been defeated in congress; she would try again in Kansas. In accordance with this purpose, "The Emigrant Aid Company" was formed in Massachusetts. Its purpose was to encourage and aid emigration to Kansas. Many leading men joined in the movement. Amos A. Lawrence, of Boston, a man of wealth and honor and large influence, was prominent among those who gave the movement not only their sanction, but their active coöperation. These men never faltered in the long struggle, but were always ready with voice and purse to help the cause along.

The interest was not confined to New England, but was general and widespread. The rising tide of anti-slavery sentiment was rapidly centering upon one practical point: "Slavery must not secure another foot of the public domain." Men anxious to check slavery felt that here was the opportunity to do something effective. They could not vote in congress, but they could go to Kansas, and vote, and that would accomplish the same thing. Even before the bill passed this thought began to mature, and people here and there were preparing for what they saw was coming.

Early in May, 1854, the Barber brothers, Thomas W. and Oliver P., with Samuel Walker and Thomas M. Pearson, made a tour in the territory with a view to settlement. They had all been "boys together" in Franklin county, Pennsylvania, but the Barbers now lived in Indiana. They came to Westport, Missouri, by public conveyance. Here they hired a half-breed Indian to take them over the territory with his team. They spent a night at "Blue Jacket Crossing" on the Wakarusa, and passed over what was to be the site of Lawrence, passing up the spur of the hill south of where the university now stands. They went up as far as Topeka where there was an old-fashioned rope ferry; they then went across the prairies to Fort Leavenworth and then back to their home. The Kansas-Nebraska bill passed while they were in the territory. All four afterwards removed to Kansas, and were largely instrumental in inducing others to come.

The most systematic and extensive movement, however, was made in New England. "The New England Emigrant Aid Company," which had been chartered by the legislature of Massachusetts in April, was then called "The Massachusetts Emigrant Aid Society." But afterwards a new charter was obtained for "The New England Emigrant Aid Company." The men engaged in it, Eli Thayer, Amos A. Lawrence, and others, began their work at once, arousing public interest and making arrangements to facilitate emigration to Kansas. As early as June, 1854, they sent Dr. Charles Robinson, of Fitchburg, and Mr. Charles H. Branscomb, of Holyoke, to explore the territory and select a site for a colony. Dr. Robinson was just the man for such a mission. Besides being in full sympathy with the ideas of Mr. Thayer, he knew the methods of the frontier. In 1849 he went to California with the gold seekers, and was a prominent actor in the stirring scenes which characterized the early history of that state. In those turbulent times he had been severely wounded, and had been put under arrest and kept in prison for several months. But he and his associates finally won the day, and California was saved from the rule of the thieves. He was just the man needed in the new emergency. He was cool of counsel and brave of heart, and knew the conditions he had to meet. In going to California he had passed over Kansas. He went by what was afterwards known as the "California Road." This road began at Westport, crossed the Wakarusa beyond Franklin, and wound up the spur of the hill just southeast of the state university. It then passed along the high prairie which divides the valley of the Kansas river from that of the Wakarusa. Dr. Robinson and his party climbed the hill along this spur, and looked off over what was afterwards the site of Lawrence. They marked the beauty of the spot and the magnificence of the view. Whether they thought then of what might afterwards occur is not known; but when the time came to select a location for the first colony, Dr. Robinson remembered this view from the hilltop, and this doubtless had much to do in the final decision. When he was asked, therefore, to go and explore the country with a view to locating colonies, it was not altogether an unknown land to him. Neither was pioneering altogether a new experience to him. He knew something of the men and methods of pioneer life. On arriving in Kansas, Mr. Branscomb and some others passed again over the Lawrence town site, while Dr. Robinson went up the Missouri river to Leavenworth and other points.

While these two gentlemen were exploring the territory, their friends were getting ready to send out the first party of emigrants. There were only twenty-nine in this first party, but they went out to prepare the way for others, and to show that the thing could be done. They were accompanied as far as Buffalo by Eli Thayer himself, the founder of "The New England Emigrant Aid Company." We quote a few paragraphs from his "Kansas Crusade:"

"The pioneer colony left Boston July 17, 1854. Immense

crowds had gathered at the station to give them a parting God-speed. They moved out of the station amid the cheering of the crowds who lined the track for several blocks.

"The emigrants remained in Worcester the first night, and received a suitable ovation. Several of the leading citizens called upon them, and applauded their patriotic devotion, and pledging remembrance in any emergency.

"The next day we were met in the evening at Albany by a good number of citizens who welcomed us with great cordiality. The next day we were cheered at all the principal stations as we passed on our westward journey. The president of the Monroe County Bible Society made an address, and presented the colony with a large and elegant Bible."

They crossed Lake Erie in the steamer "Plymouth Rock," and went by way of Chicago to St. Louis. Here they were met by Dr. Robinson, who gave them the benefit of his experience. He procured transportation for them on board the steamer "Polar Star," and they left St. Louis July 24th and arrived at Kansas City the Friday evening following, July 27th. The journey from here is well described in a letter by Mr. B. R. Knapp, published in the Boston *News*, and dated August 9, 1854:

"We prepared ourselves at once for starting. An ox team was purchased to transport the baggage and at ten o'clock Saturday evening we started on foot for our destination across the prairie. We traveled as much as possible during the night as the weather was very hot during the middle of the day. We saw occasionally a log house as we passed along, inhabited by farmers, of whom we obtained milk, etc. On the evening of Sunday we encamped on the lands of the Shawnee Indians. On Monday morning we started early, and in the evening arrived at the Wakarusa river, within ten miles of our destination. Here we camped, and the next day reached our new home. Here we established our camp, and pitched our twenty-five tents, which made a fine appearance though somewhat soiled. On Wednesday the second day of August, we went to work setting up our claim to the lands, and preparing for permanent settlement." The following are the names of this first party: E. Davenport, A. Holman, Ben. Merriam, J. F. Morgan, A. H. Mallory, J. W. Russell, E. Conant, F. Fuller, G. W. Hewes, Dr. S. C. Harrington, A. Philbrick, J. D. Stevens, E. White, W. H. Hewes, John Mailey, Sam'l F. Tappan, D. R. Anthony, H. Cameron, G. W. Hutchinson, George Thatcher, J. M. Jones, Dr. John Doy, A. Fowler, G. W. Goss, August Hillpath, O. Harlow, Arthur Gunter, J. C. Archibald, B. R. Knapp.

This party arrived August 1st. They ate their first meal on the hill where the old University building now stands. Of course they held a "meeting" and "organized." Someone has said that "wherever two or three Yankees are met together there they hold a meeting and organize." The meeting chose Ferdinand Fuller as chairman. They were in good position to

"View the landscape o'er,"

which they proceeded to do. They also had some speeches, and discussed the merits of the location and the best methods of procedure. The situation seemed to please them, and they voted to "stay here." They named the hill on which they met "Mount Oread," a name which it bears "unto this day." They remained on the hill a day or two, and then moved down, and camped near the Kansas river a little west of where the bridge now crosses that stream. The members of the party spent several days "claim hunting," and selected claims all around the proposed town site. After this was done, about half the party returned east, with the intention of bringing their families in the spring.

The second party of emigrants left Boston the last of August. It was a much larger party than the first, having sixty-seven members when leaving Boston. They received accessions on the way, swelling their numbers to one hundred and fourteen. There were eight or ten ladies in the company, and several children. There were several musicians, among them Joseph and Forest Savage from Hartford, Vermont. These musicians had their instruments with them, and enlivened the journey with music whenever opportunity offered. Before starting they assembled in the Boston and Worcester station in Boston, and sang and played Whittier's "Hymn of the Kansas Emigrant," which became a sort of national hymn to the colonists. These musicians became afterwards the nucleus of the "Lawrence Band" and were its main reliance for many years. They did noble service in stimulating an interest in music in the early times.

The following is Whittier's "Song of the Kansas Emigrant:"

"We cross the prairie as of old
　The fathers crossed the sea,
To make the West, as they the East,
　The homestead of the free.

"We go to rear a wall of men
　On Freedom's southern line,
And plant beside the cotton tree
　The rugged northern pine.

"We're flowing from our native hills
　As our free rivers flow,
The blessing of our mother land
　Is on us as we go.

"We go to plant the common school
　On distant prairie swells,
And give the Sabbaths of the wilds
　The music of her bells.

"Upbearing, like the ark of God,
　The Bible in our van,
We go to test the truth of God
　Against the fraud of man."

The second party arrived at Lawrence or "Wakarusa," as it was then called, September 9th. They had been led by Charles Robinson, who was afterwards the first governor of the state, and by Samuel C. Pomeroy, who was one of the first two United States senators. It contained a number of men who were afterwards prominent in Kansas affairs, and who will be remembered with interest by all old settlers. The following is a partial list of the members of the party: James F. Ayers, Joseph W. Ackley, S. F. Atwood, Lewis H. Bacon, Edwin Bond, F. A. Bailey, Owen T. Bassett, Susan Bassett, H. N. Bent, William Bruce, Mrs. Bruce, Mrs. Bond, F. L. Crane, Joseph H. Cracklin, Willard Colburn, Mrs. Colburn, Jared Carter, Ed. Dennett, J. S. Emery, George F. Earle, Milan Grant, Mrs. Grant, Levi Gates, Mrs. Gates, George Gilbert, Joel Grover, Azro Hazen, H. A. Hancock, O. A. Hanscom, W. A. Hood, Franklin Haskell, Lewis Howell, W. H. Hovey, R. J. Hooten, S. N. Hartwell, C. Hobart, Alfonso Jones, H. A. Fick, Mrs. Jones, Wilder Knight, Mrs. Knight, Ed. Knight, G. W. Knight, Miss Knight, D. B. Trask, W. Kitcherman, E. D. Ladd, J. A. Ladd, Luke P. Lincoln, Lewis L. Litchfield, Lewis T. Litchfield, Mrs. Litchfield, Otis H. Lamb, Samuel Merrill, J. S. Mott, John Mack, J. N. Mace, Mrs. Mace, J. H. Muzzy, Caleb S. Pratt, S. J. Pratt, Samuel C. Pomeroy, A. J. Payne, Charles Robinson, Thomas F. Reynolds, E. E. Ropes, Charles W. Smith, Joseph Savage, Forest Savage, Jacob Strout, Mrs. Strout, Matthew H. Spittle, A. D. Searl, F. A. Tolles, J. B. Taft, Owen Taylor, Mrs. Taylor, John Waite, S. J. Willis, Mrs. Willis, Sol. Willis, E. W. Winslow, Silas Wayne, Mrs. Wayne, Ira W. Younglove, J. Sawyer, Mrs. Carter. Rev. S. Y. Lum, Mrs. Lum, and Miss Anna Tappan, arrived about the same time by a different route, and were reckoned with the second party. Mr. Lum preached the first sermon preached in Lawrence, a few days after his arrival.

When the second party arrived they met the members of the first party and soon agreed upon terms of union with them in laying out the town. The members of the party were

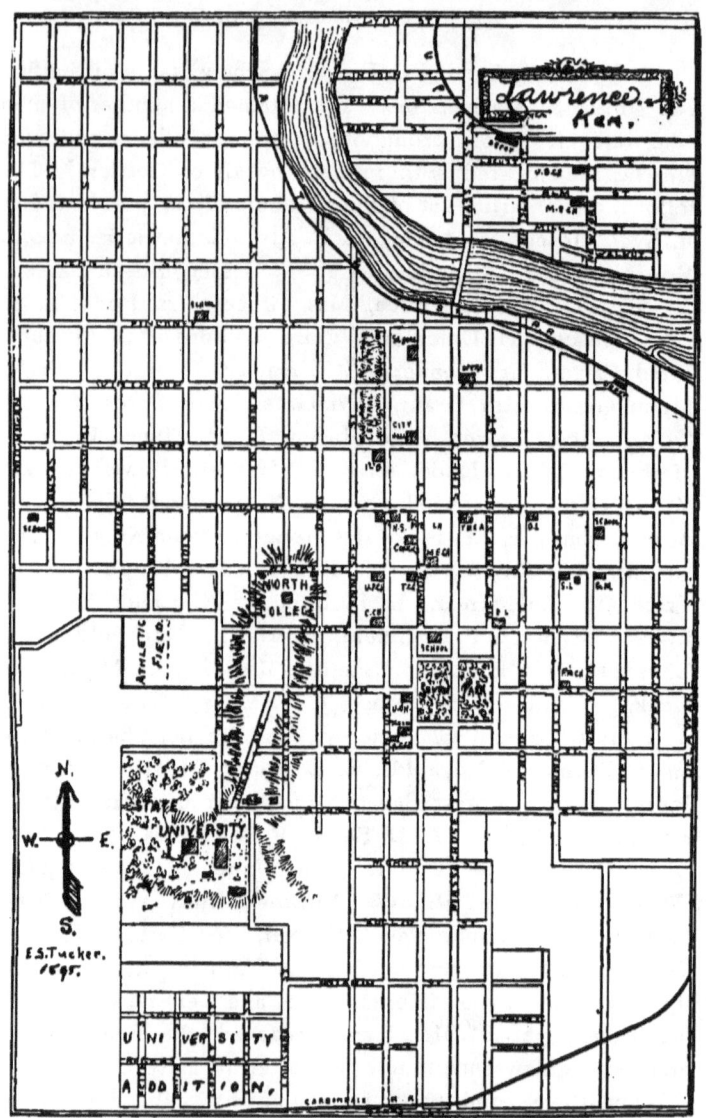

MAP OF THE CITY OF LAWRENCE.

soon scattered here and there seeking claims for themselves. September 18th a meeting of the settlers was held to effect a town organization. The necessity for this arose from the fact that there were no laws regulating such matters. The only thing they could do was to set up a sort of voluntary municipal government. This meeting adopted a constitution and agreed upon rules for the choice of claims. The next day officers were chosen, and a full city government set up. Dr. Charles Robinson was chosen president; Ferdinand Fuller, vice-president; Caleb S. Pratt, secretary; Levi Gates, treasurer; E. D. Ladd, register of deeds; A. D. Searl, surveyor; Joel Grover, marshal. The councilmen were Messrs. J. S. Emery, J. F. Morgan, Franklin Haskell. S. C. Harrington, A. H. Mallory, Samuel F. Tappan, S. P. Lincoln, S. J. Willis, N. T. Johnson, Joseph H. Cracklin. At an early meeting of the council the principles of the Maine law were proposed, and adopted almost unanimously. Thus Lawrence commenced its being as a prohibition town.

September 20th another public meeting was held by members of the first and second parties. Terms of agreement were arranged and unanimously adopted, by which they were to lay out the town together. It was agreed that the choice of shares should be sold to members of the town association. Time was allowed for payment, and the proceeds were to constitute a fund for public improvements. The choices were sold at prices varying from fifty cents to over three hundred dollars. The fifty-six claims sold aggregated the sum of $5,040. At the end of the year the association gave up the notes, and the obligation was cancelled and the money never called for. In the distribution of shares, lots were reserved for a college, for schools, for state buildings, and for other public purposes.

At midnight of this same day, September 20th, the surveyor, A. D. Searl, with Charles W. Smith and three others, went out upon the high ground on Massachusetts street, near the river, and took the observations necessary to establish the meridian line. September 25th the surveyor commenced the survey of the town, and marked off the lots and streets and reservations essentially as they stand today.

The name of the town had not been determined upon. It had been called Wakarusa, Yankee-town, and New Boston. After a full discussion it was decided to give it the name of Lawrence, after Amos A. Lawrence, of Boston. Mr. Lawrence was one of the first men of means to endorse the movement for the settlement of Kansas in the interest of freedom. He was a man of large wealth and belonged to one of the most distinguished New England families. He was also a man of wide personal influence. He was treasurer of "The New England Emigrant Aid Company," and a very liberal contributor to its funds. A little later he gave some twelve thousand dollars to help found a college at Lawrence, which ultimately became a part of the endowment of the state university. His interest in Kansas, and especially in Lawrence, never faltered. His father and uncle were Abbott and Amos Lawrence who were long distinguished in business and political circles in eastern Massachusetts. Abbott Lawrence had been a member of congress several times, and was minister to England for a number of years. Amos A. Lawrence inherited the wealth, and reputation, and business capacity of the family. He also inherited their public spirit and large liberality. The naming of the first free state town in Kansas after him was a very fitting recognition.

The following letter from Mr. Lawrence, written for the Old Settlers meeting but not received in time for that meeting, shows something of the spirit of the man and of the condition of the times. It has never before been made public. It was sent in response to an invitation from the secretary, Mr. Charles W. Smith, to be present at the meeting:

"(NEAR) BOSTON, August 16th, 1877.
" *To the Old Settlers' Association:*

"DEAR FRIENDS:—Your kind and pressing invitation, signed with your own hands, to be present at your yearly meeting, came close on that of the chancellor of the university to be present at the dedication of the new building. The same causes which keep me here, and made me decline the former, force me reluctantly to decline yours. If there are any faces on earth I wish to see they are yours.

"You are good enough to say that 'free Kansas is indebted to no man more than yourself in her days of darkness and trial, and many, very many, of our people desire to see your face, and welcome you to our state.' For the last I thank you with all my heart. But as to the first, permit me for once to differ from you, and direct your notice to others who rendered much greater service.

"Eli Thayer preached the 'Kansas Crusade.' He originated and organized the 'Emigrant Aid Society' in opposition to the plans of southern statesmen and politicians. Early in 1854, several months before the passage of the Kansas-Nebraska bill, he wrote the charter of that company, and secured its passage through the Massachusetts Legislature, of which he was a member. He it was more than any other who turned the tide of northern emigration that year, and made Kansas a free state. He traversed the northern states, and aroused the people, depicting the glories of that country, and urging the emigrants not to turn away from it, but to go on and possess it. He never faltered in his faith, and he inspired confidence everywhere.

"There was Charles Robinson, whom you chose your leader and governor. He was to you in that day what Moses was to the Israelites. When the action of the government was adverse to your interests; when Reeder and Geary were removed; when Atchison, the acting vice-president, left his seat in the senate to lead the border ruffians, and to drive you out with fire and sword, it was Robinson more than any other man who held the people firm in their allegiance to the United States. He had to fight not only the enemy but his friends. He was the representative of law and order, and so under Providence the public sentiment of the country was kept in your favor.

"You know who helped the cause there. Besides those who are now members of the association, there were many devoted men and women, who will never be known abroad; some of whom laid down their lives; and all of whom endured hardships and privations. Let us thank God for the good results and take courage. He governs the nations and individuals.

"And now good friends, for the present farewell. We may hope to meet on some other occasion. At any rate the time is not far distant when we may hope for a reunion which shall be forevermore. With great respect and affection, I am and shall ever remain,

"Yours,

"Addressed to   "AMOS A. LAWRENCE.

"C. W. SMITH, Lawrence, Kansas,

"*Secretary of the Association of Old Settlers.*"

Rev. Charles B. Boyington, of Cincinnati, in a book written about this time, describes Lawrence as she then appeared:

"A few tents were pitched on high ground overlooking the Kansas and Wakarusa valleys; others were scattered over the level bottom lands below, but not a dwelling besides could be seen. It was a city of tents alone. We had a comfortable night's rest in Dr. Robinson's tent, and in the morning were introduced to the only boarding house on the hill. Two very intelligent ladies from Massachusetts had united their forces and interests and taken boarders. In the open air, on some logs of wood, two rough boards were laid across for a table, and on wash-tubs, kegs and blocks, they and their boarders were seated around it. This was the first boarding house in the city of Lawrence. All were cheerful, hopeful and full of energy, and the scene reminded me of Plymouth Rock."

These energetic people now began to build the town, living in tents meanwhile. They built under disadvantages. One of these disadvantages was the lack of lumber. A sawmill had been promised, but had not arrived. Another mill was purchased later in the season, but was not put in operation for several months. In the meantime winter was coming on, when tents would not be as comfortable as in the hot days of summer. The people adopted many devices to shelter themselves. The first house built was a log cabin, about fourteen feet square. It stood not far from the river being nearly where Pierson's mill now stands. It was still in existence until a few years ago. It was not a very good specimen of even a log cabin. The logs were small and the openings between them were large. There had not been the careful matching which usually characterizes log cabins in the woods. But log cabins even of this inferior kind could hardly be numerous in a prairie country. Other methods were better suited to the situation. The sod house, which has since played such an important part in the settlement of the treeless plains, was not yet fully evolved. Sods were sometimes used for walls, but not for the entire structure, as has been the case in later years. A style of building became quite common, which seems to have been almost peculiar to Lawrence and to that time. It was called "the hay tent." It was built by setting up two rows of poles, then bringing the poles together at the top and thatching the sides with prairie hay. The house was all roof and gable. The windows and doors were at the ends. The gables were built up with sod walls. The "Pioneer Boarding House" was of this sort. It was fifty feet long and twenty feet wide. Here the first sermon was preached by Rev. S. Y. Lum. Some trunks were used for a pulpit, and the beds and boxes of the boarders served as seats. Here Plymouth Church was organized, October 15th, 1854. This building answered all public purposes, as well as furnishing room and board for the people. This building was burned during the autumn and the "St. Nicholas" was built in the same way, and thrown open to the public. In addition to its walls of poles and hay, this house was banked up with sod to the height of three or four feet, and was lined inside with cotton cloth. It was the leading hotel. All the aristocracy of the place boarded there. The only frame house built the first season was that of Rev. S. Y. Lum. There being no saw-mill, no boards could be obtained. As a substitute for clapboards they resorted to "shakes." A "shake" is made by sawing off blocks of timber about thirty-two inches long, and splitting them somewhat after the manner of making shingles. These "shakes" were nailed on the studding like clapboards. If nicely split and well put on they made a very fair wall. The wind, however, found its way through them in the winter time in a manner that provided abundant ventilation. With these different styles of architecture, and with the tents that remained, the people passed the first winter quite comfortably. It was a very mild winter, and they thought they had found the American Italy.

CHAPTER II.

Reinforcements.—The Disgust of the Kid-gloved Contingent.—First Sabbath Services.—The First Funeral. Town Site Troubles.—"Shoot to Hit."—First Election for Delegate to Congress.—Judge Wakefield.—The First School.—Three Newspapers.—Winter in Tents and Cabins.

Three or four other parties came from the east during the first season, about seven hundred and fifty persons in all. These were by no means all who came. Immigrants came singly or in groups from different parts of the country. A number of prominent free-state men were on the ground when the first party from Boston arrived. On the other hand, several of those who came in these parties, became disgusted when they saw the true situation. This was especially true of the third party who arrived early in October. The movement by this time had attracted wide attention, and the colonists had sent back glowing accounts of the country. These accounts were interpreted by a vivid imagination, and a number of soft-slippered people such as they would call "tenderfeet" in Colorado, enlisted, who expected to find an earthly paradise. When they came and found only a few tents and a few thatched hovels, their disgust knew no bounds. They were looking for hotels with all the modern conveniences, and expecting to find good positions waiting for them in large business establishments. After exhausting their vocabulary in denouncing the leaders who had "deceived them" and induced them to come to such a barbarous place, and the people of Lawrence for not providing for them in a more appropriate way, they turned on their heels and "went back to their folks." But most of those who came were of different stuff, and were prepared to "endure hardships as good soldiers." Even these had all the hardships they cared for before they were through. But they did not falter as difficulties increased, but

"Their courage rose with danger."

Andreas in his history quotes from a letter in the Boston *Recorder* describing the first funeral in Lawrence. The letter is dated October 5th, 1854.

"Last Sabbath was my first *prairie Sabbath;* it was the first Sabbath our parties had assembled for the 'hearing of the word.' Rev. Mr. Lum, sent us by the American Home Missionary Society, preached very acceptably. The place of meeting was one of the large receiving and boarding houses. We have two nearly adjoining each other, each of them about 20 by 48 feet, covered and thatched with prairie grass, very warm and very good. We had a large and attentive audience. Rev. Mr. Boynton, of Cincinnati, sent us two boxes of books and pamphlets, which I distributed at the interval to a very eager crowd. All our people as well as others, miss their home papers and books, and are very anxious to get anything to read.

"Though the Sabbath was delightful as my *first prairie Sabbath*, still there was one cloud that settled dark upon us; we had to open our *first prairie grave.* The call was for one of our own party, a near neighbor of mine, Moses Pomeroy, a fine young man, an only son, leaving parents and two sisters to mourn his loss. I have just finished long and very minute letters to each of them. Mr. Pomeroy left the party in Illinois. He joined Dr. R. and myself upon the following Tuesday at St. Louis, and came up the river with us. He said to me that all of his Illinois friends were sick of a fever, and after he was taken sick, he sent for me to come and see him, for he had got an Illinois fever. I went to see him on Thursday evening, September 28th, and found Dr. R. and Dr. H. in attendance. I saw he was very sick, and at his

LAWRENCE, KANSAS, 1854-55.

MASSACHUSETTS AND VERMONT STREETS NORTH FROM WINTHROP STREET (IN FOREGROUND) TO RIVER. FERRY LANDING AT PIER ON NEW HAMPSHIRE STREET.

1. First house built in Lawrence; used for Paul R. Brooks' store.
2. *Kansas Free State* office.
3. *Herald of Freedom* office.
4. Emigrant Aid office.
5. First postoffice, and Paul R. Brook's store; C. W. Babcock, postmaster.
6. S. N. Simpson's land and lumber office; also used for Emigrant Aid office; first Sabbath School, two served services and prayer meetings.
7. Hoyt's residence.
8. First hotel, Pioneer House, Lichfield & Barson, proprietors.
9. S. N. Simpson's residence.
10. J. G. Sands' harness shop.
11. Chas. Stearns' eating house.
12. First church; S. Y. Lum, pastor.
13. Emigrant Aid saw mill.
14. T. Sampson's meat market.
15. S. N. Simpson's residence.
16. St. Nicholas House; S. Fry, proprietor.
17. Miller & Elliott's printing office.
18. S. and F. Kimball's residence.
19. Ferry; Baldwin Bros. proprietors.

request sat by him all night and ministered to his wants. Friday morning I was very busy at our settlement. At evening he sent for me again. In company with Mr. Searl of our place, I stayed also Friday night. In the morning we were all fearful he would die. I was absent during the day. At evening Dr. R. and myself went again to see him. We both sat with him till three o'clock Saturday morning, when he quietly breathed his last. He had his reason and was very thankful for all our kindness to him. He had fallen among the kindest of friends, but they could not save him.

"Sabbath evening at four o'clock his funeral was attended in our New England way, services very solemn and impressive at our grass church. All our large family followed in solemn procession to the grave, and just as the sun was setting in a golden west, and all nature sinking to repose, we gently laid him down to the long sleep of the tomb."

As has been intimated the first Congregational Church was organized October 15th—the first church of any kind in Kansas except among the Indians. The church was formed in the "Pioneer Boarding House." Rev. Mr. Lum explained the object of the meeting, and a committee was appointed to draft rules. The creed and constitution were adapted from those of Mount Vernon Church, Boston. S. C. Pomeroy wrote them off, using the crown of his beaver hat for a desk; Mr. Joseph Savage held the inkstand for him, and Mr. O. A. Hanscom held the candle. They voted to name it Plymouth Church on account of the close parallel between the Kansas settlers and the pilgrims at Plymouth.

The only serious troubles the colonists met the first season were from claim difficulties. It is not easy at this distance to determine how much of this trouble arose from political reasons, and how much from misunderstanding and perhaps greed. The political situation aggravated all other difficulties, and was doubtless responsible for a great many difficulties of its own. When the Kansas bill passed the people of the South expected to take possession of the territory. They urged those on the border to "move right over," and take their slaves with them. They said "two thousand slaves settled in Kansas would make it a slave state." But the southern people did not have the "courage of their convictions." They did not dare take their slaves over. There never were but a handful of slaves in Kansas, and these were on the border where they could be easily withdrawn. But southern people determined to take possession of Kansas, and as soon as the bill was passed the men in the border counties of Missouri began to rush over, and stake off claims. In a few weeks the whole region was claimed under the pre-emption laws by persons residing in Missouri. They paid no attention to the terms of the law, but each man marked off the land he wanted, drove a stake down and wrote his name upon it, and went back home. This gave them no title and no claim because it did not comply with the law. But they agreed among themselves to shoot any man who interfered with them. When the real settlers came two months later they found many embarrassments. They might travel fifty miles and not see a human habitation or a human face, but if they attempted to claim a piece of unoccupied land, they found it already claimed by somebody in Missouri. This man had not complied with the law, and had secured no title, but then he had a revolver and a bowie knife, and in the unwritten code of the border these stood for law and right, and pretty much everything else. Many of these prior claims had been made before the country was open to settlement, or before the Indian title was extinguished, but these were "trifles light as air" in the minds of the men who were a "law unto themselves." They were all banded together, and pledged to stand by each other. Law or no law, they were determined to "keep the abolitionists out of Kansas." An end like this justified any means, as they viewed things.

The Lawrence dispute was somewhat peculiar. Gov. Robinson in his "Conflict" gives a full and clear account of it from which this account is condensed. When the town site of Lawrence was first selected it was occupied by a Mr. Stearns who had improved a quarter section and was living upon it. The Emigrant Aid Company bought his claim for $500, and the ground was supposed to be clear. After taking possession, however, other claimants appeared and insisted that the town company should vacate for them. Among these other claimants was John Baldwin, a noisy, blustering fellow, who had others back of him who were wiser than he, and who were putting him forward. He established himself a few rods from the Stearns cabin which the town company had bought. The agent of the company, Dr. Robinson, proposed to let the matter rest till the question could be referred to the land office, or to the courts, where the rights of each could be legally determined. But this was not satisfactory to John Baldwin and his set. Their purpose was to drive off the free-state men, and prevent the founding of a free-state town. They had no case in law, and could only hope to succeed by bluster and force. The first conflict is described in Andreas' history as quoted in Robinson's "Conflict":

"In the meantime Baldwin had associated with him Messrs. Babcock, Stone and Freeman, men of means and influence, and put the business in the hands of a speculator named Starr, who proceeded to lay out a rival city, which he named Excelsior, on the claim; Mr. Baldwin and the Lawrence association both occupying tents upon it. * * * On the 5th of October a wagon containing several armed men appeared in the vicinity of the New England tent. Hostilities were commenced by a woman (a sister of Baldwin, it was stated) who speedily packed the obnoxious tent with its contents into the wagon, the men with their rifles standing guard. As soon as they were discovered by the Yankees, who were at work in the neighborhood, the city marshal, Joel Grover, rushed to the rescue unarmed, followed by Edwin Bond with a revolver. The latter seized the horse by the bridle, ordering the surrender of the property. Others coming up, they allowed the tent to be replaced, but threatened that they would have two hundred Missourians on the spot in a short time. That night the Lawrence settlers organized what they called the "Regulating Band," to be ready for the next day's fray. Soon after dinner on the 6th the Missourians * * * began to assemble in the neighborhood of Baldwin's tent, but open hostilities did not commence until four o'clock, when the gage of battle was hurled at the Yankees in the shape of the following note:

"KANSAS TERRITORY, October 6th.

"DR. ROBINSON:—Yourself and friends are hereby notified that you will have one-half hour to move the tent which you have on my undisputed claim, and from this date desist from surveying on said claim. If the tent is not moved in one-half hour, we shall take the trouble to move the same.

"(Signed) JOHN BALDWIN AND FRIENDS.

"The following reply was instantly returned:

"*To John Baldwin and Friends:*

"If you molest our property you do it at your peril.

"C. ROBINSON AND FRIENDS."

E. D. Ladd, the first postmaster of Lawrence, tells the remainder of the story in a letter dated October 23, 1854, and published in the Milwaukee *Sentinel:*

"Prior to the notice they had assembled to the number of eighteen, mounted and armed, at Baldwin's, the aggrieved man's tent, on the claim and about twenty rods from our camp. On notice being served, our men, those who were at work about and in the vicinity, to the number of about thirty, stationed themselves about ten rods from the contested tent, the enemy being about the same distance from it. Subsequent to the notice a consultation was held at our position between

Dr. Robinson and a delegate from the enemy's post, which ended in the proposition of Dr. Robinson * * * to submit the question in dispute to the arbitration of disinterested and unbiased men, to the adjudication of the squatter courts now existing here, or to the United States court; and on the part of the enemy that on the termination of the notice they should proceed at all hazards to remove the tent. If they fell in the attempt our fate was sealed, our extermination certain, for three thousand, and if necessary thirty thousand, men would immediately be raised in Missouri to sweep us and our enterprise from the face of the earth. It was all expressed of course in southwestern phrase, which I will not attempt to give. * * * Well, the half hour passed, and another quarter, the enemy occasionally making a movement as if about to form for the execution of the threat, then seating themselves on the ground for further consultation. While thus waiting John Hutchinson asked Dr. Robinson what they should do if they should attempt to remove the tent. Should they fire to hit, or fire over them? Robinson replied that he would be ashamed to shoot at a man and not hit him. Immediately after this reply a man who had been with the free-state men, and till then supposed to be one of them, went over to the other party, which soon after dispersed. It was supposed at the time that the report of the spy brought the "war" to an end for that day. After the band had mounted and dispersed the principals and principal instigators avoided our neighborhood. Some of the more honest dupes, seeing the absurdity of their position, and the reasonableness of our proposition, came up to us and had a social chat, and went off with a determination never to be caught in such a farce again."

This little encounter did not end the matter, but there was no fighting. The Missourians did not care to encounter men who would "shoot to hit." But they kept up the disturbance for a long time and missed no opportunity of annoying the settlers. Once some of them undertook to tear down Dr. Robinson's house, but a few men, G. W. Deitzler, S. N. Wood and S. N. Simpson, who were in the habit of "shooting to hit," rushed to the rescue, and the ruffians got out of range. After a while the title to the Lawrence town site was quieted, but not without a long struggle and a good deal of bitterness.

The first election held was for a delegate to congress, November 26. Not much interest was taken in it, though the influx of voters from Missouri gave a hint of what might be expected in more important elections. The little town of Douglas, not far away, with only fifty legal voters, cast two hundred and eighty-three votes, thus more than out-voting Lawrence with many times the population. At Lawrence the larger portion of the votes were cast for Judge J. A. Wakefield, who lived but a few miles away. He was a plain, honest man, a hearty free-soiler, and a unique character, such as are only developed amid the peculiar conditions of those early times. He had served under Lincoln in the Black Hawk war, and had waded through swamps where "the men sank up to their knees and the horses sunk in furder." He was enthusiastic, earnest and honest, and in speech was most amusing when most serious. William A. Phillips, in his "Conquest of Kansas," thus describes him:

"As a free state man, the judge is unquestionably reliable. He is a western man, and no abolitionist. But, as he explained in a speech we once heard him make, he was 'a free-soiler up to the hub—hub and all.' The judge is a character in his way. His public speeches and private conversation are characterized by a style and enunciation decidedly provincial, and his grammar sets up a standard somewhat independent of Lindley Murray. But he is sound and shrewd in his opinions, and honest to the core." In a speech made during the campaign the judge said he was born in South Carolina, raised in Kentucky, he had lived in free states, and had been a pioneer all his life. The judge received the greater portion of the vote at Lawrence, and the vote at Lawrence was the greater portion of the vote he received. General J. W. Whitefield, the pro-slavery candidate, was elected by a large majority, more than half his vote being imported from Missouri.

On the sixteenth day of January the first school was opened. Mr. E. P. Fitch was the teacher. There was no law by which taxes could be levied, so the people maintained the school by voluntary contributions, and threw it open to all the children. It was a free school, so far at least that no charge was made for attendance. The school was not large but the work done was good. Lawrence was bound to begin right, and she began with a free school. Mr. E. P. Fitch taught the school for about three months, and then others took it up. It was not easy to maintain a school, but there was no year without one.

A Bible class was formed the first Sunday in October. There would have been a Sunday school formed also, but there were not children enough. As other parties arrived, however, there were more families among them, and the first Sunday in January a Sunday school was formed, of which Mr. S. N. Simpson was superintendent, and after him Mr. C. L. Edwards. A little after this a mission Sunday school was formed a few miles east of town. These schools were held wherever a place could be found for them, and were often interrupted by the disturbed state of affairs.

It is not easy to determine which was the first newspaper established in Lawrence. There were three, each claiming to be the first, and each being able to make its claim good, if you will follow its own line of proof. The first number of the *Herald of Freedom* was dated at Wakarusa, October 21, 1854. It was edited and printed, however, at Conneautville, Pennsylvania, and 21,000 copies distributed from there. The material was then packed and sent to Lawrence. It was delayed on the way, and the second number of the paper appeared in January. Mr. G. W. Brown had meanwhile moved to Lawrence, erected a building of unseasoned boards in which he set up his printing office. The paper was ably conducted, and for a time had a large circulation at the east.

The last of September John Speer and his brother J. L. Speer came from Ohio to Lawrence. They prepared the copy for a paper, and tried to get it printed in an office at Kansas City. But the proprietors being pro-slavery refused to do the work. They then went through a similar experience with the Leavenworth *Herald*. Mr. John Speer returned to his home at Mendina, Ohio, and issued the paper from that place October 15th. He returned at once to Lawrence and issued the first number of the Kansas *Tribune* January 5, 1855. Mr. Josiah Miller visited Kansas in August of 1854, with a view of establishing a paper. Like the others, he was hindered in getting his material on the ground. At last he was able to issue the first number of the Kansas *Free State*, dated January 3, 1855, being the first paper actually printed in Lawrence. The paper announced that it was published from an office that had neither "floor, ceiling nor window sash." Mr. Miller had associated with him Mr. R. G. Elliott, who afterwards held important positions.

The coming of three such men to Lawrence at the same time and on the same errand is significant. They were as different as men could be, and yet all were moved with the same purpose. Mr. Brown was a man of experience and of various resources. He was a good writer, and his paper was handsome and well filled. He was self-willed, however, and strong in his antagonism, and often bitterly personal. After a few years he abandoned journalism and returned to the practice of his profession in another state.

John Speer was an easy-going, good-natured man, but a

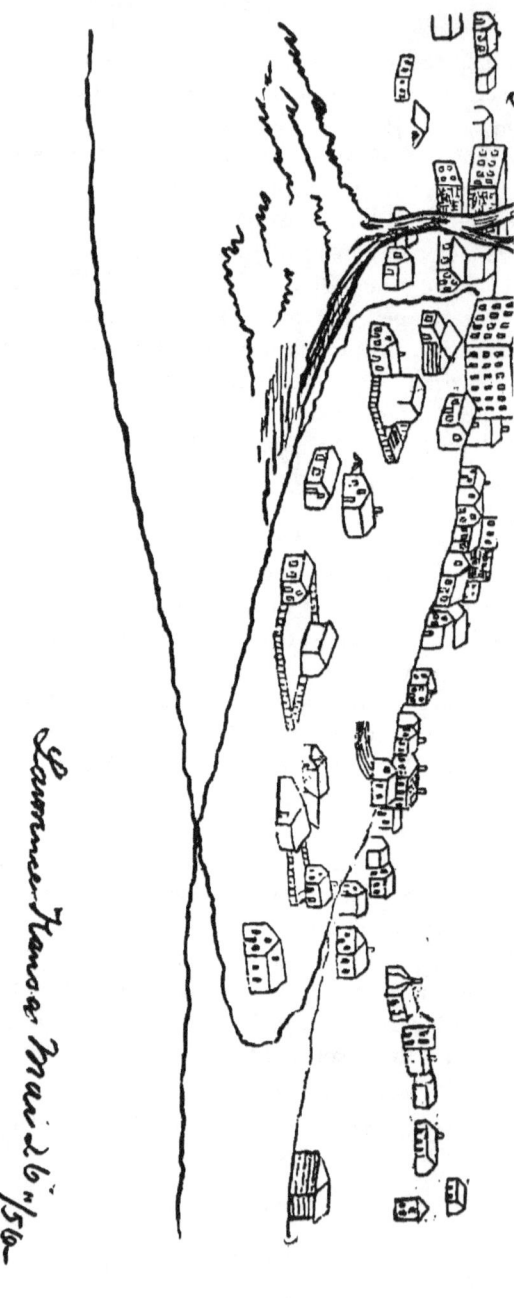

The above cut is a fac-simile of a pencil drawing found in the corner stone of the old Unitarian church, which was demolished in May, 1893. The sketch is supposed to have been made by Miss Lucy Wilder, afterwards Mrs. B. W. Woodward, on the day the corner-stone was laid. The view is of Lawrence as it was then, from near where North College now stands, or more probably from the site of the church.

sturdy friend of human freedom. He made no pretense to literary polish, but was a very fluent and effective writer. He had a wonderful memory, and could recall at any time the minutest details of all his large experience and wide range of miscellaneous reading. He was a strong politician and a master in the arts of political management. He has had a large and varied experience as a newspaper man in Kansas and may be called one of the veteran editors of the state. He is still living, honored for his long service in the interest of Kansas, and in the cause of freedom.

Josiah Miller was different from either of these. He belonged to a class which was one of the unrecognized elements in the Kansas problem. He was an anti-slavery man from the South. It was common to consider all immigrants from the South as in favor of slavery. But many of the most determined opponents of slavery were from the South. Mr. Miller's family were of Scotch descent and of the Covenanter faith. They brought with them all the love of freedom, and all the indomnitable persistence for which that people have been remarkable. They settled in South Carolina, and though able to own slaves never did own any. Robert H. Miller, the father of Judge Miller, had got himself into trouble through his anti-slavery proclivities. Their minister had said something unfavorable to slavery and had been treated to a coat of tar and feathers, one of the favorite arguments with the pious defenders of the patriarchal institution. Mr. Miller undertook to prosecute the assailants, but his attorney was poisoned, and the case was thrown out of court. Soon after he was set upon by a lot of roughs and beaten almost to death. Trained in such a school, young Josiah Miller grew up without any great love for the peculiar institution of his native state. After graduating at the state university of Indiana and studying law, he threw himself into the Kansas struggle. He was a scholarly man and an able lawyer. He took a prominent part in the stirring events which followed. In the summer of 1856, he was siezed by some of Col. Buford's men and tried for treason to his native state, South Carolina. His life was in peril for a time but he was released from prison after a few weeks. In 1857 he was elected probate judge of Douglas county, when the probate court covered a good part of the judicial business of the county. He was a member of the first state senate in 1861, and as chairman of the judiciary committee, suggested the motto on the state seal,

"Ad Astra per Aspera."

The coming of these men on the same errand, from different parts of the country, and without any knowledge of each other, is an illustration of the wide-spread interest Kansas had excited. They all came at about the same time, met almost the same hindrances, and got out the first issue of their papers within a week of each other. The papers were filled with interesting matter, and would have done credit to any eastern town. Of course Lawrence was not large enough to support three such papers. But the interest in Kansas all over the country gave them a large eastern constituency. Everybody was seeking information as to Kansas affairs.

The colonists were kept busy during the autumn preparing for winter. The cold weather came on quite early and caught them in a very poor condition to face it. A letter written at this time describes some of their experience.

"It is quite cold for the 12th of November. Yesterday we were greeted by a pretty severe snow storm for which we were hardly prepared, our house being in no better condition to receive such a guest than an orchard with the bars down. This morning I crawled from under my buffalo skin after having slept as soundly as anyone could suppose, who could see the pile of snow I had for my bed. I kindled a fire in a rough stone fire place, but the smoke rolled in upon us at such a rate that we were compelled to remove the fire, not to the middle of the floor, but to where the middle of the floor would have been, if we had a floor. By doing this we could get to the windward of the fire and thus avoid the smoke. If you could only see a true picture of us now, as we are seated upon a trunk before the fire, with our feet extended to keep them warm, and a large tea chest at our back with the lid raised to break the wind, and a buffalo pelt drawn closely about us, and each taking good care to get his share, you might be quite as good-natured in enjoying the picture as we are in enjoying the reality."

After this severe storm passed over, the weather became mild again, so mild at Christmas that people sat with the doors and windows open. This fine weather continued till late in January, when there was another cold spell. But on the whole it was a delightful winter, and Providence seemed to have tempered the blast to the shorn lambs. They passed the winter very comfortably

CHAPTER III.

Spring.—Election, March 30th, 1855.—Excitement in Missouri.—An Army of Voters Invade Lawrence.—Missouri Voters Elect a Kansas Legislature.—Slavery Triumphant and Exultant.—Free-state Men Despondent, then Indignant.—What Shall We Do?—Dr. Robinson's Policy.—"Bogus Legislature" Repudiated.

In the spring of 1855 there occurred an event which largely gave shape to the history of the next two years. This was the election of the first territorial legislature. As the Organic Act allowed the people to determine their own domestic institutions, the first legislature might establish or exclude slavery by law, and so might settle the whole question. Governor Andrew H. Reeder ordered the election to be held on the thirtieth day of March. As a preliminary to this election he ordered a census taken in February of the people of the territory. According to this census, Kansas then had a population of 8,601, of whom 2,905 were voters. This number was probably increased before March 30th, as immigration began very early, and quite a number of actual settlers came into the country before the election. But there were not enough to make any material change. The district in which Lawrence was situated had 369 voters, according to the census.

Both sides understood the importance of this election, and put forth their strongest efforts to carry it. Whoever secured the first legislature would make the first laws. A pro-slavery legislature could establish slavery and pass laws protecting slave property. Then the people of the south could come with their slaves, and slavery would actually exist in Kansas. If once a considerable number of slaves were settled in Kansas, it would be very difficult to dislodge them. On the other hand if the free-state men secured the legislature, they would establish freedom by law. Pro-slavery men could come to Kansas still, but they would not dare bring their slaves. This would practically settle the question for freedom. The canvas, therefore, was a lively one, and all felt that the contest was vital. The pro-slavery people, however, carried on their canvas in Missouri. They were not disposed to trust to the doctrines of popular sovereignty, of which they had boasted. They proposed to go over and help settle the question. For weeks before the election, the border counties of Missouri were all astir. Meetings were held and flaming speeches made, and the excitement knew no bounds. There were secret societies, called Blue Lodges, in which the main purpose was to control Kansas for slavery. The members were bound together by pledges, and armed for the battle. The plan advocated in all these meetings was to have the members of these lodges march into Kansas on the day of election, take possession of the polls, and vote, and so get control of the legislature. They proposed to go in sufficient numbers to secure their end beyond all doubt, and they proposed to go thoroughly armed so as to overcome all resistance. They would depend on numbers and bluster and threats to carry the scheme through. The "plan of the campaign" was perfectly laid. It was arranged that bands of Missourians should enter every election district in Kansas, and enter in sufficient number to out-vote the settlers. Some of the speeches by which they "fired the southern heart," sound strange in these quieter days. General Stringfellow, in a speech at St. Joseph, said:

"I tell you to mark every scoundrel among you that is the least tainted with free-soilism or abolitionism, and exterminate him. I advise you, one and all, to enter every election district in Kansas, in defiance of Reeder and his vile myrmidons, and vote at the point of the bowie knife and revolver. Never give or take quarter from the rascals."

Every man was urged to go who could, and those who could not go themselves must contribute money to pay the expenses of those who did go.

When the day of the election arrived they marched into Kansas like an invading army. They came in large companies or in small squads, according to the size of the district they proposed to enter. It was not a movement of what would be called "the roughs," though they were rough enough. It had the sanction of the leading men of western Missouri. The leading spirit of the movement was David R. Atchison, who had served two terms in the United States Senate, and was one time acting vice-president of the United States. The company that came to Lawrence was led by Colonel Samuel Young, a leading lawyer of Boone county, and Claiborne F. Jackson. Colonel Young afterwards removed to Lawrence, and was very much respected—an able Lawyer and a cultured gentleman. Claiborne F. Jackson was governor of Missouri at the opening of the civil war. It was not a burst of ignorant passion, but the deliberate purpose of the leading men of Missouri and of the South. Kansas must be secured for slavery by fair means or foul. When men's deepest passions are stirred, it often happens that the cultivated and refined become as rough and brutal as the coarse and vulgar. They came to Lawrence one thousand strong, March 29th, the day before the election, and camped in the ravine near the town. The report of the congressional committee, which investigated the affair, gives a very vivid description of the scene at Lawrence:

"The evening before, and the morning of the day of the election, about one thousand men arrived at Lawrence, and camped in a ravine a short distance from the town, and near the place of voting. They came in wagons (of which there were over one hundred) or on horseback, under the command of Colonel Samuel Young, of Boone county, Missouri, and

Claiborne F. Jackson, of Missouri. They were armed with guns, rifles, pistols and bowie knives; and had tents, music and flags with them. They brought with them two pieces of artillery, loaded with musket balls.

"The evening before the election the Missourians were called together at the tent of Captain Claiborne F. Jackson, and speeches were made to them by Colonel Young and others, calling on volunteers to go to other districts where there were not Missourians enough to control the election, as there were more at Lawrence than were needed. On the morning of the election the Missourians came over to the place of voting from their camp, in companies, or bodies, of one hundred at a time. Mr. Blanton, one of the judges, not appearing, Colonel Young claimed that as the people of the territory had two judges, it was nothing more than right that the Missourians should have the other one to look after their interests. Robert A. Cummins was elected in Blanton's stead because he considered that every man had a right to vote if he had not been in the territory but an hour. The Missourians brought their tickets with them. Not having enough they had three hundred more printed in Lawrence the evening before and on the day of election. They had white ribbons in their buttonholes to distinguish them from the settlers.

"When the voting commenced, the question of the legality of the vote of a Mr. Page was raised. Before it was decided, Colonel Samuel Young stepped to the window where the votes were received, and said he would settle the matter. The vote of Mr. Page was withdrawn, and Colonel Young offered to vote. He refused to take the oath prescribed by the governor, but said he was a resident of the territory. He told Mr. Abbott, one of the judges, when asked if he intended to make Kansas his future home, that it was none of his business; if he were a resident then he should ask no more. After his vote was received, Colonel Young got upon the window sill and announced to the crowd that he had been permitted to vote, and they could all come up and vote. He told the judges that there was no use swearing the others, as they would all swear as he had. After the other judges had concluded to receive Colonel Young's vote, Mr. Abbott resigned as judge of election, and Mr. Benjamin was elected in his place.

"The polls were so much crowded till late in the evening that for a time they were obliged to get out by being hoisted up on the roof of the building, where the election was being held, and passing out over the house. Afterwards a passageway was made through the crowd by two lines of men being formed, through which voters could get to the polls. Colonel Young asked that the old men be allowed to go up first and vote, as they were tired with the traveling, and wanted to get back to camp. During the day the Missourians drove off the ground some of the citizens, Mr. Stearns, Mr. Bond and Mr. Willis. They threatened to shoot Mr. Bond, and made a rush after him, threatening him. As he ran from them, shots were fired at him as he jumped off the bank of the river and escaped."

The Missourians mostly started for home as soon as they had voted. A few remained till the next day. According to the census taken in February, the district contained 369 legal voters. The whole number of votes cast was 1,034. A careful examination of the poll lists showed that 232 of these were legal votes, while 802 votes were cast by non-residents. What was done in Lawrence was done everywhere, and while the census showed only 2,905 legal voters in the territory, there were 6,307 votes cast. It was a clean sweep, Missourians electing the entire legislature with one exception. There was no denial of the invasion, but the pro-slavery press boasted of it as a great victory. Abolition had been rebuked in its stronghold.

VIEWS OF LAWRENCE IN EARLY DAYS.

An appeal was made to Governor Reeder to set the election aside. He at first promised to do so, but his courage did not hold out. The pro-slavery people threatened his life if he ventured to go behind the returns. He was already beginning to feel that the administration at Washington was being alienated from him. He could not depend on their support. He contented himself, therefore, with ordering new elections for the districts that had entered protests. This could not accomplish anything as it still left the legislature in the hands of the men elected by imported votes. It did not lessen the hate of the pro-slavery people, and it did not take the power out of their hands. As is common with half measures, it pleased nobody and accomplished nothing.

The settlers hardly knew where to turn next when Governor Reeder failed them. It seemed for a time as if the case was closed. A pro-slavery legislature would enact pro-slavery laws, and they must live under them for at least two years. By that time slavery might be fastened on the territory beyond reversal. The southern papers boasted that now the abolitionists must either leave Kansas or consent to live in a slave state. The news of the outrage spread over the country on the wings of the lightning, and stirred the wildest excitement and indignation throughout the entire North. It was something that had no parallel in the history of the country. A body of invaders from another state had stolen a legislature, and there seemed to be no appeal.

But after the first shock was over the people began to inquire what they could do next. They had come to make Kansas free, and they were not the sort of people to be turned from their purpose by a single rebuff. What could they do to forestall the consummation of this great crime? They could not think of submitting to it, and allowing it to gain its end. Gradually the conviction grew that the legislature and its laws must be repudiated. The legislature had been elected by fraud, and could only be a fraudulent affair. It had been elected by citizens of Missouri in violation of all law, and by an outrage unparalleled. To submit to it would be to allow the crime to secure the fruit it sought. The whole country would justify them in taking such a position. Dr. Charles Robinson first suggested the policy of repudiation as soon as it was known that Governor Reeder would give them no effective relief. The suggestion seemed wild at first, but the more people thought about it the more it came into favor. Martin F. Conway had been elected to the legislature. In a letter to Governor Reeder he resigned his seat, and in doing this gave public expression to this policy of repudiation.

"Instead of recognizing this as the legislature of Kansas, and participating in its proceedings as such, I utterly repudiate it as derogatory to the respectability of popular government and insulting to the virtue and intelligence of the age. * * * Simply as a citizen and a man, I shall, therefore, yield no submission to this alien legislature. On the contrary, I am ready to set its assumed authority at defiance, and shall be prompt to spurn and trample under my feet its insolent enactments, whenever they conflict with my rights or my inclinations."

This all happened before the legislature had met, it being deemed important to repudiate the legislature itself as an imposition and a fraud, without regard to the laws it might enact. It was a fraud in itself. June 8th a convention was held in Lawrence to consider what they had begun to call the "bogus legislature." This convention provided for a larger convention to be held on the 25th of June. This second convention was large and represented nearly every settlement in the territory. Its sessions were protracted and its discussions very earnest. Its decisions shaped the policy of the free-state men for two years. The following are some of its resolutions:

"*Resolved*, That we are in favor of making Kansas a *free territory*, and as a consequence a *free state*.

"*Resolved*, That we urge the people of Kansas to throw aside all minor differences, and make the freedom of Kansas the only issue.

"*Resolved*, That we claim no right to meddle with the affairs of the people of Missouri, or any other state, and we do claim the right to regulate our own domestic affairs, and, with the help of God, we will do it.

"*Resolved*, That we look upon the conduct of a portion of the people of Missouri in the late Kansas election as an outrage on the elective franchise and our rights as freemen, and in as much as many of the members of the legislature owe their election to a combined system of force and fraud, we do not feel bound to obey any law of their enacting."

Dr. L. W. Spring in his history of Kansas says that "between the 8th of June and the 15th of August, 1855, seven conventions were held in the city of Lawrence, all but one in the interest of the policy of repudiation." It was essential that the policy should be well understood, and that free-state people should be a unit in the matter. It was a daring position to assume and a very difficult one to maintain, hence these frequent conventions for consultation. Thus the whole people came to understand the policy, and the whole people became united in upholding it.

For popular impression, perhaps, the celebration of the Fourth of July was more effective than these conventions. It was determined to celebrate it in fitting style in Lawrence. Great preparations were made and a large crowd assembled. Some people walked sixteen miles to attend. Two military companies had been organized and had been armed with Sharpe's rifles, and were out in uniform. The ladies presented them with a beautiful silk flag, amid great enthusiasm. Dr. Charles Robinson made the oration and used the occasion very adroitly to foster and defend the policy of repudiation, which he had been the first to suggest. He pictured the Missouri invasion and the capture of the legislature by nonresident voters in vivid terms, and denounced the outrage as something not to be endured. He declared that the people of Kansas would never submit to these invaders from a neighboring state.

"I can say to Death, be thou my master, and to the Grave, be thou my prison house; but acknowledge such creatures as my masters, never! Thank God, we are yet free, and hurl defiance at those who would make us slaves.

> "'Look who will in apathy, and stifle they who can,
> The sympathy, the hopes, the words, that make man truly man,
> Let those whose hearts are dungeoned up with interest or with ease,
> Consent to hear, with quiet pulse, of loathsome deeds like these.
>
> "'We first drew in New England's air, and from her hardy breast
> Sucked in the tyrant-hating milk that will not let us rest,
> And if our words seem treason to the dullard or the tame,
> 'Tis but our native dialect; our fathers spake the same.'

"Let every man stand in his place, and acquit himself like a man who knows his rights, and knowing, dares maintain. Let us repudiate all laws enacted by foreign legislative bodies, or dictated by Judge Lynch over the way. Tyrants are tyrants, and tyranny is tyranny, whether under the garb of law or in opposition to it. So thought and acted our ancestors, and so let us think and act. We are not alone in this contest. The whole nation is agitated upon the question of our rights. Every pulsation in Kansas pulsates to the remotest artery of the body politic, and I seem to hear the millions of freemen, and the millions of bondsmen in our own land, the patriots and philanthropists of all countries, the spirits of the revolutionary heroes, and the voice of God, all saying to the people of Kansas, 'Do your duty.'"

The speech and the occasion produced a profound impression not in Lawrence alone, but in all the territory. More than any one thing, perhaps, it helped to unify the people on the bold policy they had adopted, and which they maintained with unbroken front to the end of the conflict.

While all this was being done to bring people into harmony of thought in regard to the policy of repudiating what they called the "bogus legislature," the free-state leaders were preparing for the emergency in another way. They knew the pro-slavery leaders were desperate men, and bound to carry their point by any means, fair or foul. To repudiate their legislature, and their laws, would involve collisions, and possibly bloodshed and civil war. These men would not be thwarted now without a severe struggle. The free-state men must be prepared to meet force with force. As soon as the result of the March election was finally determined, the free-state leaders sent to their friends in the east for arms. George W. Deitzler was sent to Boston to lay the matter before the friends of free Kansas. Only two persons knew of the object of his mission. New arms were needed for self-defense. Amos A. Lawrence and others, before whom Mr. Deitzler presented the case, at once saw the seriousness of the situation. Within an hour after his arrival in Boston, he had an order for one hundred Sharpe's rifles, and in forty-eight hours the rifles were on their way to Lawrence. They were shipped in boxes marked "books." As the border ruffians had no use for books, they came through without being disturbed. A military company known for many years afterwards as the "Stubbs" was organized, and was armed with these rifles. Other boxes of "books" rapidly followed these, and other companies in Lawrence and in the country were armed with them. The fame of these guns went far and wide, and produced a very salutatory effect. They who recognized only brute force came to have a great respect for the Sharpe's rifles. A howitzer was procured in New York through the aid of Horace Greeley, and shipped to Lawrence. This howitzer played quite a part in the after struggle, and had a history of its own that some one familiar with it ought to write up.

Meanwhile the "bogus legislature," about which all this stir was being made, assembled and begun their work. They met at Pawnee July 2nd, but adjourned to Shawnee Mission, where they re-assembled July 12th. They excluded all those elected at Reeder's special election, and admitted all those chosen March 30th. There was only one free-state member left in the whole lot, and he soon became disgusted and left. They had things entirely their own way, and as they had been elected by Missouri votes, they proposed to "make Kansas in all respects like Missouri," as one of their number phrased it. To save time and toil, they adopted the Missouri code of laws, simply directing the clerk to make the necessary verbal changes to adapt it to Kansas. In the matter of slavery, however, they favored Kansas with special legislation. As slavery in Kansas was in peculiar danger, it must be protected by laws peculiarly searching and strong. In this matter they acted like men whose reason had left them. They enacted a slave code so absurdly severe that it would have been broken down of its own weight:

"SECTION 1. If any person shall entice, or decoy, or carry out of this territory, any slave belonging to another, * * * he shall be adjudged guilty of grand larceny, and on conviction thereof shall suffer death.

"SEC. 2. If any person shall aid or assist in enticing, carrying away, or sending out of the territory, any slave belonging to another, * * * he shall be adjudged guilty of grand larceny, and on conviction thereof suffer death.

"SEC. 3. If any person shall entice, decoy, or carry away out of any state or other territory of the United States, any slave belonging to another, * * * and shall bring such slave into this territory with the intent to procure the freedom of such slave, the person thus offending shall suffer death.

"SEC. 11. If any person shall print, write, publish, or circulate * * * within the territory any book, magazine, hand-bill or circular containing any statements, arguments, opinions, sentiments, doctrine, advice or inuendo calculated to promote a disorderly, dangerous or rebellious disaffection among the slaves in this territory, or to induce such slaves to escape from their masters, or to resist their authority, he shall be guilty of a felony, and be punished by imprisonment and hard labor for a term of not less than five years.

"SEC. 12. If any free person, by speaking or by writing, assert or maintain that persons have not the right to hold slaves in this territory, or shall introduce into this territory, print, publish, write or circulate, or shall cause to be introduced in this territory, any book, paper, magazine, pamphlet or circular containing any denial of the right of persons to hold slaves in this territory, such person shall be deemed guilty of felony, and punished by imprisonment at hard labor for a term of not less than two years."

If anything were needed to confirm the free-state men in their attitude towards the "bogus legislature," the conduct of the legislature itself furnished it. The outrageous invasion of March might have been forgotten if the legislature itself had been moderate and fair. But first of all they broke with Governor Reeder because he would not acceed to all of their demands. Then they purged themselves of free-state members wherever any pretext could be found for doing so. Then they enacted a slave code more severe than was found in the slave states themselves. By the twelfth section of that bill it was made a penitentiary offense to express an opinion adverse to slavery. Self-respecting free-state men must either leave the territory or repudiate such laws. As the legislature itself was elected by non-resident votes, they pronounced the whole concern a fraud, and repudiated the legislature and its laws. As the work of the legislature went on, the idea of repudiation was being matured. The numerous conventions in Lawrence grew more and more distinct in their tone as the spirit and work of the legislature became more and more manifest.

It has sometimes been asked what good was accomplished by this policy of repudiation? In reply it may be said, it practically nullified the laws passed by the usurping legislature. While these laws were not repealed, and were technically the laws of the territory, they were without effect. They were not respected by the people, and were only executed by force. This was particularly true of the laws regarding slavery. Whatever the courts might have decided as to the right to hold slaves in Kansas, no slave holders dared bring their slaves into the territory, while the laws protecting slavery were repudiated by two-thirds of the people. The result was that no slaves were brought into Kansas during the two years of excitement that followed. Riches take themselves wings and fly away, but this form of riches would be very apt to take themselves feet and run away. If the free-state men had acquiesced in this fraudulent legislature, and had submitted to its laws, those laws would have gone into full operation, and two years would have brought in a sufficient slave population to settle the question at issue. The policy of repudiation no doubt saved Kansas to freedom.

Along with the policy of repudiation another movement was set on foot as a sort of "companion piece." That was the movement for a state government. Whenever the policy of repudiation was mentioned, the first question was "what are you going to do next?" The answer was: "Form a state government and apply to congress for admission to the union." Other states had been received without an enabling act, and they proposed to plead these precedents. The matter was broached very early, and was probably in mind when the policy of repudiation was first suggested. It was at first distantly hinted at in the various conventions, and then boldly advocated. At the convention held at Lawrence, August 15, the subject was discussed, and was evidently the thought of most of the free-state men. A delegate convention was called to meet at Topeka, September 19th, to take steps toward forming a state government. This convention provided that members of a constitutional convention should be elected October 9th. There were over twenty-seven hundred votes cast at this election, and the convention thus chosen assembled at Topeka, October 23rd, and framed what was known as the Topeka Constitution. This constitution was the rallying point of the free-state men for two years.

No serious attempt was ever made to put this constitution in operation. It was sent to congress and adopted in the

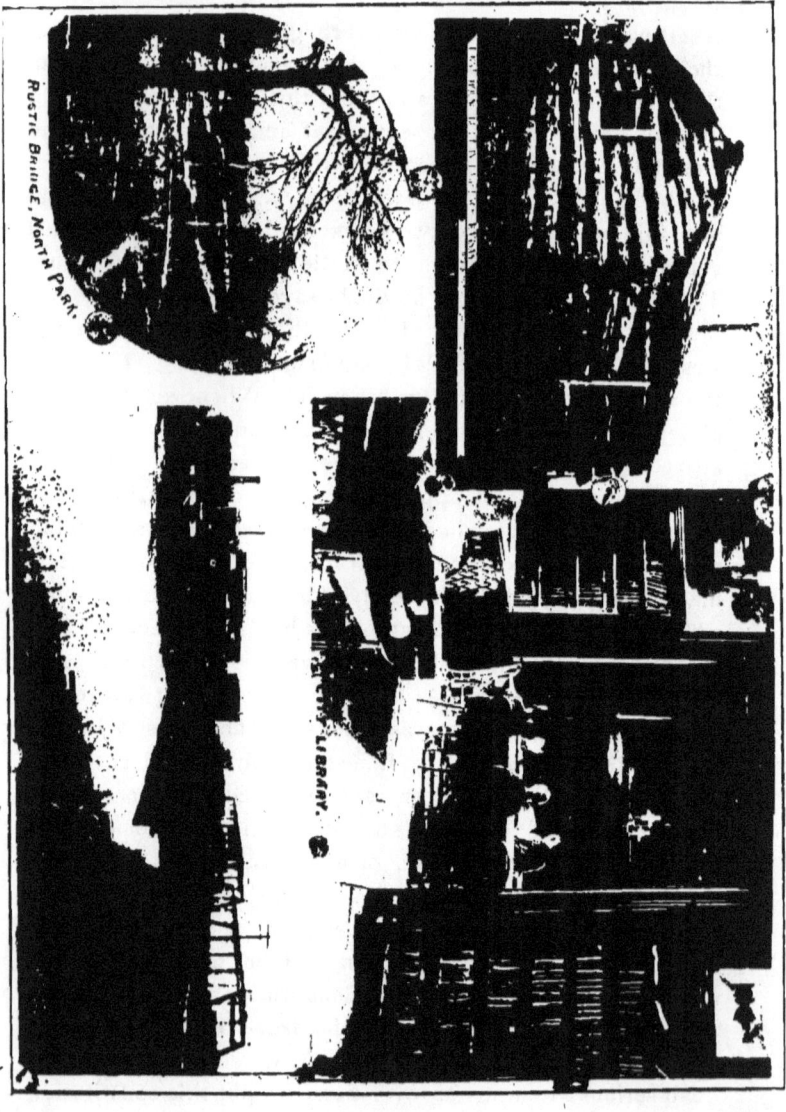

LAWRENCE: THE FIRST BUILDING, THE CITY LIBRARY, PARK, RIVER AND BRIDGE.

House but smothered in the Senate. The people of Kansas did not, however, abandon it. Though never in operation it was a vital part of their policy. It was the positive side of the policy which repudiated the bogus laws. Though the officers never took their seats, the whole movement served as a bond of union to the free-state men. As Hon. T. Dwight Thacher said at the quarter-centennial celebration at Topeka in 1866: "The Topeka Constitutional movement held the people together through a stormy period." "Without it the free-state forces must have drifted, been demoralized, and probably beaten."

The Shawnee legislature and the Topeka Constitution may not seem to belong to a sketch of the town of Lawrence, but they were so closely interwoven with all the after history that a great deal that happened in Lawrence during the next two years would not be intelligible without some knowledge of these more general events. Lawrence was the headquarters of the free-state party, and the center of the free movement. A good proportion of its early history could not be understood apart from that movement. The most exciting events in the history of the town were directly connected with the bogus laws, and the free-state policy respecting them.

Several other things happened this same summer which it is necessary to know in order to determine what occurred at Lawrence later on. As soon as it was found that Governor Reeder would not go the full length with the "bogus legislature," the pro-slavery leaders began to plan for his removal. They sent on complaints to Washington detailing their side of the controversy, and sent on their smoothest talkers to use their personal influence. The result was that Reeder was removed in less than a month from the meeting of the legislature, and ceased to act as governor August 15th. The secretary of the territory, Daniel Woodson, became acting governor, and signed all the laws which the legislature had passed. He

was in full sympathy with the pro-slavery party, and was as
eager as any of them to carry out their policy. Hon. Wilson
Shannon, of Ohio, was appointed governor, and arrived about
September 1st. He was an able man, and had been governor
of Ohio, minister to Mexico, and member of congress. He
was a man of character and was fair-minded, but he was in
full sympathy with the administration at Washington, and put
himself in the hands of the men in Kansas he supposed to be
the friends of the administration. This was unfortunate in
two respects. In the first place his own views of the situation
took a partisan coloring, and in the second place, the free-
state men were led to class him with their enemies, and very
naturally were suspicious of him and avoided him. He heard
only one side of the story. He knew nothing of the men on
the other side, or of the motives which governed them. He
entirely misjudged their character, and under-rated their
caliber. He allowed a reception in his honor at Westport
before he entered Kansas at all, and then had a formal reception at Shawnee Mission, in which the pro-slavery men and
pro-slavery policy was painted in glowing colors. Every
effort was made to commit him fully to the pro-slavery cause,
and to prejudice him against the free-state people. These
last were denounced as traitors, who had repudiated the laws
of the territory and who were ready to resist them whenever
an opportunity offered. The pro-slavery men called themselves the "law and order" party. They had gained control
of the legislature by illegal means, and then organized themselves into a "law and order" party to enforce the enactments
of this fraudulent legislature. The convention at which the
"law and order" party was formed chose Gov. Shannon for
its president. Thus he became more and more committed to
the one-sided policy which antagonized more than half the
people of the territory.

The people were divided into two very distinct parties with

antagonistic policies. The pro-slavery party was determined to enforce the laws passed by the Shawnee legislature. The free-state men repudiated that legislature and were determined never to recognize its enactments. The pro-slavery men had the forms of law, the officers of the law and the courts of law on their side, with the governor and national administration back of them. Their policy was to force a conflict and compel the free-state men either to recognize the bogus laws or resist them and suffer the penalty. Andreas, in his history, page 115, says:

"The law and order party were determined to bring the revolutionists to swift punishment as soon as overt acts should make them subject to the penalties prescribed for the violation of the laws. This was no easy matter, as they kept, as far as possible, aloof from the legal machinery devised for the government of the territory. They brought no suits into its courts; they attended no elections called by its authority; they paid no attention to its county organization; they offered no estates to its probate judges; they tried no causes and made no complaints before its justices of the peace; they paid no tax levies made by the authority of the late legislature. Yet they were careful to do no act which should lay them liable to the laws they contemned. They settled their disputes by arbitration, or by other means that might avoid litigation; they had town organizations and police regulations for the preservation of order; courts to settle squatters' claims; and all other appliances necessary for the regulation of small communities peaceably inclined. They could build, manufacture, buy and sell, establish schools and churches; but they would not be guilty of the crime of making Kansas a slave state."

This was emphatically the condition of things at Lawrence. The people were fully determined to repudiate the bogus laws, and were just as much determined not to violate them.

They would not recognize them, and they would not violate them. They would simply let them alone, and mind their own business. They would not incorporate the town under these laws. A citizens committee maintained a free school by voluntary contributions instead of taxes. Another committee looked after the good order and cleanliness of the place. They settled their disputes among themselves, and submitted to any inconveniences rather than appeal to the laws they repudiated. At the same time they were all particularly careful not to come in conflict with the laws, and to do nothing which might be construed into a violation of law. Being all intelligent and well disposed, and being also all of one mind, they did not have much trouble in carrying out this policy. They would have carried out this policy to the end if the other side had not been determined to force a conflict. They were watching for the slightest pretext to bring on a collision. The free-state men knew this. They knew that in spite of all their care a collision was bound to come sooner or later. While, therefore, they sought to avoid a conflict, they were prepared for it. As has been already said, several hundred Sharpe's rifles were procured early in the summer. Military companies were organized in Lawrence and in the country around about, and full preparations made for defense in case a conflict was forced upon them. Embankments were thrown up at exposed points and the town put in position to stand a siege.

CHAPTER IV.

THE CONFLICT BEGUN.—THE DOW MURDER.—THE BRANSON RESCUE.—SHERIFF JONES APPEALS TO THE GOVERNOR.—THE GOVERNOR CALLS OUT THE MILITIA.—MISSOURI RESPONDS TO THE CALL.—THE WAKARUSA WAR.—THE ARMY AT FRANKLIN.—PREPARATIONS FOR DEFENSE.

There was no serious trouble at Lawrence during the summer. There were many outrages in other parts of the territory. Where the sentiment was divided there were frequent collisions. Where pro-slavery sentiment was predominant free-state men were in constant peril. A man named Kelly was beaten nearly to death by a pro-slavery bully in Atchison. Rev. Pardee Butler, a preacher of the Christian Church, denounced the outrage in the streets of Atchison, and was siezed by a mob, his face was painted black, and he was bound upon a raft and sent floating down the Missouri river. He escaped after floating down a few miles. Some time afterwards he was siezed again. The mob were disposed to hang him, but finally were content to give him a coat of tar and feathers, and let him go. As these outrages and many more were approved by a large portion of the "law and order" party, no attempt was made to punish the perpetrators of them, although they were well known and made no attempt to conceal themselves or their crimes.

Thus far no difficulty had occurred at Lawrence such as the "law and order" party were waiting for. They were only watching for an opportunity to bring on a collision which would compel the citizens either to recognize or resist the laws of the bogus legislature. If they recognized those laws they would be humiliated; if they resisted them the whole force of the territorial government would be brought to bear to subdue them. But so wisely did they manage their repudiation that no occasion was given for interference. They simply ignored the laws and were a law unto themselves. The fact that the people of Lawrence were well armed and strongly entrenched, made the "law and order" people all the more careful to wait till they had a good case. They were thus compelled to wait till late in the autumn before the coveted opportunity came.

The occasion came at last, as all things come to those who wait. It was somewhat far-fetched, but it served the purpose. "It was not as wide as a church door, but it served." It all grew out of a claim dispute. Charles W. Dow and Franklin M. Coleman occupied adjoining claims at Hickory Point, about ten miles south of Lawrence. Dow was a free-state man and Coleman was a pro-slavery man. They quarreled about their claims and often had high words. The sympathy of the neighbors ran according to political affiliations. One day, November 21st, Dow was at Coleman's cabin, talking over the inevitable subject in the inevitable temper. As he started to go home, Coleman shot him dead in the road. That night Coleman fled to Westport, Missouri, and was protected by his pro-slavery friends. The cold-blooded murder naturally produced great indignation among the free-state men. They held a meeting a day or two after to express their indignation, and to devise means to bring the murderer to justice. The meeting was composed mainly of friends and neighbors of Dow, who occupied claims as he did and were exposed to similar treatment. Very naturally they expressed themselves strongly, and were not in a mood to be trifled with. Among these neighbors and friends was an old man named Jacob Branson. Dow lived in the same cabin with him, and Branson thought a great deal of Dow. Branson was a quiet, peaceable man, who never made anybody any trouble. But the brutal murder of his friend stirred the quiet depths of his nature, and he expressed his indignation without stint. He said "if I could draw a bead on Coleman with his rifle, he would not breathe the pure air of this planet another minute."

One of the friends of the murderer Coleman, named Buckley, professed to be greatly alarmed at the violent tone of the meeting, and especially at the violent expressions of Jacob Branson. He claimed that his life was in danger, and he swore out a warrant for Branson's arrest. The warrant was put in the hands of Samuel J. Jones, who had been appointed by the Shawnee legislature as Sheriff of Douglas county.

Jones was one of the characters of those times. He was postmaster of Westport, Missouri, and did not live in Kansas. He had identified himself with her interests, however, by leading a company from Missouri to vote on the memorable thirtieth of March. He went to Bloomington, and led his company in, taking possession of the ballot box of that precinct. He was a mixture of courage and cowardice, of bold bravado and obsequiousness. No appointment could have been more offensive and insulting to the people of Douglas county. He was appointed on purpose to insult and humiliate them, and to provoke them to some sort of resistance that might warrant an attack upon them. The people of Douglas county had got even with their persecutors thus far by so keeping the peace or arranging their disputes among themselves, that they had never called for the services of the obnoxious sheriff. His office seemed in danger of being lost in "innocuous dissuetude." To this man the murderer had fled, and had been taken into custody by him, not for punishment but for protection from the people he had outraged.

At last the day came when he could be avenged on the people of Douglas county who so thoroughly despised him. The warrant for the arrest of Branson was put in his hands to serve. On the night of November 26th he took some fifteen men and went to Branson's house to arrest him. It was about eleven o'clock when they arrived at the cabin. They knocked at the door, but before any reply could be made, they burst the door open and rushed in. They dragged Branson out of his bed, and made him dress himself in a hurry. Mrs. Branson demanded their authority but they told her they would attend to that. They took Branson out, placed him on a mule, and started for Lecompton by the way of Lawrence. Mrs. Branson felt sure they would kill her husband as soon as they had him fully in their power.

The free-state men in the neighborhood were advised of the writ for Branson's arrest. They had grounds to fear that he would be disposed of as soon as Jones and his posse got him in their hands. When they heard of the intended arrest, a number of them came together determined to rescue Branson if possible before he could be harmed. The rescue was arranged and conducted by Major J. B. Abbott, a man who lived in the neighborhood, a brave man and a man of prominence for many years afterwards. He was assisted by S. N. Wood, of Lawrence, who had come from the same section of Ohio as the murdered man, Dow. Wood was one of the characters of the times, a man of infinite nerve, and as calm and cool in such a matter as he would be in any common affair. There were two others present who lived in Lawrence, Samuel F. Tappan and Samuel C. Smith. The rest were all neighbors of Branson, living on farms near his. By eleven o'clock some fifteen men had gathered at Abbott's house to attempt to save Branson. They were armed with all sorts of weapons. Some of them had rifles; some of them had shotguns; and some of them had pistols. They had come with anything they hapened to have in the house. One or two had no weapons whatever. One of these picked up two large stones which he clutched in his hands in a way which showed his intensity of purpose, and illustrated the determination of the whole company.

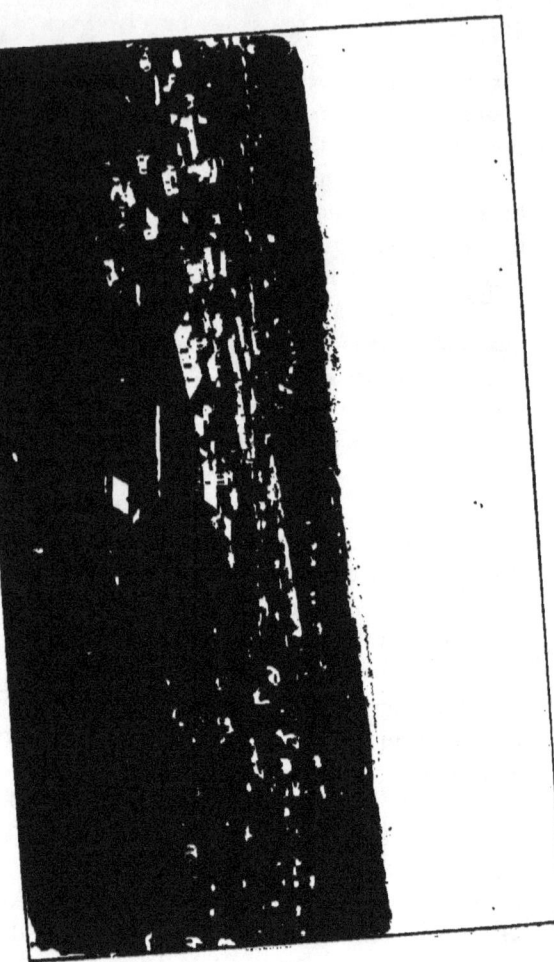

LAWRENCE IN 1866.

This view, taken from the north point of Mt. Oread in 1866, shows the city as it looked then. The building of most prominence shown in the picture will be recognized as the Central School. In the block opposite are distinguished the Presbyterian Churches of which was just completed. the Old and New Schools, the business portion and North Lawrence in the distance.

They hardly knew what to do or which way to go. It was entirely uncertain what road Jones and his party would take, and in the night it was impossible to see them any distance. But while they were wondering what to do, some one burst into the house and said: "They are coming." S. N. Wood, one of the party, wrote a vivid account of the rescue a short time after.

"Pell-mell we rushed out of the house and got into the road ahead of them. They halted within two rods of us. A moment was passed in silence when one of their party said: 'What's up?' Abbott asked, 'Is Branson there?' Branson replied, 'Yes, I am here, a prisoner.' S. N. Wood said, 'If you want to be among your friends come over here.' One of their party said, 'If you move we will shoot you.' Said Wood, "Come on, let them shoot if they want to. If you shoot, not a man of you will leave alive.' Branson attempted to ride to us; he was on a mule. 'Whose mule is that?' 'Their's.' 'Get off and let it go.' Wood left the ranks, kicked the old mule and told it to go back to its friends. Arms were aimed and cocked on both sides, but just as Branson left the ranks, one of the opposite party lowered his gun with the remark: 'I aint going to shoot.' Jones then advanced on horseback, said his name was Jones, that he was sheriff of Douglas county, that he had a warrant to arrest old man Branson, and he must serve it. He was told, 'we knew no Sheriff Jones; we know a postmaster at Westport, Missouri, by that name but we knew no Sheriff Jones.' Jones still said he had a warrant to arrest Branson and he must do it. S. N. Wood said he was Branson's attorney, and if he had a warrant to arrest him he wanted to see it, and see if it was all right. Jones said he had it, but refused to show it. Wood asked if it had been read or shown to Branson. Jones admitted that it had not. He was told that until he produced the warrant, Branson could not go with him. At least an hour was spent in parleying, when Jones and his company bid us good night and rode away."

The rescue occurred near Blanton's bridge, some five miles south of Lawrence. The rescuing party were all from the neighborhood, except three who were from Lawrence. The rescue occurred at about one o'clock in the morning, some two hours after the arrest. It was afterwards learned that Jones and his party had spent the intervening time at the house of a pro-slavery man, rejoicing at their success. They honored the event in the approved border ruffian style, drinking whiskey and carousing.

After Jones had gone the rescuers were in a quandary. They had Branson, but were puzzled to know what to do next. They began to realize that the situation was serious. They had taken a prisoner out of the hands of an officer of the law. Jones and his friends would make the most of it. It added fuel to fire already kindled, and furnished him the occasion he had been seeking so long to make an onslaught on the free-state men, and either compel them to recognize the bogus laws under which he held his appointment, or else actually resist them and expose themselves to the penalties. The company of rescuers at once discussed the situation. They knew this was not the end, and was probably only the beginning. They at once decided to go into Lawrence and tell the story to Dr. Charles Robinson, whose cool head and clear sense were always relied upon in times of real difficulty.

They reached Lawrence in the gray of the morning, and proceeded at once to Dr. Robinson's house. Mrs. Robinson, in her book written soon after, describes the appearance of the men as they drew up before the house in the morning twilight.

"I shall never forget the appearance, in simple citizens dress, some armed and some unarmed, standing in unbroken line, just visible in the breaking light of a November morning. The little band of less than twenty men had walked ten miles since nine o'clock the previous evening. Mr. Branson, a large man of fine proportions, stood a little forward of the line, with his head slightly bent, which an old straw hat hardly protected from the cold, looking as though in his hurry of departure from home he took whatever came first."

As soon as Dr. Robinson came to the window they told him their story. They set before him all the details of the arrest and the rescue, and of the threats Jones had made on being foiled of his purpose. After a few minutes thought the doctor replied to them. He said in effect that it was a serious affair, and would no doubt be used by their foes as a pretext for attacking Lawrence, and if possible destroying it. They had only been waiting for an occasion, and this would furnish it. A prisoner taken from the hands of the officers of the law would be called an insurrection. The militia would be called out ostensibly to sustain the officers, really to destroy Lawrence. There was but one thing now to be done. The affair had occurred several miles from Lawrence. Only three Lawrence men were concerned in it, and they were on their own responsibility. The people of Lawrence knew nothing about it. They could not be held responsible for an act of which they did not know until several hours after its occurrence. The perpetrators must take care of themselves and keep out of the way. If Jones and his posse came to the town to make arrests they would simply find no one to arrest. They must find the men who committed the deed and arrest them. At a meeting of citizens later in the morning Robinson's views were endorsed. It was the universal opinion that as the town of Lawrence, as such, had nothing to do with the affair, its citizens could not be held responsible for it.

The meeting appointed a committee of safety who were empowered to defend the town in case any attack was made. Everyone felt very certain that it would not be long before the services of the committee would be called for. Dr. Robinson was placed at the head of the committee, and they proceeded at once to put the town in a condition for defense. Thus far Lawrence had not been identified with the affair. A resolution approving the rescue was rejected.

The events which followed seemed to indicate that the whole thing was a plot. The arrest of Branson was made on purpose to provoke a rescue. Branson had committed no crime. He had simply denounced the murder of a member of his family. The whole country was excited about the murder. The arrest of Branson would inflame them to a fever heat. Jones proposed to take him through Lawrence. After making the arrest he waited two hours at a pro-slavery man's house to give time for the news to get out. When confronted by an equal number, poorly armed, he surrendered his prisoner without firing a shot, simply muttering vengeance. It was just what he was waiting for. A prisoner had been taken by force from the officers of the law. They had repudiated the laws before; now they had resisted them and overcome the officers of the law. It was a trap and the free-state men had fallen into it.

Jones lost no time in making the most of his opportunity. He went to Franklin, a little pro-slavery settlement four miles east of Lawrence. Thence he sent out his dispatches. His first dispatch was sent to Colonel A. G. Boone at Westport, Missouri, and his second to the governor. The governor must call out the militia, but Colonel Boone must furnish the men from Missouri. Hence it was important that the Missouri allies should be advised as soon as possible. The dispatches narrated the particulars of the rescue in extravagant terms, and claimed that there was an organized effort to resist the laws. He needed three thousand men to assist him in making arrests of criminals who were hiding from justice and were being protected by armed men in

Lawrence. Governor Shannon at once issued a proclamation declaring the free-state men in rebellion and calling out the militia of the territory to aid in the enforcement of the laws. In his order to General Richardson he said the laws had been resisted and that there was an armed force at Lawrence in open rebellion. He had been advised that houses had been burned in Douglas county and whole families turned out onto the open prairie. Sheriff Jones had warrants for the men who were committing these crimes, but he needed three thousand men to enable him to execute these warrants. He ordered General Richardson to collect as large a force as possible, and proceed without delay to Lecompton and report to S. J. Jones, sheriff of Douglas county, "and render him all the aid in your power in the execution of any legal process in his hands."

But the "Kansas militia" did not respond in very large numbers. It was not expected that they would. The call had to be made to the Kansas militia, but the Missouri militia was expected to do the most of the responding. While all the public proclamations were made to the Kansas militia, secret means were taken to secure a large force from Missouri. Daniel Woodson, the secretary of the territory, sent a private note to an official in Jefferson City, asking him "to call out the Platte County Rifles; but whatever you do, do not implicate the governor." In all these secret notes they add, "Do not compromise the governor." The proslavery press made frantic appeals and published the wildest accounts of the situation in Kansas.

The Missourians were already organized, and company after company moved towards Lawrence. There were four hundred men from Jackson county and an equal number were called out from Weston and St. Joseph. While, therefore, the Kansas militia responded only in small numbers, their lack of zeal was more than made good by the readiness of these

Missouri friends to rally to the defense of law and order in the neighboring territory. They seemed as eager to come up and restore order as they had been to come and vote a few months before. They seemed ready to do any sort of service for the new-comers. They had furnished a legislature to make their laws for them, and now they were ready to furnish an army to enforce those laws. Of the hundreds of armed men, therefore, who responded to the call for the "Kansas militia," all but fifty or so came from over the line.

None of these men who were so eager to subdue rebellion thought it worth while to inquire if there was any rebellion, or any resistance. Even the governor in calling out the militia, had not thought it worth while to inquire whether the statements on which he based that call had any foundation. As a matter of fact there had been no general resistance to the execution of the laws. The rescue of Branson was a solitary case, and belonged to the neighborhood where it occurred. There had never been any resistance in Lawrence, and there would not have been. Sheriff Jones could have come into Lawrence at any time, and made any arrests for which he had any legal authority. He was several times in Lawrence alone while he was making these extensive preparations to subdue the town. No one had any thought of molesting him, or interfering with him. But he was determined to force a conflict and humiliate the place, if not destroy it.

The Missouri allies were not slow in coming to the aid of their friends in Kansas. They were just "spoiling for a fight," and were waiting for a call. They came from all directions and in all ways; in companies, squads and singly. They only wanted a chance to "wipe out" that "abolition nest" at Lawrence. In a day or two some fifteen hundred men had gathered at Franklin, and along the Wakarusa, just clamoring to be led up to the hated town. They claimed to be acting as territorial militia though confessedly from Missouri. They had been organized and drilled at home and were all ready for the fray. It was much easier than to raise and equip a force in Kansas. The militia of Kansas was a myth while that of Missouri was a stubborn fact—very stubborn, it might be added. A force from pro-slavery Missouri would be more ready to do the bidding of the pro-slavery leaders than any that could be organized in Kansas. They camped mostly at Franklin, while detachments were stretched along the line of the Wakarusa. They expected to be led at once to Lawrence, but as they drew nearer they were disposed to hesitate. They had heard large stories about the Sharpe's rifles with which they understood the Yankees were armed. The rapidity with which they could be discharged and loaded, the great range at which they could do execution, and the terrible havoc of their bullets, had been told them in all degrees of exaggeration. William A. Phillips, correspondent of the New York *Tribune*, visited the camp. He claimed to be a mere traveler going through the country to see what was to be seen. He engaged them in conversation, and they became quite communicative. They were very anxious to know about those Sharpe's rifles. He told them they were "loaded by machinery," and told them they could be fired "ten times a minute." They asked him how far they would carry. He said he did not believe all the stories about them. There were a great many big yarns afloat about the guns. He did not believe they would carry a ball much more than a mile with any degree of accuracy. So the story went around the camp that there were a thousand men in Lawrence, armed with these terrible guns, which were "loaded by machinery, and would kill a man a mile away." The rumor did not tend to hasten an attack.

But they kept up their bluster and their threats. Whenever their courage flagged at hearing such stories as we have referred to, they could always get their courage renewed at so much a flask. If their personal courage failed, the artificial kind was plentiful, and served their purpose just as well so long as no enemy was in sight. They soon invested Lawrence, guarding all the fords of the Wakarusa, and having a camp to the west on the Lecompton road. They ransacked the country for supplies, and corn cribs and hen coops suffered severely from the nightly attacks of these brave men. They kept the whole country in a state of terror, and many people abandoned their homes and sought safety in town. The attack on Lawrence, however, was still delayed. Every day they clamored to be led up against the devoted place, but every day, for one reason and another, they decided to wait till morning. These whiskey soaked heroes were fond of telling the affrightened women and children what they were going to do when they "once got into Lawrence." But every night they came back to camp, and Lawrence was spared "just one day more."

The besieged meanwhile had not been idle. They knew the Branson rescue would be used as a pretext for calling the Missourians in to harrass and humiliate the free-state men. The committee of safety began to arrange for the defense of the town. The free-state men all over the territory became aware of the situation, and the various military companies came in to help their friends in Lawrence. About five hundred men came in thus from various points. It was not an easy matter to feed such a multitude. As in an earlier emergency, they had pretty much "all things common." The most unfortunate were those who had something. All the resources of the place had to be put under contribution. Dr. Spring in his history says of this time:

"There was a general observance of decorum and order. Most of the citizens made a virtue of necessity, and contributed freely what must have been rudely confiscated. In a

VIEW OF LAWRENCE IN 1895 FROM ROOF OF OPERA HOUSE.

single instance a little outbreak of violence occurred, expending itself in the sack of a small tailor shop. One night during the siege, according to the story of a clerk, about twenty men, armed with revolvers, invaded the premises, and extinguished the candle by firing a tobacco box at it. 'Before I could light a candle,' the clerk continued, 'everything in the store was taken from the shelves and carried away.' A young woman who had the misfortune to keep a hotel, the Cincinnati House, in Lawrence during the impecunious era of the siege, wrote a few days after its close: 'It looked strange to see the street paraded from morning to night by men in military array; to see them toil day and night throwing up entrenchments, to see them come in to their meals, each with a gun in his hand, sometimes bringing it to the table. How we toiled to feed the multitude, seldom snatching a moment to look on the strange scene and often asking, what are the prospects today.'"

The Free-State Hotel was not finished, but it was used for military purposes, and was made quite comfortable as headquarters. Several of the companies used it as a "barracks" for the accommodation of the "army." The soldiers spent their time during the day in throwing up earth works at the most exposed points. These earth works were circular, and some of them one hundred feet in diameter. The largest was at the crossing of Massachusetts and Pinckney streets, a little east of where the jail now stands. This was intended as a place of refuge for the women and children in case of an assault. It was built of hewn timbers, banked up with earth, and a deep trench dug all round it. It was five feet high. Another was at the crossing of Massachusetts and Henry streets. A third was near New Hampshire street, north of Henry. Two others were west of Massachusetts street, one of them on Kentucky street commanding the ravine. The enclosure at Massachusetts and Henry streets was arranged for cannon. Each of these defenses was in charge of an officer, and had a contingent of troops assigned to its defense. Thus the little community was entrenched on every side, and everything made ready for whatever might occur. There were fully six hundred men within the entrenchments, and two hundred or more were armed with Sharpe's rifles. In the afternoon of each day there was parade and drill, with band playing and flags flying from all the principal points. Towards evening there would be a general gathering, and different persons would exercise the inalienable right of an American citizen and make a speech. After others had spoken Jim Lane would be called out, and would work the crowd up to the fighting point. Then Dr. Robinson would come forward and calm the frenzy and advise moderation and patience. To "suffer and be strong" was a favorite phrase with him. As night came on the "guard was mounted," and every approach to the town had its sentinel. These sentinels were posted in the outskirts and sometimes reached almost down to the enemy's line. It was not uncommon for the pickets of the two armies to meet. William A. Phillips, in his "Conquest of Kansas," gives an instance of this kind:

"One night when the free-state patrol approached the forks of the road where they were ordered to go, they met the enemy's patrol about twenty strong. One or two officers of the general's staff had volunteered that night, and General George W. Dietzler was in command of the guard. As they approached the place the leader of the enemy's guard shouted,

"'Halt! Who goes there? Give the countersign.'

"'We have no countersign for you. We are the Lawrence guard.'

"'The Lawrence guard will file to the left,' said the border ruffian chief, and his own command drew off the road while we filed by them. The two companies thus passed each other, there being little more than the road between them."

The guards were under strict orders to avoid a conflict. If there was to be any fighting, the other side must take all the responsibility of it. As the border ruffians tried every way to provoke a quarrel, this policy was sometimes quite exasperating. But it was evidently the wiser as well as the more humane policy.

In the day time there was less strictness. People came and went very much as they pleased. Many members of the other camp came into town at different times. Sheriff Jones himself was often in town, and was never interfered with. He made no attempts to make any arrests. He doubtless would have been glad if there had been violence offered him, as that would give him a new occasion for calling in his friends from Missouri to help him. There was policy in thus allowing these officers free access to the town. The excuse Sheriff Jones gave for calling out the militia was that he could not serve a writ in Lawrence, and that he needed three thousand men to assist him. Yet he and other officers could come into the town freely, and never were molested. The troops had been given him for a specified purpose, to aid him in making arrests. But there was no thought of resisting any arrest he might attempt to make. If he could only provoke the free-state men to violence he would have a case. But they steadily refused to be provoked, so they spoiled his case every time.

During the progress or the "siege" it was learned that a twelve pounder howitzer had arrived at Kansas City for Lawrence. Captain Thomas Bickerton and two young men named Buffam went to Kansas City with teams to bring it up. When they arrived at Kansas City they found the commission merchant cross and unaccommodating. He wanted to know what was in the boxes before he would let them go out of his warehouse. One of the Buffam boys took an axe and broke into one of the boxes and said he believed it was a carriage. The merchant looked into the opening and saw the wheels, and was satisfied. The men then loaded their wagon with the "goods," and started for Leavenworth across the Delaware reserve. When they had crossed the Kansas river, they found the bluff leading up to Wyandotte very steep, and their heavily loaded wagons were "stuck." A company of border ruffians passed by, and they asked them to help. They said they were on their way to Leavenworth with goods, and the hill was too steep for their teams. Leavenworth being a good pro-slavery town all suspicion was removed, and the men put their shoulder to the wheels, and helped the Yankees up the hill with their cannon. As soon as they were well out of the Delaware reserve, they turned up the Lawrence road and made the best time they could towards the beleaguered city. When they drew near, word was sent to the free-state leaders, and twenty armed men were sent out to meet them, and the whole outfit was brought safely into town.

About the same time it was feared the ammunition would run short. There was a lot of powder and ammunition for Sharpe's rifles at the house of a free-state man on the Santa Fe road. The problem was how to get it into town. At last two ladies, Mrs. S. N. Wood and Mrs. G. W. Brown, offered to get it. They went out in a buggy and were not molested. After reaching their destination they stowed the powder and caps and other things among their clothing and started back. The ruffian pickets were too gallant to molest ladies, and allowed them to pass the lines, and they brought their load triumphantly into town. The ladies helped in many other ways besides feeding the multitudes. Thus the whole population joined in the defense. There was nothing else to be done, and nothing else was done. The siege began about December 1st and continued about a week. The general response of free-state men everywhere to "help Lawrence" was very encouraging. They had come from all parts and in every conceivable manner, on foot, on horseback and in wagons; singly and in squads and companies. Companies came in from Bloomington, Palmyra, Ottawa Creek, Osawatomie and Topeka. The coming of a well armed company from Topeka was the occasion of great enthusiasm and a source of much encouragement. Localities were forgotten in the common danger. To let Lawrence fall was to expose all these settlements to a similar fate. It was one of those events which helped to bind the free-state men together, and prepare them the better for the long conflict that was coming. No matter where they lived they were all here for a common purpose, and they worked together to a common end. They began to understand the gravity of the conflict, but no one was inclined to draw back. The more serious the conflict the more firm was their resolve. "Their courage rose with danger."

CHAPTER V.

GOVERNOR SHANNON ALARMED.—TELEGRAPHS THE PRESIDENT FOR REGULAR TROOPS.—THEY DO NOT COME.—THE GOVERNOR VISITS LAWRENCE—CONFERS WITH THE FREE-STATE MEN.—A TREATY OF PEACE.—THE MILITIA GO HOME.—A LOVE FEAST AT LAWRENCE.—THE MURDER OF BARBER.—OLD JOHN BROWN.

Governor Shannon soon began to see that he had raised a storm that he could not control. He had called out the militia to aid Sheriff Jones in enforcing the laws. But no resistance had ever been offered to any regular legal process. Jones often went through Lawrence, and could have served any legal writ he might have. There never had been any resistance in Lawrence. The rescue of Branson had occurred several miles from Lawrence. The citizens of Lawrence knew nothing of it. When Governor Shannon called out the Kansas militia the response came from Missouri. Of the fifteen hundred men camped at Franklin not over two hundred were from Kansas. They had come, too, for a purpose of their own. They had come to destroy Lawrence. They were eager to make an attack. They clamored to be led out to battle. They would have raised the black flag and marched without orders had they not conceived a wholesome fear of the Sharpe's rifles with which the defenders of the town were armed. They were a lawless lot, many of them. They roved about the country committing depredations, and a collision between the two opposing forces was liable to occur any day. The picket lines confronted each other, and a stray shot might at any time precipitate a conflict. Only the firm determination of the free-state men not to give any possible excuse for violence prevented serious results. Governor Shannon saw something of the danger and was anxious for a settlement. General L. J. Eastin, editor of the Leavenworth *Herald* and commander of the northern brigade of the Kansas militia, wrote to the governor. He told him "the outlaws," as he called them, were strongly intrenched at Lawrence and were well armed. They had cannons and Sharpe's rifles, and numbered about a thousand men. It was not going to be easy to dislodge them. The militia was disorganized and poorly armed. He advised the governor to call on the authorities at Fort Leavenworth for government troops. This might overawe "the outlaws" and prevent bloodshed. The governor at once telegraphed the president, stating the condition of things, and asking authority to call on the regular troops at Fort Leavenworth. He sent a dispatch also to Colonel E. V. Sumner, who was in command at the fort, to hold himself in readiness to march at once on receipt of orders from Washington. Colonel Sumner replied, under date of December 1st, as follows:

"I do not feel that it would be right in me to act in this important matter until orders are received from the government. I shall be ready to move instantly when I receive them. I would respectfully suggest that you make your application extensively known at once, and that you countermand any orders that may have been given the militia until you receive the answer."

The colonel seemed to understand wherein the real danger lay. The real danger lay in the lawlessness of the "posse" which Sheriff Jones had gathered about him at Franklin. The governor accepted the suggestion. He wrote to Jones ordering him to refrain from any attempt to serve writs until the answer should come from Washington. But Jones did not relish the idea of submitting his action to the inspection of such a man as Colonel Sumner. He knew that he had no case which would stand for a moment in the eyes of a clearheaded, fair-minded man like him. He replied to the governor from the "Camp at Wakarusa," under the date of December 3rd, that the volunteer forces at that point and at Lecompton were growing weary of inaction. He feared that they would remain but a few days longer unless a demand was made for the prisoner. He thought he should have a sufficient force to serve the writs by the next day. He was not disposed to disobey the governor's order, but he really thought the demand should be made just as soon as a sufficient force had been collected to enforce it. He added that the force at Lawrence was not nearly as strong as had been reported. He said he had sixteen writs to serve against persons in Lawrence. He could not give all the names as the writs were in his office at Lecompton. He said he had heard that the men who had aided in the rescue of Branson had been run out of town and probably could not be found.

Governor Shannon received word from Washington that orders would be sent to Fort Leavenworth putting the United States troops there at his disposal. He was anxious Colonel Sumner should not wait for the formal orders, but move at once on the strength of his information. But Colonel Sumner refused to move until the orders were actually received. The orders never came and Colonel Sumner did not move. It has never been known why the orders promised by the president were never sent. Governor Robinson, in his "Conflict," suggests the most probable explanation. Jefferson Davis was secretary of war. The pro-slavery leaders were anxious to bring about a conflict in Kansas. Technically the law was on their side, and the power was on their side. A conflict would embarrass and perhaps crush the free-state movement. Jefferson Davis doubtless knew the situation and was in the secret of the pro-slavery counsels. He therefore never sent the orders which had been promised by the president.

While this was going on, the committee of safety at Lawrence were not idle. They wished to avoid a conflict, although

ABRAM WILDER.   OLIVER BARBER.

LYMAN ALLEN.   WESLEY DUNCAN.

EARLY KANSAS PIONEERS.

they were preparing for it. So long as the two armies lay side by side a conflict might occur at any hour. They knew that the governor had been misinformed and that there was no just reason for assembling so large a force on their borders. It was a continual menace and peril. They determined to lay the case before the governor, and appeal to him for protection. They wrote to the governor, therefore, and sent the letter by a select committee consisting of G. P. Lowry and C. W. Babcock.

"*To His Excellency, Wilson Shannon, Governor of Kansas Territory:*

"SIR: As citizens of Kansas territory we desire to call your attention to the fact that a large force of armed men from a foreign state have assembled in the vicinity of Lawrence, and are now committing depredations upon our citizens, stopping wagons, opening and appropriating their loading, arresting, detaining and threatening travelers upon the public road, and that they claim to do this by your authority. We desire to know if they *do* appear by your authority, and if you will secure the peace and quiet of the community by ordering their instant removal, or compel us to resort to some other means and to higher authority."

(Signed by the committee.)

It was no easy matter to reach Governor Shannon. All the roads were guarded and all lines of communication closed. Lowry and Babcock had to work their way through the lines of the border ruffians as best they could. They were halted several times and detained, but they were equal to the emergency. Each time they beguiled the pickets and were allowed to pass on. At last they reached the governor at Shawnee, and presented him their letter. Their interview is set forth in G. P. Lowry's testimony before the congressional committee.

"We got to Shawnee Mission a little after sunrise, and presented our letter to Governor Shannon. * * * Governor Shannon said that he would answer the letter, and we went out while he was doing so. When we returned we had a long conversation about these affairs. The governor said there had been sixteen houses burned by free-state men, and women and children driven out of doors. We told him we were sorry he had not taken the pains to inquire into the truth of the matter before he had brought this large force into the country, which perhaps he could not get out again; that this information was wholly false, and nothing of the kind had happened. We told him what we knew of our personal knowledge, of men from Missouri being there. He was not inclined at first to admit that there was anybody from Missouri there. He made a general argument against the free-state men, and quoted their resolutions passed at different meetings in regard to the territorial laws. We explained to him that the territorial laws had nothing to do with this case. We were getting ready at Lawrence to fight for our lives, and the only question was whether he would be a *particeps criminis* to our murder, or the murder of somebody else, if we should all be slaughtered. We explained to him that the rescue, upon which he based his proclamation, took place a number of miles from Lawrence; that there were but three persons living in Lawrence who had anything to do with it, and they had left the town and were not there at all; that from what we could judge from the force at Wakarusa, at Lecompton, and in the country about, from their own declarations, they intended to destroy the town for a thing in which they had no part or parcel.

"We took our own individual cases as instances. We had not been present at the rescue; we did not undertake to have any sympathy with it, or talk about it at all. But if we submitted to the force which he had called in, all our throats would be cut together—the innocent and the guilty—if there were any guilty.

"He denied that these Missourians were here by his authority; that he had anything to do with them, or was responsible for them. He said he had communicated with Colonel Sumner at Fort Leavenworth, and had sent an express for him to meet him that night at Delaware Ferry, and go with him to the camp on the Wakarusa. He said he should go to Lawrence and insist upon the people obeying the laws and deliver up their Sharpe's rifles. We denied his right, or the right of anybody else, to make any such condition of a community, or make any such demand of them, until it had been shown that they had resisted the laws, which they had not done. There had as yet been no proceedings in Lawrence under the territorial laws. He had no right to presume that there would be any resistance to them when they were instituted. He gave up that point after some argument. I asked him why he insisted on the giving up of the Sharpe's rifles, and if he intended to demand, too, western rifles, shot guns and other arms. He said he did not intend to demand other than Sharpe's rifles, but he intended to demand them because they were an unlawful weapon. After some time he said they were dangerous weapons, to which I agreed. I then told him if he had any such ideas in his head as that, he had better stay away and let the fight go on. I thought the thing was not feasible, and he would do no good by coming here, if those were his terms. I told him he might as well demand of me my pocket-book, or my watch; and I would resent the one no more than the other. I told him I did not consider myself safe, or that General Robinson or Colonel Lane would be safe, in going before our people with any such proposition.

"He then gave us the letter and we started to Kansas City to change horses."

Governor Shannon now began to "see men, as trees, walking." He saw at least that he had acted without investigating the grounds of his actions. The rumors of free-state outrages he had accepted as true. He now found they were false. He had called a great army to enforce laws which had not been resisted. Whatever the people of Lawrence had said about the territorial laws, they had not resisted them, for no attempt had been made to put them into operation. They certainly had not merited extinction at the hands of a mob, and they were only doing what any set of men would do: defending their lives. He saw that his hasty proclamation had brought a lot of Missourians into Kansas, and sectional passions, as well as hate, had been appealed to. A bloody conflict was likely to occur, and he would be held responsible for the consequences. His first work was to get rid of the sheriff's posse without any further depredations. This was not an easy thing to do. Many of them were border desperadoes full of bad whiskey and worse passions. They had come swearing that they would "cut the heart out of some abolitionist" before they went back. While they shrank from confronting the Lawrence rifles, they were not disposed to be foiled in the purpose for which they came.

Now that the governor began to understand the situation, he was anxious to avert any further violence. He repaired at once to the Wakarusa camp to endeavor to persuade the men to go home, and let peaceful measures be tried. He arrived at the camp on the evening of December 5th. He found that many of the officers had come to a "realizing sense" of the awkwardness of the situation, but the rank and file were still of the idea of "helping Jones wipe out Lawrence." They had been waiting from three to five days, living on what they could steal of the people, and drinking up their stock of whiskey. They were not disposed to go back till they had finished their work. The governor was anxious to have Colonel Sumner with him to help in the negotiations, and to enforce the conclusions they might reach. His letter to him was as follows:

"WAKARUSA, December 6, 1855.

"COLONEL SUMNER, First Cavalry, U. S.:

SIR:—I send you this special dispatch to ask you to come to Lawrence as soon as you possibly can. My object is to secure the citizens of that place as well as others, from a warfare which, if once commenced, there is no telling where it will end. I doubt not that you have received orders from Washington, but if you have not the absolute pressure of this crisis is such as to justify you with the president, and the world, in moving to the scene of the difficulty.

"It is hard to restrain the men here (at least they are beyond my power, or soon will be) from making an attack on Lawrence. The presence of United States troops at Lawrence would prevent an attack, save bloodshed, and enable us to get matters arranged in a satisfactory way; and at the same time secure an execution of the laws. It is peace, not war, that we want, and you have the power to secure peace. Time is precious; fear not that you will be sustained.

"With greatest respect,
"WILSON SHANNON."

Colonel Sumner had received no orders from Washington, and he was too much of a soldier to move without orders. He therefore very courteously but firmly declined.

After conferring with the officers at the Wakarusa camp, Governor Shannon sent word to Lawrence that he wished to visit that place in the interests of peace, and asked for an escort. An escort was furnished, consisting of leading citizens of the place, led by G. P. Lowry. The governor was accompanied by Colonel Boone, of Westport; Colonel Kearney, of Independence, and General Strickler, also of Missouri. He entered Lawrence December 7th and went at once to the rooms of the committee of safety at the Free-State Hotel. The committee of safety was represented by Dr. Charles Robinson and Colonel James H. Lane. The interview lasted over an hour. He heard the whole story from the free-state standpoint, and found that he had been entirely misled as to the condition of affairs. He suggested that a memorandum of a treaty be drawn up which could be presented to the other camp as a basis of settlement. He also urged that they surrender their arms as a condition and pledge of peace, but this they refused to do.

He returned to the camp at Wakarusa, and insisted that

no movement should be made while negotiations for peace were going on. The men in camp were almost in a state of mutiny, and were threatening to raise the black flag and march on Lawrence, orders or no orders. But the governor insisted that the officers must repress any such movement, as an "attack on Lawrence, in the present state of negotiations, would be most unjustifiable."

Having done all in his power to impress his views on the officers, and to quiet the ugly temper of the men, he returned to Lawrence in the evening to complete the work. He had drawn up a paper as a basis of a treaty, and the free-state leaders had also drawn up one. With a few verbal changes that presented by the free-state men was accepted by the governor. The governor accepted it for himself and the leaders of the invading army, and Robinson and Lane for the people of Lawrence. The "treaty" was as follows:

"TREATY OF PEACE.

"WHEREAS, there is a misunderstanding between the people of Kansas, or a portion of them, and the governor thereof, arising out of the rescue at Hickory Point of a citizen under arrest, and other matters; and

"WHEREAS, a strong apprehension exists that said misunderstanding may lead to civil strife and bloodshed; and

"WHEREAS, it is desired by both Governor Shannon and the citizens of Lawrence and its vicinity to avoid a calamity so disastrous to the territory and the union, and to place all parties in a correct position before the world, now therefore it is agreed by said Governor Shannon, and the undersigned citizens of the territory now assembled, that the matter be settled as follows, to-wit:

"We, the said citizens of said territory, protest that the said rescue was made without our knowledge or consent, but if any of our citizens were engaged in said rescue, we pledge ourselves to aid in the execution of any legal process against them; that we have no knowledge of the previous, present or prospective existence of any organization in said territory for resistance against the laws, and that we have not designed, and do not design, to resist the legal service of any criminal process therein, but pledge ourselves to aid in the execution of the laws, when called on by proper authority, in the town or vicinity of Lawrence, and that we will use all our influence in preserving order therein; and we declare that we are, as we ever have been, ready at any time to aid the governor in securing a posse for the execution of such processes: Provided that any person thus arrested in Lawrence or vicinity, while a foreign force shall remain in the territory, shall be examined before a United States judge of said territory in said town and admitted to bail; and provided further that Governor Shannon agrees to use his influence to secure to the citizens of Kansas territory remuneration for any damage sustained, or unlawful depredations, if any such have been committed by the sheriff's posse in Douglas county; and further that Governor Shannon states that he has not called upon persons resident in any other state to aid in the execution of the laws, and such as are here in this territory are here of their own choice, and that he has not any authority or any legal power to do so, nor will he exercise any such power, and that he will not call upon any such citizen of another state who may be here: That we wish it understood that we do not herein express any opinion as to the validity of the enactments of the territorial legislature.

(Signed)

"Done in LAWRENCE, KANSAS,
December 8, 1855.

"WILSON SHANNON.
"C. ROBINSON.
"J. H. LANE."

The agreement was very adroitly drawn, and the last clause in regard to the territorial legislature, left it an open question as to what was meant by "legal processes" and "proper authorities." Each side could put upon these phrases the interpretation which suited them. When it was read to the people of Lawrence, therefore, they all assented to it, and the "treaty" was ratified as far as they were concerned.

The next point was to secure its adoption by the invaders at Franklin. This was the principal object of the treaty, to persuade these ruffians from Missouri to go home. This was no easy matter. They came up with a great deal of bluster, and had swaggered around for a week, boasting the great things they were going to do. To go home without doing anything, and acknowledge themselves outwitted, was very humiliating.

Governor Shannon was extremely anxious to affect a settlement. He realized that the difficulty would be with the invading army. They were beyond his control, and the officers had little authority. Discipline was little more than a form and the whole multitude was coming to be a disorganized mob. Governor Shannon had arranged to have a joint meeting of the leaders of each side. He asked that a delegation from Lawrence go with him to Franklin and meet with the leaders of the opposite party. Lane and Robinson went with him, when he took the treaty, to explain more fully the attitude of the free-state men. This meeting is best described in Governor Robinson's own language, as found in his "Conflict:"

"At the meeting, in an unfinished building, Governor Shannon led off with an explanation of the settlement, giving the position occupied by the citizens of Lawrence. After him Colonel Lane attempted to speak, but his opening so offended the thirteen militia captains that they started to leave the room, saying they did not come to be insulted. The governor begged them to remain and hear Dr. Robinson. Lane did not proceed, and Robinson in a few words explained the action of the citizens of Lawrence, saying that no attempt had ever been made to serve any process by any officer, real or pretended. Jones was appealed to by a military captain to know if Robinson told the truth. Jones replied that he did. 'We have been damnably deceived, then.' As to the Sharpe's rifles, Robinson appealed to them to say if they would as American citizens submit to be deprived of their constitutional right to bear arms, or if they would respect any people who would submit. The leading men saw their predicament, and said: 'Boys, it is no use. They have got us. We can do nothing this time.' The conference ended with a pressing invitation to remain to supper. This Robinson and Lane, as it was getting dark and a cold north wind

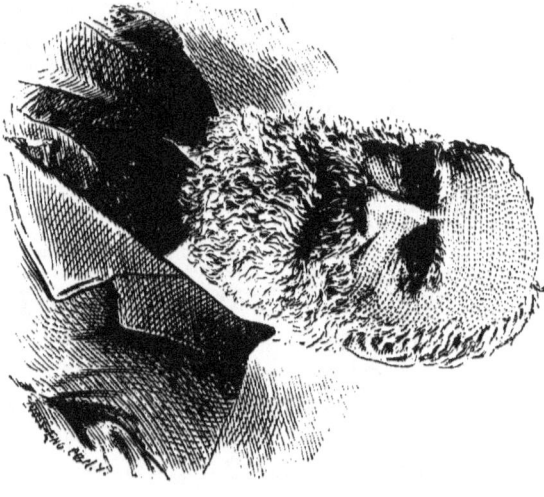

MILITARY LEADERS IN BORDER-RUFFIAN DAYS.

had arisen with heavy sleet, tried to decline. But they said Governor Shannon and party had dined with Robinson, and no refusal would be accepted. When supper was over it was so dark no object was visible, and the sound of the horses' hoofs on the hard ground was the only guide. A solitary horseman started to escort the visitors through the line, but he proceeded only a few hundred yards when he said good-night, and left his charge to get through the lines as best they could. At this Lane said: 'Hurry up. This means assassination. They mean to kill us.' He started his horse on a run. * * * Deep gullies had been washed in the road at this point, causing the travelers to turn sharply to the right to avoid them. As Robinson's horse was on the left, his horse ran into one of these gullies, while Lane's horse escaped. The horse fell with great force, and for some minutes was unable to rise. No damage was done, however, except the delay."

Sheriff Jones and his friends were very sullen at the turn affairs had taken. All the hot-heads were very bitter at the governor for interfering, and there was a good deal of grumbling in the invaders' camp. But the old saying that "fortune favors the brave" was again made good. The weather had been delightful during the whole week, so that many of the soldiers on both sides were in summer clothes. But on Saturday, December 8th, the day of the treaty, there was one of those sudden changes for which Kansas is noted. The wind veered to the north, and in the evening a tremendous sleet storm set in—a regular Dakota blizzard. Though Dakota was not then known, her blizzards were as terrific as they have been since. The cold became so intense that the zeal of the Missourians was cooled off, and even "Dutch courage" was found to be a poor defense against ten degrees below zero. The blustering braggarts of a sunny afternoon

"Now folded their tents like the Arabs."

and scud for home. They might defy the governor's proclamation, but when the north wind joined with the governor, they yielded and fell into line for the home march, or more properly the home rush.

Governor Shannon returned to Lawrence after peace was assured highly pleased with the outcome of affairs. In the evening the ladies arranged a sort of banquet in his honor. They all did their best to make it pleasant for the governor. Although it was Sunday evening, and Lawrence was a sort of Puritan town, neither the stillness of the Sabbath nor the austerity of Puritan customs characterized the banquet. Dr. Robinson and a large portion of the people of Lawrence were teetotalers, yet there is a tradition that tea was not the only drink furnished. At all events the governor was delighted, and said it was the "happiest day of his life." Lawrence people were also happy. But the course of true love never did run smooth, and some boulders were thrown into the course of this current. Right in the midst of this delightful "era of good feeling" a report was brought in that the Missourians, instead of going home as the governor had ordered them, were marching on Lawrence and were going to "wipe it out." The thing was not at all unlikely, and when the report came to the governor's ears he was very much disturbed. He knew these fellows had no very kind feelings towards him. If they came he would fare no better than the hated abolitionists.

"What shall we do?" said Robinson.

"Call out your men and defend the town as best you can."

"But the charge against us has been acting without authority, and defying the law."

"I will give you authority," the governor said.

He at once wrote out the following paper:

" *To Charles Robinson and J. H. Lane:*
"You are hereby authorized and directed to take such measures and use

the enrolled forces under your command in such manner, for the preservation of the peace and property of the people of Lawrence and vicinity, as in your judgment shall best secure that end.

"(Signed) WILSON SHANNON.
"LAWRENCE, December 9, 1855."

The foe did not come. It was a very common feeling that the free-state men did not expect him. It was the common opinion that the report came from another room in the hotel, and was intended to accomplish just what it did accomplish. When Governor Shannon learned several days after that a hoax had been perpetrated on him for the sake of securing the order he had written for Robinson and Lane, he "let his angry passions rise," and expressed himself in some vigorous English.

Monday evening, December 10th, there was a grand peace party at the Free-State Hotel. Governor Shannon did not remain, but a number of the invaders were there as invited guests, and among them Sheriff Jones. The hotel was illuminated, a long table was spread, the band played, and speeches were made by Robinson and Lane and many others. The festivities continued until far into the night. The next day, Tuesday, the soldiers were dismissed and went home rejoicing. The companies from a distance were cheered by the Lawrence people as they passed out.

The only casualty of the siege was the killing of Thomas W. Barber. Andreas, in his history, gives an account of this murder, which is perhaps as near the truth as it is possible to get:

"Thomas W. Barber, with his young wife, had taken a claim just north of the Wakarusa, seven miles above Blanton's bridge, about eight miles southwest of Lawrence, and perhaps a mile on the road between the Bloomington settlement and that town. He had gone up to the defense with the rest of the Bloomington free-state men, contrary to the wishes of his wife, who had strong premonitions, which she expressed to him, that he would never return alive. On Tuesday noon, December 6th, all being quiet, but the town being still in a state of siege, he started to visit his wife, in company with his brother, Robert, and his brother-in-law, Thomas M. Pearson, both members of the same company, and having claims near his. His companions had revolvers. They were all mounted, and had ridden some three miles out of Lawrence when they discovered a party of horsemen, numbering ten or twelve, approaching them from the direction of Lecompton. It afterwards proved to be a party from the camp near that place on their way to the Wakarusa camp. Two of the party, George W. Clarke, government Indian agent for the Pottawatomie Indians, and James Burnes, known as Colonel Burnes, a merchant of Westport, Missouri, left the main party, rode across so as to confront them in their road, and ordered them to halt. Angry words were bandied, the Barbers refused to turn back at the command of the highwaymen, who obstructed their way. Pistols were drawn on both sides, and shots fired. Thomas Barber, the only unarmed man, received a shot in his side. He rode a hundred yards, told his brother, with a faint, sickly smile, that 'that fellow hit him.' He rode swaying in his saddle supported by his brother a little further, then slipped off in the dust, and died a little later in the road. His brother and Pearson, fearing further violence, fled, leaving the body in the highway. The credit of the murder was claimed by both Clarke and Burnes. Neither of them knew which fired the fatal shot. Clarke said to an acquaintance three days after, 'I tried to kill him, and if it was not me, I wish it had been.' History will rank them as a brace of murderers, it matters not who gave the *coup de grace.*"

When the body of Barber was brought to Lawrence the settlement was at fever heat. Only the cool counsel of Robinson and other leaders prevented the armed men from rushing out and attacking the invaders in their camp and avenging the murder of their comrade. The body of Barber lay in the hotel the next day when Governor Shannon came to confer with the committee of safety. He was much moved by the sight, and it had much to do with his eagerness to bring about a peaceful settlement.

The funeral of Thomas W. Barber was one of the closing features of the campaign. The military companies attended and the scene was very solemn and impressive. Dr. Robinson pronounced a funeral oration which is interesting as showing the temper of the times. The oration was published later in the *Herald of Freedom*. The following extract will show the tenor of the speech:

"By whose act do the remains of the lamented Thomas Barber now await interment at our hands? By whose hand is his wife made a widow? By whose instrumentality are we made to mourn the untimely fall of a brave comrade and a worthy citizen? Report says Thomas Barber was murdered in cold blood by an officer, an officer of the government, who was a member of the sheriff's posse, which was commissioned by the governor, who is backed by the president of the United States. Was Thomas Barber murdered? Then are the men who killed him, and the officials by whose authority they acted, his murderers. And if the laws are to be enforced, then will the Indian agent, the governor, and the president, be convicted and punished for murder. There is work enough for the law and order men to do, and let us hear no more about resistance to the laws, until this work is done. If all Missouri must be aroused, and the whole nation convulsed to serve a peace warrant on an unoffending citizen, may we not expect some slight effort to bring these capital offenders to justice?"

No effort was ever made to bring these "capital offenders to justice," and they not only remained at large, but boasted of their deed as something to be proud of.

Another incident of the Wakarusa war is alluded to by Prof. L. W. Spring in one of the most eloquent passages of his book. Having spoken of the general satisfaction with which the treaty of peace was received, he quotes an exception.

"A single voice was raised in solemn and public protest against the peace. After the treaty and its stipulations had become known; after the speeches of felicitation on the happy subsidence of troubles which threatened to engulf the settlement, had been made, an unknown man—tall, slender, angular; his face clean shaved, sombre, strongly lined, of Puritan tone and configuration; his blue-gray eyes honest, inexorable; strange unworldly intensities enveloping him like an atmosphere—mounted a dry goods box and began to denounce the treaty as an attempt to gain by foolish uncomprehending make-shift what could be compassed only by shedding of blood. Since that day the name of this ·unknown man, plucked down from the dry goods box with his speech mostly unspoken, has filled the post horns of the world—Old John Brown."

This was the first appearance of old John Brown among the free-state men of Kansas. His sons had come to Kansas the year before, to make themselves homes in the new country. They were so annoyed and harrassed by marauders from Missouri that they wrote to their father for arms to defend themselves. The old man had been for years a foe of human slavery. He concluded it was time to strike a blow for freedom. So he came out to Kansas to join his sons, and arrived some weeks before the Wakarusa invasion. When he heard of the siege of Lawrence, he started with his four sons for the place to join in the defense. He arrived the day Governor Shannon came to confer in regard to peace. He was welcomed and put in command of a company. He did not like the treaty of peace. He thought the miscreants should have been driven away by bullets, and taught a lesson, and not parleyed with. But the people were too glad to be relieved from the strain and peril, and refused to listen to him.

John Brown was one of the unique characters which the Kansas struggle drew out. He was a man by himself. Very few of the free-state men agreed with him in his policy or action. Many of them were in constant fear that he would precipitate a conflict by some rash deed. He came to Kansas because he hated slavery, and his hatred of it was as a fire to his bones. He had a further thought than the freeing of Kansas. As he said to Governor Robinson once, "he wanted to strike a blow at slavery." A little incident in his early life may throw light on his later conduct. In 1837 the family lived on a farm in the Western Reserve, Ohio. They were members of the village church near by. When Elijah P. Lovejoy was killed at Alton by a pro-slavery mob, the news reached the village on the evening of the week-day prayer meeting. The members of the church all being intensely anti-slavery, the killing of Lovejoy became the theme of the meeting. John Brown and his father were present. After the meeting had proceeded some time, the elder Brown arose and offered a marvelous prayer. He seemed to take the case right up to the heavenly court, and lay it before the Righteous Judge. Everybody was electrified by the prayer. At its conclusion John Brown arose and made a vow, that "he would devote his life to unceasing hostility to human slavery." One is reminded of the boy Hannibal, taken by his father into the Carthagenian temple, and made to swear eternal enmity to Rome. Thirty years later that vow echoed on the plains of Italy in the tramp of conquering legions. And the vow of this young man in the village church in Ohio echoed, eighteen years later, on the plains of Kansas, and a few years later still echoed again in the tramp of armies, who sang;

"John Brown's body lies mouldering in the grave
While his soul goes marching on."

CHAPTER VI.

A Hard Winter.—Conflict Takes a New Form in the Spring.—The Courts Come to the Rescue.—Judge Lecompte's Charge.—The Grand Jury's Indictment.—High Treason.—The Sacking of Lawrence.—Burning of the Free-State Hotel and Printing Offices.

The year 1855 had been a year of much progress in Lawrence. Immigration flowed in continually, and many improvements were made. The hay tent seems to have disappeared, and the shake shanty and the log cabin took its place. There were even a few fairly built frame houses erected, and some of stone or "concrete," as it was called. The people were more comfortably housed than they were the year before. Still there was a good deal of exposure and a good deal of suffering, as many new-comers were but very inadequately sheltered. Most of the business houses were temporary affairs made to serve the occasion. The most substantial improvement was the building of the Free-State Hotel on the site of the present Eldridge House. It was built by the Emigrant Aid Company at a cost of about $20,000. It was fifty feet front and seventy feet deep, three stories high, with a basement story. It was of stone and quite solidly built. It was begun in the spring of 1855, but not completed until the following spring. The roof was on at the time of the Wakarusa war, and it furnished an excellent shelter for the troops and headquarters for the leaders. It rendered important service even in its unfinished condition.

Three churches were formed during this year, 1855. In the spring of that year Rev. Ephriam Nute was sent out by the American Unitarian Association, and commenced holding services in the open air. About the same time Mr. E. B. Whitman, a man who had been prominent in educational

WILSON SHANNON,
Territorial Governor '55-56.

CHARLES ROBINSON,
First Governor of Kansas.

C. W. BABCOCK,
President Territorial Council.

SOLON O. THACHER,
Tem. Chairman Constitutional Convention

MEN WHO MADE KANSAS HISTORY.

affairs in Massachusetts, came to Lawrence and joined with Mr. Nute in the work of developing a Unitarian Church. They took steps towards securing a house of worship, but the troubles of the summer prevented their doing much at that time. Mr. Nute was quite prominent in public affairs. He was a man of fine address, great energy, and was perfectly fearless in speech and conduct. His spirited letters to eastern papers did much to increase the public interest in the Kansas question.

The Methodists commenced services in Lawrence late in the fall of 1854, and a class was formed in the following spring. But the class became scattered and soon disbanded. During the summer, however, Rev. L. B. Dennis succeeded in making a permanent organization. They held their services in the open air under one of the trees in Central Park. Here the church was formed, and here they continued to worship during the summer. Later in the season they secured a room in the "Union House," and the following summer they worshiped again in a tent.

The Baptist Church was formed June 25th, 1855, and included the following persons: J. S. Emery, M. M. Hammond, S. Jones, Rebecca W. W. Jones, W. F. Herrick, Lydia A. Herrick, Elizabeth Parks. They worshiped in the private homes of the members for several months, and then in more public rooms and halls as they could secure them.

The times, however, were not favorable for church work or church growth. The disturbances kept the minds of the people in a continual ferment all summer, and little else was thought of beyond the public defense. All the religious services were compelled to adapt themselves to the exigencies of the times. They were held here and there as was found possible, and sometimes they were entirely suspended for weeks together. It was no unusual thing for church services to be interrupted by a call for the men to rally for the defense of the town. At other times the women and children only met, the men being away on duty. One of the pastors of this period writes: "All the public buildings are turned into barracks, the preaching hall with the rest, and nothing is thought of but the best means of defense."

The same happened in regard to the schools. The people were determined to have a free school whenever possible. Mr. E. P. Fitch opened a school in January of this year, 1855, and Miss Kate Kellogg opened a school in June and continued three months. But the disturbances so thickened later on that no further effort was made in this line until the following year.

There had been much more progress in the unifying of the community than in the enlarging of it. They were all inspired by a common purpose, and they were all confronted by common danger. These two causes drove the community together in a peculiar way. They felt the need of each other's sympathy in a way that created a peculiar bond, and the companions of those trying times ever after had a strong interest in each other. They knew each other better than citizens of older communities after years of association. They were so dependent on each other, both for protection and friendship, that the common jealousies and cliques and classes that usually play so large a part, had little chance to develop. In a very peculiar way and in a very unusual degree they were a unit, understanding each other and helping each other. Their attitude towards the territorial laws made them unusually considerate of one another. They did not recognize the territorial laws, and so could not appeal to the territorial courts. They had to settle their differences among themselves. This made them very careful to avoid differences and disputes. It put them all "under bonds to keep the peace."

Another peculiarity of this time was the identity of interest in town and country. As far as community of feeling was concerned, the country about Lawrence for fifteen miles was simply an extension of Lawrence itself. They had all come for one purpose, and they all had one cause. Their attachment to the common cause was stronger than any local attachment. They were all one community, and whether they happened to live inside the limits or outside made little difference. They had come to make Kansas a free state: that was the common bond. Where they should live was a secondary consideration. Some of them remained in town, and others went out into the country; but they were none the less one people, with one chief purpose. As far as interest and loyalty was concerned, Lawrence had just as good citizens ten miles out as in the center of town. They were all one compact people. To the westward, for example, the Barbers, Thomas Pierson, Captain Walker, Charles W. Smith, and many others, were just as loyal to Lawrence and just as ready to rally to her defense as if they lived within the limits. To the east and south it was the same way. Major J. B. Abbott, a man of rare courage and coolness, lived beyond the Wakarusa. He was born a leader, and did a great deal of valliant service. He was a sort of outpost to Lawrence. They began to touch Lawrence when they came to where he lived, and were very apt to feel something of the force of Lawrence as well. Then still further out there was Thadeus Prentice, an original character, who in appearance might be considered a companion piece to Jim Lane. He had a rare faculty of getting news. If any mischief was brewing in his direction, he would somehow get wind of it by a sort of instinct, by a sort of sixth sense. Whenever he felt that there was something in the air of this kind, he would mount his horse and ride into Lawrence. Whenever the people saw the tall, gaunt figure of "Thad. Prentice" coming down the street, they knew that it was "tidings, my Lord, tidings." He always came in with a smile, greeting his friends on the street as he passed. He had many quaint expressions which came to seem like a part of him. If everything was favorable he would reply to the questions asked him, "Oh, everything is lovely and the goose hangs high." These are but a few of those who, all around Lawrence, were just as much interested in her defense as those who lived within the town limits.

Up to December 8th the winter had been very mild. On the evening of that day a cold rain set in, which soon changed to sleet and snow. From that on the winter was very severe, said by some to be the severest ever known in the history of Kansas. The settlers were poorly prepared to face such a winter. The previous winter had been so mild that the need of protection against cold was not understood. The houses were open and exposed. Log cabins poorly chinked and shake shanties with gaping sides were a poor defense against a genuine northwester. The wind found its way through openings in the sides, and the snow sifted through the loosely constructed roof. It was no unusual thing to find six inches of snow on the floor in the morning. One lady said that water often froze upon her shawl as she stood over a hot stove cooking breakfast. Colonel Sam Walker says in a letter "that they often had to go to bed to keep from freezing." The severity of the winter had one favorable effect. It put a stop to all military movements, and if the people were cold they were quiet. They did not have to stand guard by night, nor march against the foe by day. They did not have much, but they were not in constant fear of having what little they had stolen.

A letter written by Captain Sam. Walker during this winter may be taken as illustrating the common condition:

"I failed to complete my log house before the winter of 1855-56 set in. The sides were up, roofed, and partly plastered when the Wakarusa war interrupted work. On my return home, on the conclusion of peace, the cold was so severe that nothing more could be done, and we had to shift the best we could till warmer weather. Our cabin had no floor, but we were as well off in this particular as most of our neighbors. Chinks and fissures abounded in roof and gable, as the green slabs with which they were covered warped badly. Seven of us made up the family, five children mostly small. At times when the winds were bleakest we actually went to bed as the only escape from freezing. More than once we woke in the morning to find six inches of snow in the cabin. To get up and make one's toilet under such circumstances was not a very comfortable performance. The wolf was never very far from our door during that hard winter of 1855-56."

Though the settlers were not molested during this severe weather, they knew the quiet was only temporary. The opening of spring would bring a renewal of hostilities. The hordes that had left Franklin so sullenly did not propose to drop the controversy. They saw they had made a mistake, and the free-state men had profited by it. Next time they would plan more wisely. They would not be caught in court again without a case. All over Missouri and the south preparations were going on to push the controversy to a successful issue for slavery. The shrewdest men in the land were planning together for the summer campaign. The general idea was to make it so uncomfortable for the free-state men that they would flee the country, and so that others would not come.

The line of attack was not hard to determine. The free-state men occupied a position that was difficult to maintain. They knew that the Shawnee legislature had been elected by Missouri votes. They pronounced its enactments an imposition and a fraud. They determined to ignore them and as far as possible to nullify them or destroy their effect. The laws were of the most extreme pro-slavery type. They not only protected slave property, but punished all acts and expressions against slavery with great severity. They could not even discuss the subject without becoming liable to criminal prosecution. Their only course was to ignore these laws and practically nullify them. Then nobody would dare to bring any slaves into Kansas. If there were no slaves in Kansas, slavery would not really exist, even though the laws did recognize it. In two years there would be another election, and by that time the free-state men felt they would be strong enough to take possession of all the machinery of government and shape the laws to suit themselves. If they could only keep things as they were till the next election, immigration from the north would do the rest.

The pro-slavery people, on the other hand, strove to force an immediate issue. They laid their plans to compel the free-state men to recognize the bogus laws, or else resist the officials charged with their enforcement. The problem of the free-state men was to ignore the bogus laws and yet avoid a collision. They might suffer violence, but as far as possible they were to avoid doing violence. Above all they were to avoid any collision with the authority of the United States.

Another element entered into the problem which must be mentioned that the whole situation may be understood. That element grew out of what has been referred to as the "Topeka movement." The free-state policy had its negative side in the rejection of the bogus laws. It had its positive side in the adoption of the Topeka constitution. During the autumn of 1855 the free-state people held a constitutional convention at Topeka which framed a state constitution. They then sent it to congress and asked to be received into the union as a state. The house of representatives passed the bill admitting Kansas as a state, but the senate rejected it. Thus the movement failed in congress, but it was kept alive in Kansas as a rallying point of defense. An election was held in January for state officers, and Dr. Robinson was elected governor. The legislature then chosen met in March and organized, and Governor Robinson sent in his message. No attempt was made, however, to put the state government into operation. But the thought was to do this if the situation became intolerable. The occasion never came and the Topeka government and constitution never went into effect.

As spring opened the policy of the pro-slavery men began to manifest itself. It was a deeply laid, shrewd scheme. It went on the assumption that the attitude of the free-state men toward the bogus laws was rebellion, and that the actors in the Topeka free-state movement were guilty of treason. They proposed to have the free-state leaders indicted for high crimes, and either have them arrested or compelled to flee from the territory. This will give a general clue to the new line of attack, and will show the animus and purpose of the violent proceedings which followed.

One of the difficulties of such a position as the free-state men were trying to maintain is that somebody is liable to go beyond the bounds defined by those who marked out the policy, and commit some deed which is abhorrent to them all, and which compromises them all. This happened several times during the Kansas struggle, and made that struggle much more severe and embarrassing. Such a thing happened just at the juncture of which we are speaking. The free-state men often had occasion to pray, "Save us from our friends." April 18th Sheriff Jones came into Lawrence to arrest some of the Branson rescuers. He did not succeed, and appeared again the next day and tried to arrest Samuel F. Tappan, but Tappan struck him in the face and escaped. This was as good a thing as Jones wanted. He now applied for a posse, and the governor gave him an officer and ten soldiers. April 23rd he appeared in town thus supported and arrested a number of citizens on various charges, most of them for "contempt of court" in not assisting him to make arrests on his previous visits. He was particularly offensive and insolent, and remained in town over night. While he was in the tent of his military posse, someone in the darkness outside shot him and wounded him. The man who fired the shot disappeared, but the citizens disavowed the act and offered five hundred dollars reward for the arrest of the assassin. Still they were held responsible for the crime, and it was used with great effect in stirring the passions of the pro-slavery people. It has never been known how severe a wound Jones received. He was reported in the pro-slavery papers as "foully murdered," "mortally wounded," "struck down in the night." As he was able to lead in the sacking of Lawrence less than a month after, his wound could not have been so very severe. But the affair was very unfortunate, as it added to the flame and placed the free-state men in a very awkward position.

The pro-slavery people brought to their aid the powerful influence of the judiciary of the territory. They had the forms of law, and they proposed to use them for all they were worth. The grand jury of Douglas county met at Lecompton early in May. Samuel D. Lecompte gave a charge which foreshadowed the new line of attack. He defined treason so as to point very plainly to the leaders of the free-state party. Among other things he said:

"This territory was organized by an act of congress, and so far its authority is from the United States. It has a legislature elected in pursuance of that organic act. This legislature being an instrument of congress by which it governs the territory, has passed laws. Those laws, therefore, are of United States authority and making, and all who resist those laws resist the power and authority of the United States, and are therefore guilty of *high treason*. Now, gentlemen, if you find that any persons have resisted these laws, then you must,

GEN. JAMES H. LANE,
First U. S. Senator from Kansas.

JOHN SPEER,
Editor Kansas Tribune, 1854-5.

under your oath, find bills against them for *high treason*. If you find that no such resistance has been made, but that combinations have been formed for the purpose of resisting them, and individuals of notoriety have been aiding and abetting in such combinations, then must you find bills for *constructive treason.*"

The mill having been set up by the chief justice, the grand jury began to grind out its grist of indictments. The first victim was ex-Governor Reeder. He was summoned before the grand jury, but he refused to obey the summons, as he was then attending the sessions of the congressional investigating committee, which was sitting in Lawrence. Deputy Marshal Fain then came to him with an order for his arrest for contempt of court. Reeder refused to be arrested, and told the marshal to touch him at his peril. This only made matters worse, as he would now be indicted for resisting an officer. He soon saw there was no escape except in flight. He fled in disguise to Kansas City, where he was concealed for several days in a friendly hotel. He was taken on board a steamboat going down the river. Going to a wooding station, below Kansas City, he jumped aboard disguised as a wood chopper. The captain of the boat of course was in the secret. He thus passed down the Missouri river and escaped safely into the free states. In the rooms of the State Historical Society at Topeka is a painting of Governor Reeder as he appeared in disguise. He is dressed as an Irish laborer, with a stick in his hand, an old clay pipe in his mouth, and an ax on his shoulder on which is suspended his "luggage" tied up in a handkerchief. It would be an expert detective who would suspect that this curious outfit was taking the distinguished ex-governor of Kansas out of the territory.

The plan of the grand jury was to proceed rapidly against all of the free-state leaders—Robinson, Lane, Wood, Brown, Jenkins, and others—and have them indicted for treason

These men would either have to leave the country or be arrested and held as prisoners. Either result would tend to demoralize the free-state men. The jury conducted their business in secret, and did not intend to have their plan made public till they were ready to execute it. But one of the jurymen, who had a warm side towards some of the free-state men, warned them of their danger. All the men connected with the defense of Lawrence, and all those connected with the Topeka state government were to be indicted. Congressmen Howard and Sherman, of the congressional committee, and Governor Robinson and others held a council that night to decide upon a line of action. It was decided, among other things, that Robinson should go east at once to lay the situation before the governors and people of eastern states, and also to be out of the way when the indictments were to be served. He and Mrs. Robinson as soon as possible took a boat at Kansas City and proceeded eastward. When they reached Lexington, Missouri, a company of men came on board, pounded at his stateroom door, and told him he must leave the boat and come ashore. He asked them why he must be detained, and they replied, that they understood that he was a fugitive from justice. He told them there was no indictment against him and he had a right to do as he pleased. But his words availed nothing. They were determined to take him. The arrest was entirely arbitrary. They had no authority whatever, but they had received word from Kansas to hold him at all hazzards, until the in dictment couldbe made out and the proper papers sent on. Mrs. Robinson was allowed to go on her journey, taking with her the papers and testimony they were bearing to eastern friends. They held the governor thus for nearly a week before the papers for his arrest were received. He was then taken back to Kansas. At Leavenworth a pro-slavery mob threatened to hang him, but were prevented from carrying out their purpose. He was then taken to Lecompton, where he and other free-state men were kept in a prison camp for several months. Among those prisoners under charge of high treason were such men as Charles Robinson, George W. Deitzler, G. W. Brown, Gaius Jenkins. Lane and Sam Wood were indicted but were out of reach. No attempt seems to have been made to arrest old John Brown. He was probably omitted because he was not a comfortable man to handle.

This wonderful grand jury distinguished itself in another line. It first indicted all the free-state leaders—some for things they had done, and some for things it was supposed they intended to do. But they were not content with searching the thoughts and interests of the heart. They turned their attention to subjects where there was no heart to search. They seemed to have discovered what some writer calls "the total depravity of inanimate things." In accordance with this principle they made the following presentment which is certainly original in the doings of courts:

"The grand jury, setting for the adjourned term of the first district court in and for the county of Douglas, in the territory of Kansas, beg leave to report to the honorable court, that, from evidence before them showing the *Herald of Freedom*, published at the town of Lawrence, has from time to time issued publications of the most inflammatory and sedicious character, denying the legality of the territorial authorities, advising and demanding forcible resistance to the same, demoralizing the public mind, and rendering life and property unsafe, even to the extent of advising assassination as a last resort.

"Also that the paper known as the *Free State* has been similarly engaged, and has recently reported the resolutions of a public meeting in Johnson county, in this territory, in which resistance to the territorial laws even unto blood has been agreed upon, and that we respectfully recommend their abatement as a nuisance.

"Also that we are satisfied that the building known as the Free-State Hotel in Lawrence has been constructed with a view to military occupation and defense, and regularly parapetted and port-holed for the use of cannon and small arms, and could only be designed as a stronghold for resistance to law, thereby endangering the public safety and encouraging rebellion and sedition to the country; and we respectfully recommend that steps be taken whereby this nuisance may be removed.

"OWEN STEWART, *Foreman*."

The Free-tSate Hotel mentioned in this presentment had just been completed and furnished. It had been erected by the Emigrant Aid Company, and was probably the best building in the territory. It was certainly the best equipped hotel. There was nothing about it of a military character, unless its strong stone walls could be so considered. There was a motive in the indictment but it does not appear in the wording of it. The great lack of Lawrence had been a good hotel. People were hindered from coming to Kansas because they could not be comfortably cared for when they got here. Now they could tell the comfort-loving emigrant that Lawrence had as good a hotel as he would find in St. Louis. He could find a roof and a room the day he arrived, and need not live out of doors till he could build a cabin. It was bound to prove an effective element in drawing free-state men to Kansas, and the whole question was one of immigration. The policy of the pro-slavery men was to keep away free-state settlers. To destroy this hotel was to remove a powerful attraction. All these disturbances had largely the same motive. They would keep the country in such a state of confusion and terror that settlers would be kept away.

The novelty of the proceedings becomes more manifest when we remember that the sheriff took the indictment of the grand jury for an order of the court. The legal process never went any further. There was no citation, and no trial and no sentence. These were trifles with which these high-minded men could not be troubled. They could not wait for formalities. The king's business demanded haste. The execution was the chief thing, and the execution anticipated all trial and all evidence. Lawrence, that foul nest of abolitionists, must be humiliated, and her free-spoken newspapers must be destroyed.

On the eleventh day of May, the United States marshal issued his proclamation. He stated that an attempt had been made to execute writs by the United States deputy marshal,

"Who was evidently resisted by a large number of the citizens of Lawrence, and there is every reason to believe that an attempt to execute these writs will be resisted by a large body of armed men; now, therefore, the law abiding citizens of the territory are commanded to be and appear at Lecompton, as soon as practicable, and in numbers sufficient for the execution of the law.

"I. B. DONALDSON,
"*United States Marshal for Kansas Territory.*"

The proclamation was posted in a few pro-slavery towns, and in Missouri. The response was so prompt that armed men began to gather before the free-state men had become aware of the proclamation. They saw at once what the thing meant. It was a plot to humiliate, or destroy Lawrence. The plan had been more carefully laid than in the Wakarusa war. The United States court had issued the order, and a United States marshal was to execute it. The people of Lawrence must tamely submit, or resist United States authority. They saw at once the seriousness of the situation, and bestirred themselves to avert the blow. The citizens held a meeting on the tenth of May and passed resolutions appealing to Governor Shannon to protect them from this army from another state. The governor replied that "there was no force around or approaching Lawrence, except the legally constituted posse of the United States marshal, and the sheriff of Douglas county, each of whom, I am informed, has a number of writs in their hands for execution against persons in Lawrence. I can in no way interfere with either of these officers in the discharge of their official duties.

"If the citizens of Lawrence submit themselves to the territoritorial laws, and aid and assist the marshal and sheriff in the execution of processes in their hands, as all good citizens are bound to do when called upon, they, or all such, will entitle themselves to the protection of the law. But so long as they keep up a military or armed organization to resist the territorial laws, and the officers charged with their execution, I shall not interfere to save them from the legitimate consequences of their illegal acts."

There was not much comfort in this letter and no hope of help from the governor. Another meeting was called of which Colonel Phillips in his Conquest of Kansas gives a report.

"The harsh partisan letter of the governor could not be regarded as anything short of a declaration of war. As the people of Lawrence were anxious to avert trouble, a meeting was held and the following action taken:

"'WHEREAS, By proclamation to the people of Kansas territory, by I. B. Donaldson, United States marshal for said territory, issued on the 11th of May, 1856, it is asserted that certain judicial writs of arrest have been directed to him by the First District Court of the United States, to be executed within the county of Douglas, and that an attempt to execute them by the deputy marshal was violently resisted by a large number of the citizens of Lawrence, and there is every reason to believe that any attempt to execute them will be resisted by a large body of armed men, therefore,

"'*Resolved*, By this public meeting of the citizens of Lawrence, held this 13th day of May, 1856, that the allegations and charges against us, contained in the aforesaid proclamation, are wholly untrue in fact, and in the conclusion drawn from them. The aforesaid marshal was resisted in no wise whatever, nor by any person whatever in the execution of said writs, except by him whose arrest the said deputy marshal was seeking to make; and that we now, as we have done heretofore, declare our willingness and determination, without resistance, to acquiesce in the service upon us, of any judicial writ against us by the United States marshal for Kansas territory, *and will furnish him a posse for that purpose*, if so requested; but that we are ready to resist, if need be, to the death, the ravages of an invading mob.

"'J. A. WAKEFIELD, *President*.'

"The resolution was forwarded to the marshal and to Governor Shannon.

"As I have said the marshal never sent a copy of his

proclamation to Lawrence. The copy that reached Lawrence was sent to me from Lecompton by one of my agents, and was received a few hours after its issue. I carried it into the chamber of the committee of safety, which held a meeting that night. Its meetings were private. Several proposals were made, but the majority were unwilling to do anything. Lieutenant Governor Roberts and Colonel Holliday were opposed to any defense being made. Holliday urged that it was a busy season, and the farmers could not be taken from their farms to sustain another siege without great loss. Others urged that the merchants and business men had advanced provisions, stores and goods during the Wakarusa war, and had got pay for only a small part, and could not advance anything more for the defense of the place.

"Deitzler and several other members of the committee were for defending the place against the marshal's posse. The discussion was vague, pointless and unsatisfactory. There was no one to take the lead. One proposal was that three or four hundred men, armed only with pistols and other side arms, should go to Lecompton, and offer themselves to Donaldson as his posse, in obedience to his proclamation, and demand from the governor a share of the public arms then at Lecompton.

"The committee determined that matters should go as they were. Roberts declared that he did not mean to go out of the territory, but should stay and be arrested.

"I mention these things because they show why the impending blow was permitted. The people as a general thing wanted the town defended, and dispensed with the old committee, and elected a new one, composed in part of members of the first. The names are as follows: W. Y. Roberts, G. W. Deitzler, Lyman Allen, John A. Perry, C. W. Babcock, S. B. Prentis, A. H. Mallory, Joel Grover. A few days after this election Mr. S. C. Pomeroy arrived from the east, where he had been on business for the Emigrant Aid Society, and was admitted a member.

"A change of ruler does not always bring a change of policy. This second committee was more pacific than the first, although selected by the people with the expectation that resistance would be made. In fact it was the federal authority employed that acted as a weight against them."

It may be added to this account of Colonel Phillips that it had been the settled policy of the state leaders not to resist United States authority. The decision of the committee not to resist does not argue any lack of courage but was in line with the settled policy of the free-state men.

The next day the committee and citizens held a joint meeting and determined to make another effort at pacification. They voted to send resolutions similar to those just quoted to the marshal with a letter as follows:

"LAWRENCE, May 14, 1856.

"I. B. DONALDSON, United States Marshal for Kansas Territory:

"DEAR SIR:—We have seen a proclamation issued by yourself, dated 11th of May, and also have reliable information that large bodies of armed men in pursuance of your proclamation have assembled in the vicinity of Lawrence.

"That there may be no misunderstanding we beg leave to ask respectfully that we may be reliably informed of the demands against us. We desire to state most truthfully and earnestly that no opposition will now or at any future time be offered to the execution of any legal process by yourself or any person acting for you. We also pledge ourselves to assist you, if called upon, in the execution of any legal process.

"We declare ourselves to be order-loving and law-abiding citizens, and only want an opportunity to test our fidelity to the laws of the country, the constitution and the union.

"We are informed also that these men collected about Lawrence openly declare that their intention is to destroy the town and drive off the citizens. Of course we do not believe that you would give countenance to such threats, but in view of the excited state of the public mind we ask protection of the constituted authorities of the government, declaring ourselves in readiness

ROBERT G. ELLIOTT,
Editor of *Kansas Free State*.

T. DWIGHT THACHER,
Editor of *Lawrence Republican*.

JOSIAH MILLER,
Editor of *Kansas Free State*.

WM. A. PHILLIPS,
Correspondent of *New York Tribune*.

EARLY KANSAS NEWSPAPER MEN.

to co-operate with them in the maintenance of the order and quiet of the community in which we live. "Very respectfully,

"ROBERT MORROW.
"LYMAN ALLEN.
"JOHN HUTCHINSON."

The reply of the marshal was not reassuring. It was both insolent and exasperating:

{ OFFICE OF UNITED STATES MARSHAL,
LECOMPTON, K. T., May 15, 1856.

"MESSRS. G. W. DEITZLER and J. H. GREEN, Lawrence, Kansas Territory:—On yesterday I received a communication addressed to me, signed by one of you as president and the other as secretary, purporting to have been adopted by a meeting of the citizens of Lawrence held on yesterday morning. * * *

"From your professed ignorance of the demands against you I conclude that you are strangers and not citizens of Lawrence; or of recent date, or have been absent for some time; more particularly when an attempt was made by my deputy to execute a writ of the first district court of the United States for Kansas territory against ex-Governor Reeder when he made a speech in the room, and in the presence of the congressional committee, and denied the power and authority of said court, and threatened the said deputy if he attempted to execute said process, which speech and defiant threats were loudly applauded by some one or two hundred of the citizens of Lawrence, who made such demonstrations that the deputy thought that he and his small posse would endanger their lives in executing the process.

"Your declaration that you will truthfully and earnestly offer now, or at any future time, no opposition to any legal process, is difficult to understand. May I ask, gentlemen, what has produced this wonderful change in the minds of the people of Lawrence? Have their eyes been suddenly opened so that they are now able to see that there are laws in Kansas territory which should be obeyed? Or, is it that just now those for whom I have writs have sought refuge elsewhere? Or, it may possibly be that you now, as heretofore, expect to screen yourself behind the word 'legal,' so significantly used by you. How am I to rely on your pledges when I am well aware that the whole population of Lawrence is armed and drilled, and the town fortified? When too I recollect the meetings and resolutions adopted in Lawrence and elsewhere in the territory, openly defying the laws and the officers thereof, and threatening to resist the same to a bloody issue, as recently verified in the attempted assassination of Sheriff Jones while in discharge of his official duties in Lawrence. If no outrages have been committed by the citizens of Lawrence against the laws of the land, they need not fear any posse of mine. But I must take the liberty of executing any and all processes in my hands as United States marshal, in my own time and manner, and shall only use such power as is authorized by law. You say you call upon the constituted authorities for protection. This indeed sounds strange, coming from a body of men armed with Sharpe's rifles and other implements of war, bound together by oaths and pledges to resist the government they call on for protection. All persons in Kansas territory, without regard to location, who honestly submit to the constituted authorities, will ever find me ready to aid in protecting them; and those who seek to resist the laws of the land, and turn traitors to their country, will find me aiding in enforcing the laws, if not as an officer, as a citizen.

"Respectfully yours,
"I. B. DONALDSON,
"*United States Marshal for Kansas Territory.*"

This reply cut off all hope of any relenting on the part of the marshal. Other efforts were made to avert the blow, but without effect. An attempt was made to induce the governor to secure United States troops to accompany the marshal instead of the miscellaneous mob which had assembled in answer to the marshal's proclamation. But the governor was not disposed even to do this much. He afterwards said he would have done this if the matter had been left to him. There remained nothing but to let events take their course. The marshal's posse had already begun to arrive before the proclamation was dated, showing that the plan was well understood, not by the marshal alone, but the pro-slavery people in Kansas and Missouri. The issuing of the proclamation was simply a form adopted to comply with the law. The word had gone out as to what was to be done, and the people began to gather. As they came they were armed with United States muskets, which had been sent for the use of the territorial militia. They had come promptly, for parties had been waiting on the border for these preliminaries of legal technicalities. They had failed in the Wakarusa war because these formal details had been carelessly attended to. They did not propose to have their plans upset again. Impatient as they were to get a blow at Lawrence, they would wait till the legal forms were complied with, rather than be balked again by the diplomacy of the shrewd Yankees.

As they came they formed camps at Lecompton, and other points, and awaited the orders of their chief. The whole country was once more in a state of terror. Travelers were stopped on the highway, people were robbed in their houses, stock was driven off, and houses were pillaged. A young man named Jones was murdered on his way home from Lawrence to his farm south of that place. Another man named Stewart, who went out with two others to secure the murderer, was also killed.

On the morning of May 21st, Marshal Donaldson with a posse of several hundred men, and some pieces of artillery, appeared on Mount Oread, the hill overlooking Lawrence. As these came under United States authority, it was decided to make no resistance. Deputy marshal Fain rode into town about eleven o'clock. The streets were very quiet. Some of the citizens were in prison, some who did not like the decision not to resist, took themselves out of the way. The deputy marshal rode up to the Free-State Hotel where the committee of safety were in session, and summoned a number of citizens to act as his posse in serving writs. He then arrested G. W. Smith, Gaius Jenkins, and G. W. Deitzler, who had been indicted for treason. The marshal and his men were invited to dine at the Free-State Hotel.

After dinner the marshal returned to the camp and told the men he had made all the arrests he desired at this time, and that they were dismissed. As soon as they were dismissed as the marshal's posse, Sheriff Jones summoned them to act as a posse for him, as he had some writs to serve. This then was their shrewd game. This mob was brought to Lawrence as the posse of the United States marshal. The people of Lawrence had determined in no case to resist United States authority. The town came easily into their possession. But an officer of the United States was limited by law and was compelled to pay some regard to decency and justice. All he could do was to make a few arrests to which the people made no objections. But as soon as the town had submitted and was helpless, he turned his posse over to Sheriff Jones who was hampered by no restrictions. The sheriff rode into town with a company of men and drew up in front of the hotel. He demanded first that all the arms in the place be given up to him. He gave the committee five minutes to decide. If the arms were not surrendered he would bombard the town. A hurried consultation was held, and it was decided to give up the cannon, and the arms in possession of the committee of safety. They told him the other arms were private property and not at the disposal of the committee.

The one cannon they possessed was hidden under a building and never could have been found by the invaders. But so anxiously nervous were they to appease the fussy sheriff and save the town, that General Samuel C. Pomeroy crawled under the building where the cannon was hidden, and dragged it out, and turned it over to Jones. But neither their promises nor their humiliation availed anything.

As soon as Jones had possession of the cannon and other arms, he proceeded to carry out his purpose to destroy the Free-State Hotel. He gave the inmates till five o'clock to get out their personal effects. When all was ready he turned his cannon upon the hotel and fired. The first ball went completely over the roof, at which all the people cheered, much to the disgust of Jones. The next shot hit the walls but did little damage. After bombarding away with little or no effect till it was becoming monotonous, they attempted to blow up the building with a keg of powder. But this only made a big noise and a big smoke, and did not do much towards demolishing the house.

At every failure the citizen spectators along the street set up a shout. At last Jones became desperate, and applied the vulgar torch, and burned the building to the ground. Meanwhile the two newspaper offices had been ransacked, the presses broken and the type thrown into the river, or scattered along the street. The mob by this time had become thoroughly reckless, and were ransacking the town. Nearly every house was entered, and many of them robbed. Trunks were broken open, clothing stolen, and everything taken off to which they took a fancy. In the evening Governor Robinson's house was set on fire and burned to the ground.

Jones was exultant. His revenge was complete. "This is the happiest moment of my life," he shouted as the walls of the hotel fell. He had made the "fanatics bow to him in the dust." He then dismissed his posse and left.

The losses sustained by the people of Lawrence and surrounding country were quite heavy. It was estimated that the value of the property destroyed and stolen amounted to nearly $200,000. A newspaper correspondent speaks of seeing some of these legalized bandits in Kansas City the next day, dressed in articles stolen at the sack of Lawrence. "They had crossed their native red shirt with a satin vest, or a narrow dress coat, pillaged from some Lawrence Yankee, or had girded themselves with the cord and tassels which the day before had ornamented the curtains of the Free-State Hotel." The committee of safety sent a statement of the whole affair to Washington afterwards, and from their paper we quote a few paragraphs. "Men endeavored by argument, and women by tears, to alter the determination of Jones, but in vain. The work of pillage had commenced. The contents of the printing offices had been scattered in the streets, and the red flag planted on the roof, first of the office of the *Herald of Freedom*, and afterwards of the Free-State Hotel. The family of Mr. G. W. Brown were driven from their home, and the immediate pillage of the hotel was prevented only by the resolute interference of a few citizens, aided by some individuals of the mob, who kept a strict guard at the doors, and insisted that the families of the proprietors should have the time promised them by Jones in which to collect their most necessary effects and leave. At last the cannons were placed and ready, and it was announced to Colonel S. W. Eldridge, that the bombardment would commence in five minutes. His wife and children were driven off between files of United States bayonets, and amidst the yells of the impatient mob. The work of pillage spread through the whole town, and continued until dark. Every house and store which could be entered was ransacked, trunks broken open and money and property taken at will. In one house over two thousand dollars in money were carried away. The house of Charles Robinson was pillaged and burned to the ground. Towards evening the forces were drawn off to their camp, and the sack of Lawrence was concluded."

To evade the pledge of the United States marshal that his posse should not enter Lawrence, they were disbanded on the hill, and then summoned to act as a posse for Sheriff Jones. The marshal dismissed them at the town limits, and the sheriff led them in.

All this was done in the name of law by men sworn to administer the law. Among the crowd were a United States marshal and his deputy, David R. Atchison, late vice president of the United States, and other men of distinction. It is but justice to say that many of these men endeavored to restrain the mob within some sort of bounds, but the mob was not of the kind that drew nice distinctions between burning down a hotel against which no wrong had been proved, and ransacking a private house or store. They were common, rough men who could not draw the distinction between crime by order of a court, and the same crime just outside the limits of that order. They could not appreciate therefore the eloquence of gentlemen who urged them to confine their outrages within the limits prescribed by the court. The result was that Lawrence suffered beyond the appointed measure, and was a pretty thoroughly demoralized community.

CHAPTER VII.

The Summer of 1856.—Outrages Everywhere.—Lawrence Invested by Pro-slavery "Forts."—The Capture of Franklin, Fort Saunders, and Fort Titus.—Titus a Prisoner.—Governor Shannon Makes Another Treaty.—Governor Shannon Resigns.—Daniel Woodson Acting Governor.

The sack of Lawrence was followed by an unprecedented condition of affairs. The whole territory was in a confusion. The summer that followed was the most exciting that Kansas ever knew. First of all came what has been known as the Potawatomie massacre. The news of the attack on Lawrence reached Osawatomie the day it occurred and while it was still being prosecuted. Old John Brown at once assembled a company of about fifty men and started for that place. Before reaching Lawrence they learned the particulars of the assault and found they were too late to render assistance. Most of the men returned to their homes, but John Brown with a small band remained. Two days later occurred the terrible tragedy at Dutch Henry's Crossing, which has never been satisfactorily explained, and which was quoted for years as the excuse for pro-slavery outrages without number. Other outrages followed on the other side and continued all summer. Captain Henry Clay Pate led a company of ruffians along the old Santa Fe trail, and robbed Black Jack and Palmyra and other places, and spread terror all about. Old John Brown, learning of his exploits, pounced upon him with a company of free-state men and captured the whole outfit. Then in turn, Colonel Sumner, with some United States troops, overhauled Brown and compelled him to release his prisoners. About the same time General Reid gathered about two hundred men in Missouri and marched through the border counties. He

COL. JAMES BLOOD,
First Mayor—1857.

A. D. SEARLE.
First City Engineer.

GEO. W. COLLAMORE,
Mayor at the time of the Raid.

DR. ALONZO FULLER,
Acting Mayor after the Raid.

LAWRENCE CITY OFFICIALS.

came to Osawatomie and let his ruffians loose there. They looted the town and finally burned it. Colonel Sumner approaching they withdrew and disappeared in Missouri. Bands of armed men of both parties moved here and there, each seeking to defend their own and to gain some advantage over the other. A number of so called battles were fought, but no great losses were sustained on either side. The men who were killed were usually attacked alone and murdered in cold blood. A drunken ruffian in Leavenworth made a bet that he would bring in the scalp of an abolitionist in less than two hours. He sallied out on the Lawrence road and met a Mr. Hoppe coming over from Lawrence in a carriage. He at once shot and scalped him, and bore the scalp into town on a pole amid the cheers of the crowds on the streets. An inoffensive German who expressed his horror at such brutality was shot dead. Mr. Hoppe was a brotner-in-law of Rev. Ephraim Nute, pastor of the Unitarian Church of Lawrence, and he and his wife were visiting there. Mr. Nute gave a very vivid account of the affair and the general condition in a letter written a week later, August 22nd, to a friend in Massachusetts:

"The horrors of ruffianism grow thicker and closer about us. My home has become a house of mourning. A brother-in-law came out to us and reached our house a week since with his wife, an own sister of mine. On Monday last he started to return to Leavenworth, leaving his wife sick. That night he was shot within a few miles of Leavenworth, and his scalp exhibited in fiendish exultation in the town.

"I have tried in vain to raise a body of men to go for the recovery of our brother's remains, to give them a decent burial, and for his effects about his person, all his money, etc. I have taken my rifle and offered to be one of fifty to go. A sufficient number responded and had pledged to go the morning after the sad tidings reached us. But it was thought best to delay until we should get answer from the officer in command of the United States dragoons camped about ten miles from here, to whom we had applied for a force to go with us. It came at night, referring us to a superior force then on the way with several companies to join Pierce's bloody officials at Lecompton. Twice have we sent, making the request of him for the protection of an escort to go with our teams to Leavenworth for provisions, and twice have been refused. There is not a single sack of flour or bushel of meal for sale in this vicinity, and we have at least two thousand men, women and children to be fed. What shall we do, what can we do, but fight our way through, with the desperation of men who know themselves surrounded by merciless savages. *This we are determined to do.* You will have a report of bloody work before this reaches you. It may be that nothing short of a massacre of the suffering people of Kansas will arouse this nation to a sense of the inconceivable wickedness of the men at the head of affairs. You may imagine the feelings with which I read the cold blooded sneers, the diabolical sport which is made of our sufferings in the Boston *Post* which I have just received. Are all the feelings of humanity, is all sense of decency dead in the minds of the men who uphold this infamous administration? Many of us have ceased to hope for anything but the foulest from the government. All that seems to be in store for us worth aspiring to is heroic martyrdom." * * *

A few days later Mr. Nute and his sister and several others went over to Leavenworth to ascertain the facts in regard to the murder of Mr. Hoppe and bring home his effects. They were all taken prisoners by a band under command of Captain Emory. Mrs. Hoppe was not permitted even to visit the grave of her husband, but was put on board a steamboat and sent down the river to her friends in Illinois. Mr. Nute, Mr. Wilder, a merchant of Lawrence, and their companions, some fifteen in all, were imprisoned in Leavenworth, and were not allowed to go home for over two weeks. Other outrages were committed in other parts of the territory.

A little earlier than this a political event had occured which increased the sense of unrest. On the Fourth of July the free-state legislature met at Topeka in Constitutional Hall. There had been rumors that they would be dispersed by federal troops. A free-state convention met at the same time to encourage the legislators, and as some thought to protect them if they were disturbed. As nothing of the kind was attempted, however, it was doubtful if there was any serious thought of such a thing. On the day of meeting Colonel E. V. Sumner appeared in Topeka with six hundred dragoons, and several pieces of artillery. As the hour of assembling drew near, the cannon were posted so as to sweep the street in front of the hall, and Colonel Sumner, with six hundred men, rode up in front of the building. He then went in and went forward to the speaker's stand. He said it was a very painful duty, but it was his duty, to order them, in the name of the president of the United States, to disperse. The members quietly went out, and the troops quietly went home. Some one asked Colonel Sumner why he brought so large a force, and if he expected to need them. He said, "No, I brought them that I might not need them." The governor about this time issued a proclamation ordering all bodies of armed men to disband, and promising protection to all without regard to party. But as there was a general suspicion among free-state men that this was meant for only one side, they all kept their arms and kept up their organizations. Neither party paid any attention to the proclamation, except as United States troops compelled compliance. The result of it all was that matters grew worse instead of better, and the excitement increased instead of subsiding.

The whole country shared the excitement, for the whole

nation was interested in the result of the conflict. Other events tended to intensify the common feeling. The day before the sacking of Lawrence Senator Charles Sumner made his great speech in the United States senate on the "Crime against Kansas." It was a terrible indictment of the national administration for its policy and the results of it. The day following, May 22nd, Preston S. Brooks struck him down with a cane, as he sat in his seat in the senate chamber. His act seemed to be but an echo of what was going on in Kansas at the same time. The whole country was in a blaze of indignation, and Kansas was the center towards which all eyes were turned. The whole North seemed to rise at once determined that Kansas should be free. There was but one way to make her free, and that was to settle the territory with free-state men. From all sections, and of all classes, immigrants moved towards Kansas. The farmer left his farm, the merchant left his store, the professional man left his office, at the impulse of an idea that had taken hold of his soul.

> "They left the plowshare in the mould,
> The sheep and herd without a fold,
> The cattle in the unshorn grain,
> The corn half garnered on the plain."

College students, just graduated, or before graduation, turned their back on the literary life they had chosen, or the professional life to which they were looking, and went to Kansas at the call of freedom. They came often without any definite idea as to what they were to do or how they were to make a living. That was entirely a secondary consideration. But they had a very decided idea as to what kind of a state Kansas must be. It was no uncommon thing to find college graduates driving an ox team through the streets of Lawrence, or cutting timber by the river, or living in some lonely shanty or dug-out

> "Far out upon the prairie."

Not in towns alone, but on claims all around, you would find the same class of people. In the loneliest cabins in the most out of the way place, you might find men who could talk to you intelligently of the latest scientific theory, or discuss the latest novel. And they did not come as adventurers to see how they would like it. But they came to stay and see the thing done. Whether they made a farm or not, whether they made a living or not, they proposed to make Kansas free. They came possessed of an idea, and they intended to make that idea effective. As a rule they were peaceable men who did not come to fight. But they were made of the stuff of which all heroes are made, and when they were compelled to fight, it was a sorry day for "the other fellow." There were rough and turbulent characters among them, and rash things and wrong things were done by them. But the great mass of free-state settlers came with honest intent to make Kansas a free state.

The pro-slavery people endeavored to meet this great uprising at the North by a counter-movement. The Missouri river had been the great highway to Kansas. There was no railroad, and the overland trip was long and tedious. The bulk of immigration came by way of the river. The Missourians determined to blockade the river, and thus stem the tide that was becoming irresistable. They thus expected to put a stop to free-state immigration to Kansas. Steamboats coming up the river were stopped and overhauled, usually with the connivance of the captain. If the captain objected it did not make any difference. Free-state passengers were taken off and sent back by the next down boat. The overland route was also blocaded, and the highways through Missouri were patrolled, and intending immigrants going overland were turned back.

As soon as this decision was known at the north it produced great consternation, as well as great indignation. It seemed as if the enemy had the key to the situation, and the rest of the country was helpless. But the discouragement did not last long. "Where there is a will there is a way." Here there were a good many wills, and they soon found there were more than one way. The Missourians did not own the earth. The blockade only turned the tide northward. The stream could not be stopped. They might as well try to stop the flow of the "Big Muddy" itself, as to stop the determined purpose of the north. Hindrances only stimulated it to more vigorous effort. A way was opened through Iowa and Nebraska, and the stream soon began to flow in a torrent along the new channel. Companies of two and three hundred strong made their way by this slow and circuitous route. It took longer but "they got there," in more ways than one. Everything that could be done to annoy and hinder was done. But it all stimulated the movement. The very attempt to stop the tide only increased its force and volume. Among these annoyances, these companies were accused of coming with hostile intent, and not as bona fide immigrants. The various companies were therefore met at the northern border of the territory by a force of United States troops and put under arrest. One writer who was with a company of some three hundred described their experiences. "When we came to the Kansas line we were met by the United States marshal and three hundred United States cavalry and put under arrest. The next day they marched us twenty-seven miles under a heavy guard. The next day, being Sunday, they marched us fifteen miles and camped on Straight creek, where in the evening we had religious services. On Monday morning we resumed our march and continued for two days when we came to the Kansas river not far from Topeka. Here we were met by the governor, and he being satisfied at our peaceful intentions set us all at liberty, and we went our various ways."

Thus the very efforts made to hinder really helped the cause. The more the way of the immigrants was blocked, the thicker and faster they came. The harder the journey the more eager people were to make it. Every outrage only stirred the popular mind more deeply, and made the common determination more strong. Every free-state man killed brought a score to fill his place. If the arguments of free-state speakers failed to move, the excesses of their opponents could not fail. It may truly be said that Kansas was made a free state by the excesses and outrages of those who sought to make it a slave state.

The bearing of all this on the history of Lawrence will be readily seen. Lawrence was the focus of the fight. The troubles she endured were a part of the general condition. She was the center of free-state operations, and consequently the center of pro-slavery hate and pro-slavery plots. She might be called the capital of the free-state party. The free-state party was more than a political organization. It was essentially a sort of second "body politic." It had a settled policy of its own, a sort of intangible organization that was effective for combined effort, but which could not be located. It had its soldiers and its officers, its arms and its unwritten laws. Its settled policy was to avoid conflict if possible, but to be prepared for defense. Its main point was to hold the ground until the preponderance of free-state immigration should settle the question at issue. It was a very shrewd policy and very difficult to maintain, but it was maintained with marvelous consistency.

After the judicial sacking of the town on the twenty-first of May, Lawrence was in a very depressed condition. Many of the people felt humiliated at the thought of having allowed such an outrage without even a show of resistance. According to the common agreement they just stood by and looked on, as the hotel and printing offices were destroyed and the town robbed. They were compelled to look on as all this was done; and also to endure the insults of the overbearing miscreants who exulted in their work, and called the citizens a pack of "cowardly Yankees." This was doubtless the wisest policy they could have chosen, but the situation was very galling. Their foes would have been delighted if they could have provoked them to resistance, and a good deal of their insolence and ostentation were for the purpose of goading them beyond endurance. Had the citizens resisted, even if they had been able to drive the marauders out of town, they would have been charged with resisting officers, and a new batch of indictments would have been issued, and a larger posse would have been secured. As it was, the ruffians were guilty of an unprovoked outrage, and had put themselves in the position of law-breakers, while professing to enforce law.

The feeling of depression was very general. The people knew not what next might come. They were not as well organized as they had been at the time of the Wakarusa war. Their trusted leaders were gone. Robinson was in prison near Lecompton. Many of their ablest citizens were in prison with him. Lane was out of the territory to avoid arrest. A great many others had left to escape indictment. Their leading men in prison, or fleeing from indictments, their beautiful hotel in ruins, their printing presses scattered, their houses broken into and robbed, and no law or courts to which they could appeal for redress, it was not strange that a spirit of despondency should settle over the community.

The troubles all over the territory found their focus in Lawrence. Bands of pro-slavery men roved about making travel dangerous and putting life in constant peril. Lawrence became invested by a system of forts, or block houses, where bands of pro-slavery men were housed, and from which they sallied on expeditions of plunder or revenge. One of these so-called forts was at Franklin, four miles east of Lawrence. Another, Fort Saunders, was on Washington creek, twelve miles southwest. A third was near Lecompton and was called Fort

REV. S. Y. LUM,
Preached first sermon.

REV. WM. BISHOP,
First Pastor of Presbyterian Church.

REV. RICHARD CORDLEY,
Pastor of Congregational Church.

REV. CHARLES REYNOLDS,
First Rector of Episcopal Church.

EARLY PASTORS OF LAWRENCE.

Titus. These forts were simply log houses, with port-holes for guns, and supplied with provisions and ammunition, and prepared for defense or siege. These three strong holds practically cut off Lawrence from help and from supplies. So close was the investment at one time, that provisions became very scarce, and there was danger of a famine from the fact that it was not possible to bring in supplies. The garrisons in these forts were continually committing depredations, waylaying travelers and robbing farms and slaughtering cattle. By August the situation in Lawrence was becoming unendurable, and they began to devise plans of relief.

August 12th Major S. D. Hoyt, a citizen of Lawrence, went to Fort Saunders to confer as to terms of peace, that both parties might cease their depredations. He was kindly received, but on his return two men accompanied him, and as soon as they came to a lonely spot they shot Hoyt dead, and left him half buried. This brutal murder so enraged the people of Lawrence, that they laid plans for the immediate reduction of these strongholds. They began with Franklin. This had always been a pestilent place. In the Wakarusa war it was the headquarters of the invading army. It was a pro-slavery settlement and the feeling towards Lawrence had been very bitter from the first. In June the free-state men had tried to reduce the place. They had attacked in the night and wasted no end of ammunition. But bullets had little effect on the heavy logs of which the fort was built. At daybreak they withdrew, leaving things pretty much as they were. But this time they had a stronger force, and a stronger provocation. The fort consisted of a block house, with a log house on either side. The free-state men made a night attack again, and began firing as before. They lay upon their faces, shielding their heads behind fences, humps of dirt, or anything that afforded a friendly shelter from the enemy's bullets. I heard one of these improvised soldiers tell his experience.

He had been brought up a quaker, but the Kansas outrages had so stirred his blood that he fell from grace so far as to carry a musket with the boys. When they came to their position, he lay down behind a fence post. At the command to fire he emptied his gun in the direction of the fort, but he said the enemy's bullets so pelted the ground about him, that he could not reload without running the risk of catching one of them. He lay still therefore. He said the bullets struck all around him, and threw the dirt in his face, and splintered his protecting fence poast, but spared his head. He said "It was the most careless shooting I ever witnessed." Whether the rest of the soldiers reserved their fire as this prudent young man did we are not advised. Whether they did or not there was little effect produced by the firing on either side. The garrison defied them. But they had underrated the resources of Yankee ingenuity. A load of hay stood in the street not far away. This they pushed towards the block house, and set fire to it. As the blazing load of hay came up against the logs, the inmates became panic stricken and cried for mercy. The free-state men then took possession, destroyed the fort, and carried off the arms and stores found therein. Among the arms was a cannon which was just the thing they needed to reduce the other forts. The only cannon the free-state men possessed had been surrendered at the sacking of Lawrence in May. One point in attacking Franklin first was to secure this cannon for use against the other forts.

The success at Franklin inspired the free-state men with increased zeal, and they began to gather from various quarters until three or four hundred men were in camp. The next point was Fort Saunders on Washington creek. They had a cannon now and could do more effective work in battering down walls. But they had no cannon balls. The piece was turned over to Captain Bickerton, the man who was so successful in bringing a cannon from Kansas City the autumn before. The first thing was to secure balls. Now the type of the two newspapers were put to a new use. In the sacking of the town in May the type had been scattered, many of them melted in the burning buildings. Captain Bickerton and his men gathered up the type and the type metal and molded them into balls for the cannon. Every time one was fired into the ruffians' stronghold the soldiers would shout, "Another issue of the *Herald of Freedom*."

When all was ready they proceeded against Fort Saunders. The refugees from Franklin had reinforced the garrison. The free-state men were under the command of Captains Shombre, Walker, Cracklin, Bickerton and others. While waiting, scouts found the body of Hoyt who had been murdered a few days before, and whose murder was the immediate cause of the attack. This so enraged the men that they insisted on moving at once. The officers had favored delay, but the men would not be restrained. The whole body marched forward at two o'clock on the afternoon of the 15th of August. The garrison fled before the troops reached the fort, leaving their guns and stores for the visitors. They also found near the fort the horse of the murdered Hoyt.

The next day they turned their attention to Fort Titus. They moved in this more speedily, as Titus and his men had been committing depredations in the neighborhood, which had exasperated the free-state men, and induced them to attempt the immediate destruction of the fort. Fort Titus was about two miles from Lecompton. It consisted of Colonel Titus' log house put in shape for defense. Here a number of pro-slavery desperadoes made their headquarters, and from this they were in the habit of sallying forth to harrass free-state men, and ravage the country. When pursued they fled to "the fort," and were safe from any ordinary attack. It was the strongest and most annoying of the three forts by which Lawrence had been invested. It was only two miles from Lecompton, which was the territorial capital, and the headquarters of pro-slavery operations. They could always rely on the support of their "friends" at the capital. Besides this it was only a mile from the camp where the free-state prisoners were kept. This camp was in charge of a company of United States soldiers under the command of Major John Sedgwick. The soldiers were there at the request of the governor, and were under orders from the territorial officials. These officials had a very peculiar way of making use of the soldiers. When pro-slavery men committed depredations the authorities at Lecompton could never get any "official" information in time to interfere. But whenever free-state men were moved to retaliate, the information came quickly and was always "official." Then a squad of troops would be ordered to go to the scene of disturbance and "preserve order." Colonel Titus had felt secure in the presence of these troops, who could reach him in a few minutes in case of attack. But his own movements and outrages were never reported in time to allow any intervention. Major Sedgwick was a soldier, and an honorable man, and he and his men had become very much disgusted with the one-sided way in which things were managed, and especially indignant at the part they were compelled to play. Major Sedgwick had also become thoroughly incensed at the insolence and outrages of Colonel Titus and his gang. Being a soldier under orders he could do nothing directly, but when he learned that the free-state men were about to take the thing in hand, and clean out the pestilent gang, he quietly told Captain Walker a few days before, that if "they wanted to gobble up old Titus and would do it quickly, he did not think he should be able to get over in time to hinder him."

Colonel Titus was from Florida. He was a typical border ruffian. In the pictures of him that have come down to us he is represented as a short, thick-set man, in his shirt sleeves, with a broad-brim slouch hat, and his pants stuck in his boots. He was a swaggering, blustering blatherskite, whose insolence was more offensive than his sword. He was a thick-necked, coarse-grained bully, and of course a miserable coward when it came to the test. He had established his fort at his house in order to harrass and annoy free-state people. He had gathered about him a gang like himself, and had been the terror of that whole region for months.

The free-state forces were now under the command of Captain Samuel Walker, as brave a man as ever lived, a man cool in counsel and wise in action. He came to be the trusted leader of the free-state men, not only on account of his skill, but because they could trust his prudence, and were always sure he would make no rash or doubtful move. He came to Kansas early in 1854 on a tour of inspection. In 1855 he returned bringing a large colony of immigrants from Ohio who settled in the territory. He himself took a claim seven miles west of Lawrence, where he lived until he moved into Lawrence itself. His claim was not very far from Fort Titus, and soon after he had located his claim this same Colonel Titus called on him and notified him that "all these nigger stealers must get out of the country." He gave him two weeks to make his exit. The next day Captain Walker called his neighbors together, and they organized themselves into a military company which they called the "Bloomington Guards." The pro-slavery plan was to drive settlers off one by one. This organization was made that they might sustain each other. The order of Titus was not enforced. This company of Bloomington Guards had eighty-six members, and they were all of the kind that are not frightened by bluster. All this drew upon Walker the special dislike of Titus. He did not attack him, but he endeavored to induce others to do so. He had printed a large hand-bill in which he offered five hundred dollars for the head of Samuel Walker, "on or off his shoulders." This hand-bill was posted up in various places with the evident intent of inducing some madcap to assasinate Walker. It was very natural, and very fitting that Captain Walker should lead the attack on Titus' fort.

This attack was made August 16th. The forces which operated against Fort Saunders August 15th moved towards Lecompton during the night and camped a short distance from the fort. Early in the morning Captain Henry J. Shombre started in advance of the main body with a company of cavalry, in order to surprise the fort. In the course of the attack Captain Shombre was shot and mortally wounded. Captain Shombre had only been in Kansas about three weeks. He came from Indiana, where he had raised a company of brave young men to come and help in the Kansas struggle. He joined Lane's party of immigrants in Iowa and came with them. He reached Topeka August 13th. Hearing of the troubles at Lawrence he started at once with his men and was present at the capture of Fort Saunders the day before his death. He was one of the finest and bravest young men that ever came to the territory, and even in the few days he was among them he won the affection and esteem of the free-state people.

After their leader fell Captain Shombre's men retired and waited till the main body had come up. When they came up they were so posted as to prevent the escape of the inmates of the fort. Firing then commenced and the men inside responded in a lively way. But the bullets of the assailants buried themselves in the logs of the fort and had no other effect. After a little the cannon captured at Franklin was brought into use by Captain Bickerton, and balls and slugs made from the type and printing presses of the *Herald of Freedom* were poured into the old building. This put a new face on the affair, and a few minutes after a white flag appeared, and the garrison of some seventeen men surrendered. Colonel Titus crawled out of his den, coatless and covered with blood. He had received two wounds, one in his hand and the other in his shoulder. He came out as meek and cringing as he had formerly been insolent. He begged piteously for his life. He had been such a terror to the whole country that the men in the free-state army had determined to kill him. Many of them had suffered from his insolence and cruelty. He appealed to Captain Walker to save him. "You have children; so have I; for God's sake, save my life!" Right before them was one of those hand-bills, offering five hundred dollars for Walker's head "on or off his shoulders." Walker saw it plastered on the walls of the cabin while he was talking to him. But Walker was as chivalrous as he was brave, and would not strike a fallen foe. Some of his men had been so wrought up by the outrages Titus had committed that it was not easy to restrain them. But Walker insisted that they must not touch him, and no man raised his gun.

The casualties of this battle were not numerous. Two of Titus' men were killed and two wounded, and one free-state man was killed and six wounded. The prisoners were taken to Lawrence and held as "prisoners of war."

The next morning Governor Shannon, Major John Sedgwick, and Dr. A. Rodrique, postmaster at Lecompton, went to Lawrence to arrange terms of peace and secure the liberation of Titus and his men. A correspondent of an eastern paper gives an account of this remarkable incident:

"Another Sunday morning treaty with Shannon. Governor Shannon, Dr. A. Rodrique, postmaster, and Major Sedgwick have just arrived from Lecompton. It is supposed that they have come to demand the prisoners. They are now closeted with the officers of the free-state forces. They cannot have the prisoners without giving the free-state party an equivalent.

"Later:—A treaty has been made, and Governor Shannon, after some opposition, has been permitted to state what it is, and to make a short speech. He said he should leave us, and he wanted to leave the territory with the people feeling better towards him, and in a quiet state, to his successor. He glorified the union and thought we had a glorious country.

"The terms of the treaty are substantially as follows:

"1. That they shall give up to the charge of Major Sedgwick, and in good condition, subject to the order of Captain Walker, the howitzer so valiantly surrendered to Sheriff Jones the 21st of May.

"2. That the prisoners then held in custody at Lecompton, those arrested by 'Squire Crane for being connected with the battle of Franklin, shall be released and brought safely to Lawrence.

"3. That all arms taken from these and other prisoners shall be given up.

"4. That the territorial authorities should use their power to break up these bands of plunderers and drive them from the territory.

"In consideration of this the free-state men were to deliver up their prisoners. They even demanded the cannon taken at Franklin. Major Sedgwick had nothing to do with the negotiations, any further than to say to Shannon that it was his duty to make an unconditional demand for the prisoners. The Franklin prisoners held at Lecompton were arrested under legal process, as they term it, yet they agreed to deliver them up. What right Governor Shannon and Dr. Aristides Rodrique had to do this perhaps a Philadelphia lawyer can tell; we can't."

After the treaty, when Governor Shannon desired to talk to the people, there was a general growl of opposition. They felt that he was responsible for their troubles, and they had suffered so much that they were greatly embittered. When the governor proposed to speak they gave a yell which drowned his voice. They were in an ugly frame of mind and the situation was alarming. Captain Walker saw the danger, and drawing his revolver he rushed in front of the crowd and shouted, "I am with you, boys, but the governor shall not be

DR. S. B. PRENTISS,
Chairman First School Committee.

DR. ALBERT NEWMAN,
Secretary First School Committee.

LATHROP BULLENE,
President of First Board of Education.

CHAS. L. EDWARDS,
Principal of First High School.

EARLY EDUCATORS AND TEACHERS.

insulted." After that everything was quiet and the governor made his speech, in substance as follows:

"FELLOW CITIZENS:—I appear before you under very extraordinary circumstances, and I ask your attention to a few remarks in relation to them. I came down here today for the purpose of adjusting these difficulties, and I regret as much as any man can the existence of these difficulties. I wish to set myself right before the people of Lawrence. I have been misrepresented through the press, and my motives have either been misunderstood or purposely aspersed, and things have been said of me which never happened. I desire now to say while I remain in office, that I have never done a single act but what I believed would best subserve the interests of the whole people. God knows I have no ill-feeling against any man in the territory.

"I am sorry blood has been shed here. In the revolution our fathers from both the North and South fought and bled together, for the same common cause, the cause of liberty, and the result was a glorious triumph, and the security to themselves and their posterity of their inalienable rights. So it was in the war of 1812; so it was in the war with Mexico, and each time the stars and stripes floated over a conquered nation. Shall we steep our hands in our brother's blood?"

Here were cries from the crowd, "Give us back Barber and others that have been murdered." "Order!" "Order!" "Law and order!" "Don't insult the governor." "Go on." The governor resumed when quiet was restored:

"I came here for the purpose of peace, to try and adjust a serious difficulty between the people now in the territory. In a few days my successor will be among the people of this territory, and I desire now to say that the few days that remain of my continuance in office will be devoted to the furtherance of peace and harmony, and to carry out the terms of the agreement which will be the final settlement of all strife."

"Let us hear the agreement," a voice cried. "I do not understand the terms." "Let us hear the terms." "Order!" "Order!" "Law and order!" After quiet was again restored, the governor stated the terms of the agreement, and concluded:

"Fellow citizens of Lawrence, before leaving you I desire to express my earnest desire for your health, happiness, and prosperity. Farewell.

This treaty was one of the most remarkable ever made, not

in its terms, but in the parties between whom it was made. A great nation, in the person of Governor Shannon, makes a treaty of peace with a committee of citizens, stipulating for an exchange of prisoners and captured property, and a mutual cessation of hostilities. The governor agreed to surrender the cannon captured at the sacking of Lawrence, and the prisoners held for participating in the various conflicts, and the free-state men agreed to surrender Titus and his men.

CHAPTER VIII.

RETALIATION.—GOVERNOR SHANNON RESIGNS.—WOODSON ACTING GOVERNOR.—MARTIAL LAW.—MILITIA CALLED OUT.—MISSOURI RESPONDS.—TWENTY-EIGHT HUNDRED MARCH ON LAWRENCE.—GOVERNOR JOHN W. GEARY ARRIVES.—APPEARS IN LAWRENCE WITH TROOPS.—THE MILITIA SENT HOME.—"THE BENIGN INFLUENCE OF PEACE."

But high as was the authority making the treaty, the free-state men soon found it was not high enough. They had treated with the governor of Kansas who represented the government of the United States, but this did not bind the powers that were making war. There was a power behind the throne, which was determined to use the throne for its own purpose or else topple the throne over. Territorial governors and judges and officials were counted as instruments to accomplish a purpose, and that purpose was to enslave Kansas. The pro-slavery party was above the territorial authorities. If they could not control them they could change them. Every governor came expecting to sustain the pro-slavery policy. Nearly every governor had his eyes opened after a short experience, and endeavored to do what was fair and just. And every governor when he came to this position was removed. It had been so with Reeder; it was now so with Shannon. Reeder had fled from the territory in peril of his life. Shannon was more conservative and more slow in coming to his conclusions, but now his life was threatened and he remained only a few days after the treaty of August 17th. It is interesting to note that ex-Governor Shannon afterwards returned to Kansas and chose Lawrence as his home, and he remained there the rest of his life, held in the highest esteem by everybody.

As was intimated above, the treaty of peace did not bring

peace. The parties making war were not bound by it. The free-state successes in capturing the strongholds about Lawrence stirred up the pro-slavery elements in Kansas and Missouri to the wildest frenzy. Exaggerated accounts of these various affairs were published in pro-slavery papers on the borders, and frantic appeals made for vengeance. It was represented that pro-slavery men were everywhere being driven from their homes, and were in danger of their lives. The fight at Fort Titus was magnified into an all-day contest in which the inmates manifested the greatest heroism, and only surrendered to the force of overwhelming numbers. Titus was a martyr to the truth in the hands of men who would tear him in pieces. They pictured the country in a state of terror, men running for their lives, women and childrdn fleeing from their burning homes. They thus sought to "fire the southern heart," and gather a force by which they could not only be avenged, but recover the ground lost. The press of the border was lurid with descriptions and frantic with appeals. Flaring headlines announced the news: "Important from Kansas;" "Civil war and rebellion;" "Women and children fleeing from their houses for their lives." It called upon the friends of slavery "to rise as one man and put an effectual quietus on the hired tools of abolition now rampant over the plains of Kansas with firebrand and sabre. * * * To strangle the demon of disunion." The whole border was aflame and sectional passion at a white heat. Everything was astir in Kansas, too. Bands of armed men, of both parties, were moving here and there, endeavoring to outwit each other, and sometimes coming in conflict with each other, but more commonly expending their valor on defenseless people.

At this point an event occured which gave the pro-slavery party an advantage, which they were not slow to improve. Governor Shannon left the territory August 21st. Then

Daniel Woodson, the secretary of the territory, became again acting governor. He was in full accord with the pro-slavery managers. He would go with them to the full length. He had no qualms of conscience, and no spasms of indecision. He believed in the pro-slavery policy, and he had the courage of his convictions. He believed the territorial laws were valid, and he was prepared to push that theory to its logical conclusion. He stopped at no half-way measures, and shrank from no appalling results. He had been secretary from the first, and had acted as governor at each interregnum. Every time he came to power the pro-slavery people had an open field, and carried things with a high hand. They could not devise any plan for humiliating the free-state people which Woodson was not ready to sanction. Had he been in power for any length of time it would have changed the whole aspect of affairs. It would have shortened the Kansas struggle. It might have reversed its result. More likely it would have driven all the free-state men to adopt the policy of John Brown, take their rifles and fight it out to "the bitter end." His term of office was each time short, and always closed just as his plans were on the border of full execution. In most cases his term of power closed just at the crisis of the emergency he had invoked.

Secretary Woodson assumed the office of acting governor August 21st. Four days later, August 25th, he issued a proclamation written with the same carmine ink used in the editorials over the border. He represented that the "territory of Kansas was infected with large bodies of armed men, many of whom have just traveled from the states, combined and confederated together, and amply supplied with munitions of war; these armed men had been engaged in murdering the law-abiding citizens of the territory, driving others from their homes, * * * holding others as prisoners of war, * * * plundering property, * * * burning down houses, * * * even robbing United States postoffices, * * * and all this for the purpose of subverting by force and violence the government established by the law of congress in the territory."

"Now therefore, I, Daniel Woodson, acting governor of the territory of Kansas, do hereby issue my proclamation, declaring the said territory of Kansas to be in an open state of insurrection and rebellion; and I do hereby call upon all law-abiding citizens of the territory to rally to the support of the territory and its laws, and require and command all officers, civil and military, and call all other citizens of the territory, to aid and assist, by all means in their power, in putting down the insurrectionists, and bringing to condign punishment all persons engaged with them, to the end of insuring immunity from violence, and full protection to the persons, property and civil rights of all peaceable and law-abiding inhabitants of the territory."

This proclamation, like most of its predecessors, was not intended for home consumption. It was intended for use across the border, and to furnish a cover under which Missourians could march in again and help to settle the affairs of their neighbors. There was a great eagerness in Missouri to respond to this appeal from the governor, and a great rush to be enrolled in the militia of Kansas territory. As Charles Robinson says in his "Conflict":

"Guerrilla bands of pro-slavery men infested the territory as if by magic. Intercourse with Leavenworth was cut off, and the beleaguered town of Lawrence was nearly destitute of provisions as well as ammunition. Men unarmed and defenseless were shot down like dogs, and in one instance at least scalped. All appeals to Woodson were in vain."

An army was gathering on the eastern border. All the "tried and true" pro-slavery leaders were in it. There was Atchison and Reed, and other large fish and small fry, all helping to increase the tumult. The army marched on Osawatomie, which, next to Lawrence, was the most hated place in the territory. They easily captured this place, and, after pillaging it, burnt the town. Six free-state men lost their lives, and nobody has ever been able to ascertain how many were killed on the other side.

But in these affairs they only "tried their 'prentice hand." Their masterpiece was to be the destruction of Lawrence. Without that their victory would be incomplete. As their force increased they prepared for the supreme effort. Lawrence, meanwhile, was poorly prepared to resist. The fortifications which had been thrown up the year before had been largely broken down. The town had been demoralized by the sacking of the place in May. The men, too, were scattered. Even the "Stubbs," the favorite rifle company of Lawrence, was just then absent on some mission at Hickory Point. The free-state men to the north and west of Leavenworth had been driven from their claims by bands of pro-slavery maurauders who were roving about the country. These refugees, under the lead of such men as Hon. F. G. Adams, now of the State Historical Society, were anxious to recover their claims and return to their homes. They called upon Topeka and Lawrence for help, and were planning to march to Leavenworth to recover their claims, and if possible deliver that town from border ruffian rule. On account of this disturbed condition towards the north, the "Stubbs" had marched over towards Hickory Point, and a series of skermishes took place. For this reason the best organized and best equipped company of Lawrence was away just at the crisis of affairs. There were only about three hundred men available about Lawrence, and not more than fifty of these were armed with Sharp's rifles.

An encouraging event, however, occurred about this time; that was the release of the free-state prisoners at Lecompton. It will be remembered that these prisoners were the leaders of the free-state cause, and many of them belonged in Lawrence, such as Dr. Robinson, G. W. Deitzler, G. W. Brown, Gaius Jenkins, and others. Amos A. Lawrence, of Boston, after whom the town was named, was an old time friend of Dr. Robinson. He was also a personal friend of President Pierce. He exerted all the influence he could bring to bear to induce the president to order the release of the prisoners on bail. After a long delay the president consented and and ordered their release. They were "turned loose," as one of them expressed it, September 10th, and went to Lawrence where they were received with great rejoicing. Having been in prison four months, however, they could not do much towards the defense of the town in the short time remaining.

Another event favorable to the free-state cause, and really the turning point of the occasion, was the appointment of John W. Geary as governor. The pro-slavery people were clamoring for a pro-slavery governor. They would have been contented with the promotion of Woodson, as he would have served their purpose. But they wanted a man who knew the situation, and one whom they could trust. They did not want another Reeder who would go over to the enemy as soon as he found the kind of work they were doing. They did not want another Shannon who should fail them just in the nick of time. They wanted a man who not only sympathized with their general purpose, but who would carry out their policy to the final issue; a man whose nerve would not give out when he came to the hard places. With such a man they felt they could drive the free-state men from the territory. The border press gave the administration any amount of good advice on this point. Their ablest editorials were constructed with a view of convincing the president and his advisers of their duty in the matter. But it fortunately happened that the administration had reasons for really desiring to quiet affairs in Kansas. In fact it was a political necessity that this should

MARY (BOUGHTON) BROOKS.

SARAH A. BROWN.

LIZZIE (HASKELL) FRENCH.

LUCY (WILDER) WOODWARD.

FIRST TEACHERS IN CITY SCHOOLS.

be done, and done at once. A presidential election was coming off in November. The Kansas troubles were working havoc in the democratic party. They were indeed becoming more disastrous to that party than to the free-state party in the territory. In fact they were bringing about that great political revolution which four years later swept the country from ocean to ocean. Even southern leaders, such as Jefferson Davis who was secretary of war, saw that it would be better to quiet Kansas for a time at least than to be hurled from power altogether and lose everything they were contending for. The choice fell on John W. Geary, of Pennsylvania. He was strictly charged that he must restore peace in Kansas at all hazards. The administration promised to support him to the full extent of its power. Governor Geary had been in the California troubles with Dr. Robinson, and knew something of what the task meant. He was a man of ability, with great executive force, and infinite conceit of himself. He was a man of good judgment and right instincts. He arrived at Leavenworth September 9th. He issued at once a proclamation. In this he stated, "that the employment of militia was not authorized by his instructions except upon the requisition of the commander of the military department.

"That an authorized regular force had been placed at his disposal to insure the execution of the laws:

"Therefore he declared that the services of such volunteer militia were no longer required, and they were ordered to be immediately discharged.

" He further commanded that all bodies of men, combined, armed and equipped with munitions of war, instantly disband or quit the territory, or they will answer the contrary at their peril."

Governor Geary reached Lecompton September 10th, and this proclamation was issued the next day. There could not be much doubt about the meaning of it. It was certainly couched in very plain English. The free-state men would have obeyed at once, if they could have been assured that it was meant for both parties. But they had been accustomed to proclamations that were intended for free-state men. Pro-slavery offenses were winked at while free-state offenders were pursued to the death. They feared to lay down their arms until they knew that the governor would require the same of the other side.

The pro-slavery army took no notice of it. They too had been accustomed to proclamations that were expected to apply only to free-state men. They moved right on, therefore, just as if no new governor had come, and no new proclamation had been issued. The army had swelled by this time to some twenty-eight hundred men. It was the largest, best organized and best equipped army that had ever come up from Missouri. Had they moved forward promptly they could have destroyed Lawrence before relief could reach the place. Procrastination proved the thief he always is, and stole their opportune time from them.

September 14th the enemy began to approach Lawrence. Preparations were at once made for defense. A body of armed men were placed on the circular earthworks at the corner of Massachusetts and Henry streets. Another on Rhode Island street, and others in other sections. The Stubbs and most of the best armed men were away, and the prospect for defense did not seem very flattering. About the middle of the afternoon the word went over the town, "they are coming." Captain Cracklin was charged with the duty of going out to see who had come and what. In a letter he tells the story of his effort:

"I went for the Stubbs but found they had disobeyed orders and left town with Colonel Harvey. I regretted this very much. I then hunted the Wabaunsee rifles. As I was returning I heard some cry out, "there they come." I stopped, turned my eyes in the direction of Franklin, and I saw a large body of horse-men going towards Mr. Haskell's. I immediately started on the run for the Wabaunsee boys and told them to follow me; and then started on a dog trot towards the cabin of John Speer, and halted a short distance from it on top of a ridge. At the time I halted, the enemy had passed into the timber beyond Haskell's. Supposing it their intention to pass into the bottom and approach the town from that direction, I concluded to wait where I was till they showed themselves, feeling sure that with them in the bottom, I would have the advantage of position, and could attack them with a plunging fire. I was disappointed, however. In a few minutes they made their appearance, coming out of the timber and heading towards us. As soon as they got in range I ordered the boys to open fire. They had not fired more than a dozen shots, when looking towards the town I saw quite a number of men on the run to our assistance. In the meantime the enemy had disappeared in a hollow or ravine. As fast as my friends arrived I placed them in line until my force amounted to fifty-eight. I sent Ed. Bond to see what the enemy was doing. We watched him until he arrived at the entrance of the ravine where the enemy were concealed, when he stopped, leveled his rifle and fired. He then put spurs to his horse and galloped back. He reported them in the ravine at a halt, some of them dismounted. I then ordered a forward movement, with my line extended as skirmishers. We had a space of half or three-quarters of a mile to cross before we would reach the ridge that separated us from the enemy. On reaching it we discovered them just going out of the upper end of the ravine in the direction of Hanscom's farm. I ordered the boys to open fire and load and fire at will. Our whole line immediately commenced blazing away. They fired several shots in return but they fell short. One of their men was seen to fall near Mr. Hanscom's fence. They put spurs to their horses and galloped towards Franklin."

This ended the contest for the day. But this was only the advance sent ahead to feel the way. The army was behind and was coming. The spirited manner in which the advance was met probably kept them from attacking in force that day. If they had done so they could easily have captured the town. But by waiting a day they lost their opportunity.

During the day dispatches had been sent to Governor Geary at Lecompton apprising him of the seriousness of the situation. He immediately sent Colonel Johnson with a force of artillery and cavalry to Lawrence. They arrived during the night, and posted their cannon on Mount Oread, while the dragoons took their place south of town. In the morning as the citizens arose, they beheld the stars and stripes floating on Mount Oread, and cannon bristling from its summit, while the dragoons lay between them and the enemy. The sensation of relief and thankfulness which came over them was something never to be forgotten. A gentleman who was there said to the writer of this that "words could not express our feelings towards those soldiers coming thus in the nick of time to our relief. United States soldiers had never helped us before. They had always been with our enemies." They were not willingly with the enemy, but they were under orders. The orders were given by the territorial authorities, and the territorial authorities carried out the policy of the pro-slavery party. If there was an annoying, exasperating process to be served a few United States soldiers were sent with the officers. Then the free-state people could do no other than submit, no matter how unjust or how malicious the process might be. Under no circumstances would free-state men resist United States soldiers. When bands of pro-slavery men were roaming about the country, plundering and murdering, and keeping the whole community in terror, the officials never knew of it till it was too late to interfere. But if free-state men undertook any counter movement, the officials learned of it with surprising promptness, and United States troops were sent "to disperse the outlaws." Many of their plans of annoyance would have failed but for the use they could make of these United States troops. Yet the troops themselves had no sympathy with the policy they were compelled to support, and often despised the work they were compelled to do. But they were true soldiers, and obeyed orders, and often did good by their impartiality, and prevented unauthorized outrages such as were often committed by volunteer posses, under the charge of territorial officers. The soldiers bore themselves admirably, and won the highest regard of all the free-state men, notwithstanding the part they were compelled to play. After all this experience it was a new sensation which the people of Lawrence felt that morning, when they saw that these brave soldiers had actually come to their assistance in the hour of great peril.

Early in the morning of September 15th, Governor Geary followed the troops and came to Lawrence. He found the men all under arms expecting the army from below. He promised them full protection, and advised them to go to their homes and resume their ordinary business. Trusting his word, they were thankful and rejoiced in the sense of security.

The governor pushed on at once for Franklin, where the invading army was encamped. Before he reached Franklin he met the advance guard already on their way. He asked them who they were, and what they proposed to do. They replied that they were "the territorial militia called into service by the governor of Kansas, and they were marching to wipe out Lawrence, and every abolitionist in the country." He informed them that "he was now governor of Kansas, and commander-in-chief of the militia," and he ordered the officer to turn his troops about, and march back to camp. There was a good deal of grumbling, and some hesitation, but they soon ordered a right about face, and conducted the governor to the main body. Dr. J. H. Gihon, Governor Geary's private secretary, gives a full description of the scene:

"There in battle array were ranged at least three thousand armed and desperate men. They were not dressed in the usual habiliments of soldiers, but in every imaginable costume that could be obtained in that region. Scarcely two presented the same appearance, while all exhibited a ruffianly aspect. Most of them were mounted, and manifested an unmistakable disposition to be at their bloody work. * * * In passing along the lines, rumors of discontent and savage threats of assassination fell on the governor's ears, but heedless of these * * * he proceeded to the headquarters of the leaders."

The governor summoned the officers together and addressed them in a very adroit way, and explained the situation and his own policy, and then ordered them to disperse. There were some mutterings, and even a suggestion that they should pitch into the United States troops, and go on and finish their job. But this was only the bluster of disappointment, and the wiser ones saw the folly of attempting to go forward. In a little while the whole army was on its way home to Missouri.

They went away in a sullen mood, and in anything but a peaceable spirit. They stole horses and cattle on the way, and made free with whatever they found. This could have been endured, for it was soon to end. But some of them did not confine their depredations to cattle and horses. A company of Kickapoo Rangers went home by way of Lecompton, crossing the Kansas river at that place, and going north. They were not in a hurry either. September 17th, two days after the army disbanded, they were going towards Lecompton some seven miles from Lawrence. Here they came upon David C. Buffam, working with his team. Buffam had come to Kansas with the second party in 1854. While guarding one of the forts in Lawrence he was accidently wounded in the thigh, and was crippled for life. He afterwards went on a farm where this gang of desperadoes found him. They wanted his horse. He protested against it, and told them "he was a cripple, a poor lame man; that he had an aged father, a deaf and dumb brother, and two sisters dependent on him, and he was dependent on his horses to make a living." His pleading enraged them, and one of them siezed him by the shoulder with one hand and shot him with the other. They then took his horse and left him to die. A few minutes after Governor Geary and Judge Cato came along where he was lying. They dismounted and came up and heard the dying man's story. The governor was so much moved that he asked Judge Cato to take the poor man's dying deposition.

On his return to Lecompton the governor had a warrant sworn out for the arrest of the murderer, and placed it in the hands of the marshal. The marshal had been remarkably vigorous in the arrest of free-state men on all sorts of charges, but he was not able to find the murderer of Buffam, and so reported. The governor by this time began to grow angry, and offered a reward of five hundred dollars for the arrest of the murderer. Some weeks after he learned that the man, whose name was Hays, was living in Atchison county, and he at once ordered his arrest, and he was indicted on the charge of murder in the first degree. But a week later Judge Lecompte released him on bail. The governor was thoroughly enraged at the unwarranted interference, and had Hays arrested again. But Judge Lecompte again released him on a writ of *habeas corpus*. This was the end of the case, as the governor saw he was dealing with men who would go to any extreme to carry their point.

Another incident which illustrated the same thing was the misfortune which befell the "Stubbs," the favorite military company of Lawrence. As was said they were not present when the Missourians came up. They had been ordered by Colonel Lane to go to Hickory Point, where a number of pro-slavery men had fortified themselves in a log house. Under the command of Colonel J. A. Harvey they and others made an attack September 14th and kept up the firing for several hours. Then the pro-slavery party surrendered. There had been one pro-slavery man killed, and several on both sides wounded. The prisoners were at once released, and the free-state men started home. On their way home they were met by a body of United States troops and made prisoners. They considered their capture as a trivial affair, and went on cheerfully with their captors. They expected nothing more serious than a little delay. But when they reached Lecompton they were put under arrest and kept as prisoners waiting an examination. They were given poor shelter and poor rations, and their examination was provokingly delayed. When an examination was at last accorded them, they were indicted for murder, and Judge Cato refused to admit them to bail. They received their trial in October. Some were acquitted, and some convicted of varying degrees of crime. Those convicted were kept in prison, and Sheriff Jones wished to subject them to still greater indignity by putting balls and chains upon them. Governor Geary, however, refused to furnish these articles of footgear, and they were spared this outrage. The officer put in charge of them, however, was kind to them, and let them go about as they pleased on their word of honor that they would return. A southern gentleman visiting Lecompton wished to see these prisoners of whom he had heard such dreadful stories. The governor pointed out to him where they were, and he walked over. Not seeing any frowning prison he inquired of two men, who were pitching quoits, where the prison was. They pointed to an old tumbled down house without windows or doors, and informed him that that was the prison. He was astonished at the prison, and said he wanted to see the prisoners.

"Well, I am one of them, and that is another," pointing to his companion.

"But do they allow convicted murderers to go about in this way, without a guard to watch them?"

"Oh, yes. They used to send a guard when we went over to the legislature, to protect us from the members; but it was too much trouble and expense, and they told us we must protect ourselves."

"But why don't you run away?"

B. W. WOODWARD,
First Druggist.

PAUL R. BROOKS,
First General Merchandise.

J. G. SANDS,
First Saddler.

ROBERT L. FRAZER,
First Jeweler.

FIRST MERCHANTS IN LAWRENCE.

"We have often been urged to do that, but these rascally legislators have been threatening to kill the governor, so we propose to stay here and watch them and protect him."

On the second day of March, 1857, the governor pardoned the whole lot, in compliance with numerous petitions to that effect. He pardoned them on the ground that "the offense for which they were convicted was committed in a political contention in which most of the people were engaged; that while others more guilty were still at large, they had been punished sufficiently already, and that their further punishment would neither subserve the ends of justice nor the interests of the territory." So after nearly six months the "Stubbs" were all at home again. They had conducted themselves manfully during the whole trying experience, and had won the entire confidence of their keepers, Captain Hampton and his men.

CHAPTER IX.

THE BOGUS LEGISLATURE AGAIN.—GOVERNOR GEARY COMES INTO COLLISION WITH IT.—HE IS BITTERLY ASSAILED BY PRO-SLAVERY LEADERS.—RESIGNS IN MARCH.—WALKER AND STANTON.—PEACE AND PROGRESS AND PROSPERITY.—LAWRENCE AND HER VOLUNTARY CITY GOVERNMENT.—MARTIAL LAW ONCE MORE.

After the "army of invasion" had left, September 15th, 1856, Governor Geary continued his effort at restoring peace and order. He commanded all bodies of armed men to disband, and promised protection to all alike. As soon as they were convinced that he meant what he said the free-state men acquiesced cheerfully in his policy. They only wanted quiet and fair play. In a few weeks order was restored, and everybody could go peaceably about his work. But the governor's attempts to administer equal justice and secure fair play for all were not well received by his own political associates. A man who insisted on fair play was not at all to their mind. They distrusted him from the first. They had not been consulted in his appointment, and their advice as to what kind of a governor was needed had been entirely disregarded. When they found him trying to give justice to free-state and pro-slavery men alike, they had no further use for him. They began at first to embarrass him, and then openly to antagonize him. During the session of the legislature the following winter he was in conflict with them continually. He sought to procure legislation that would promote peace and order, while they were aiming at legislation that would favor their own idea and desire. He vetoed several of their bills, but they passed them over his veto. The feeling ran so high that his life was several times threatened, and he began to be in constant fear of violence. To make matters worse, he began to discover that they had been working against him at Washington, and that the national administration had deserted him. When things seemed threatening and he asked for troops to maintain peace, he was coolly informed that "there were no troops available for that purpose." When he first came the administration answered all his requisitions promptly, and to the full extent. Now there "were no troops available." Of course he knew what that meant. When he first came to Kansas a national election was impending, and he was urged to "quiet Kansas at any cost." Now the election had been held, the administration had been successful, and peace in Kansas was no longer essential to them.

As pro-slavery men deserted the governor free-state men rallied about him. They even offered to furnish a military guard when United States troops were refused him. But this he wisely declined. The free-state men had predicted what the outcome would be if he adhered to his policy of equal justice. One day in the previous autumn, when he was discoursing confidently as to what he was going to do, Captain Walker, who was present, said to him, "We like your talk first rate, but I predict that you will take the underground railroad out of Kansas in less than six months." His words were prophetic. The breach between him and the pro-slavery leaders grew wider and wider, and the conflict more and more bitter. He worried through the winter, and had a stormy time during the session of the legislature. They were many of them rough men, living in a rough time, and desperate. By spring the strain of the conflict had become unendurable, and March 4th he sent in his resignation. Before his resignation became known in Kansas, he had quietly left the territory, and never returned. Only a few trusted friends knew the purpose of his departure. He feared to have his resignation known until he himself was out of reach.

Governor Geary had proved himself the man for the time.

Personally he fared just as the free-state people predicted, and just as his predecessors had fared. The moment it was discovered that he would not concede all the pro-slavery leaders demanded, they forsook him; and when they forsook him the administration at Washington forsook him also. He came to Kansas with the sound of trumpets, and with the tread of a conquering hero. He left Kansas six months later in the night, careful that even his footsteps should not be heard. He had added largely to his stock of experience, but his stock of conceit had been very materially reduced. He came with the sense of victory, and left with the sense of failure. But his administration was not a failure. It was a very marked success. He accomplished what he set out to do. He found the territory in a state of civil war and on the eve of a great calamity. He restored and maintained order throughout all the land, and in his own favorite phrase, he gave the people "the benign influences of peace." And peace was what Kansas needed. She was weary of war and worn out of the conflict. And the peace that came with his administration came to stay, and continued to reign when he was gone. There were local disturbances and local outrages after that, but the territory as a whole was quiet and its people were permitted to prosper, with no one to molest them or make them afraid.

Lawrence enjoyed to the full extent the peace that came to her when the "army" left. She had known no quiet since early spring. Much of the time business was practically suspended, and some of the time the people were in danger of famine. There could be no improvement made and no progress. These few weeks of quiet before winter, were much appreciated, and very necessary for preparation for the winter's comfort. There was not much building going on, but everybody did his utmost to repair the damages of the summer, and to get ready for the cold of winter.

After the resignation of Governor Geary, President Buchanan took a month to consider the question of a successor. April 10th he appointed Robert J. Walker, of Mississippi, governor and Frederick P. Stanton, of Washington, secretary of the territory. Walker had been in the senate a number of years, and was secretary of the treasury under President Polk. He was a man of prominence and of high character. Stanton was younger but scholarly and forceful, an able lawyer, and in every way an admirable man. He was an eloquent speaker, with a rich voice, and a fine presence. He came out at once, while Walker did not come till May. Stanton arrived at Leavenworth April 13th and issued an address setting forth "his policy," as acting governor. He was particular to emphasize the idea that the laws of the territorial legislature would be enforced. This pleased the pro-slavery crowd, but set the teeth of the free-state men on edge. They feared a renewal of the scenes of the previous year. Soon after this he went to Lawrence and addressed the people. His speech very adroitly avoided the points at issue and dealt in eloquent generalities and classical allusions. Though there were a good many college graduates among his hearers, they were less interested in the Agrarian laws of Rome than in the bogus laws of Kansas. In the midst of one of his flights of oratory they interrupted him with the question: "How about the territorial laws, governor?" He did not seem to hear the question, but sailed on. The question was repeated,
"Nearer, clearer, louder than before."

"How about the territorial laws?" "The laws must be obeyed," he replied at last. "Never, never," replied a score of voices in unison. "Then there will be war between you and me—war to the knife, and the knife to the hilt." "Let it come; let it come; we are ready." The governor closed his speech more abruptly than the rules of rhetoric advise, and went away with a feeling that he had a problem to solve.

Governor Walker arrived May 25th, and he also issued an address in which he set forth the same policy as that foreshadowed by Acting Governor Stanton. They were both clear-headed, fair-minded men, and performed their duties in an impartial way, and thus soon won the confidence of the people, and preserved the peace of the country. As with their predecessors, so it fared with them. In less than six months their attempts at impartial management brought them into collision with their own party, and they were compelled to look for support and sympathy to the free-state men.

The year 1857 was in marked contrast with that of 1856. "Order reigned in Warsaw." There were no more armed invasions from Missouri, and no attempts to overthrow the free-state cause by violence. The contest was not over, but the pro-slavery party had changed their policy and were seeking their end through other lines. The embargo on the Missouri river was removed, and all ways to the territory were open. The disturbances of the year before had turned all eyes towards Kansas, and with the opening spring the tide of immigration began to flow in a larger volume than ever. They came from all quarters and by all roads and by all methods. Some came by steamer, some by wagons, and some on foot. It would hardly be overstating it to say that three-fourths of those who came were in favor of a free state. Though a good proportion were from the south, very many even of these were not in favor of slavery. The pro-slavery cause suffered from the fact that slaveholders did not dare to bring their slaves, and consequently very few slaveholders came. The territorial legislature had passed stringent laws protecting slave property, but the attitude of the free-state men practically nullified these laws. The free-state men felt, therefore, that they only needed to wait. If they could have quiet for a year or two, the preponderance of free-state immigration would settle the question beyond dispute.

The enormous rush of immigration made times lively. It was what they called a prosperous season. All these people brought money, and they had to spend money. They all wanted to invest in some of the sacred soil of which they had heard so much. To accommodate this army of would be investors, a good portion of the territory was laid out in town-sites, and in the words of a wag "several of these had buildings on them." But whether they had buildings on them, or were marked only by the corner stakes, they were all represented on beautifully lithographed maps, from which the eager immigrant selected his lot. There were not less than a score of such town-sites within fifteen miles of Lawrence.

The tide of immigration kept rolling in. It was popular to come to Kansas, and the trip could be very comfortably made. Not only immigrants came, but multitudes of others came to see the country and to see the fun. Everybody came to Kansas, for all sorts of reasons. Her highways were thronged, her stage coaches were packed, and her towns were crowded. Not a great deal was done to develope the country. There were a great many claims but not much farming, a great deal of consumption but not much production. All these people had to live, but not many of them were making a living. They all brought money and they all had to spend money. It was a time, therefore, of "unexampled prosperity." The merchant sold no end of goods at prices that made him happy. The land dealer sold lots without limit, and so long as the tide kept up, at constantly advancing prices. The purchaser of one day became the seller of the next, and all went on swimmingly until the last man should be left "holding the bag." It was not unusual for a man to double his money in a few weeks. Money loaned at unheard of rates, to be used in unheard of bargains. Everybody was getting rich trading back and forth in property that produced no income, and had no intrinsic value.

Lawrence was in the center of all this whirl. She was the center of free-state interest, and the "capital of the free-state party." Everybody that came to Kansas came to Lawrence. As all roads led to Rome, so all roads led to Lawrence. Here immigrants came to get their bearings and their supplies. Here visitors came to begin their tours of observation. Here politicians met to discuss the situation and lay their plans. The Leavenworth *Herald*, a year later, said of this same season: "Every newly arrived immigrant, as he stepped upon the levee, shouldered his carpet-bag, and stopping long enough to inquire the way to 'Larrence,' set off towards the Mecca of his abolition pilgrimage." The contagion was universal, and no caution was proof against it. Conservative men would come from the east, shake their wise heads at the folly of these western investments, and in three weeks be as wild as the wildest. A very conservative business man of New York came out to warn his children against engaging in these reckless speculations. After remaining with them a few weeks, he was more eager to invest than they had ever been. The singular feature about this speculating mania is that those in the midst of it always think that this condition will continue. One of the most far-seeing of the promoters of Lawrence told the writer of this sketch afterwards, that at the time he had the most positive conviction that Lawrence would have twenty thousand people in two years.

As Lawrence grew she began to feel the need of a municipal government. The territorial legislature incorporated the town in 1855, but the citizens never organized under the act and were without municipal regulations or officers. In July 1857 they adopted a charter of their own, and adopted a form of municipal government. Governor Walker pronounced this act treason, and sent Colonel Cook with four hundred dragoons to suppress it. He came also himself to superintend the job. He placed the town under martial law, and cut off

GEN'L. GEO. W. DEITZLER,
First Regiment Kansas Volunteers.

COL. O. E. LEARNARD,
First Regiment Kansas Volunteers.

MAJ. EDMUND G. ROSS,
U. S. Senator 1866-71.

COL. JOHN K. RANKIN,
Aid-de-camp Staff of Gen'l. Mitchell.

EARLY MILITARY LEADERS.

connections with the surrounding country except under military inspection. The offending government about which all this commotion was made remained invisible. They sought it but they could not find it. Those who had it in charge, however, went on with their duties: looked after the sanitary condition of the town, the cleaning of streets, the hauling off of dead horses, but did all this so quietly, and so entirely by common consent, that it was not possible to make a case against them. The citizens and the soldiers were on the best of terms, and exchanged jokes continually as to their rather unusual situation. The pro-slavery papers predicted trouble as soon as any "overt act" was committed, but the people of Lawrence took good care that no "overt act" should be committed, and that nothing should be done which should furnish an occasion for military interference. After a few weeks this farce grew too broad to be continued, and the troops were removed.

CHAPTER X.

LECOMPTON CONSTITUTIONAL CONVENTION.—THE CENSUS AND APPORTIONMENT.—FREE-STATE MEN IGNORE IT.—ELECTION OF TERRITORIAL LEGISLATURE.—SHALL WE VOTE?—FREE-STATE MEN CARRY THE ELECTION.—OXFORD AND THE CINCINNATI DIRECTORY.—WALKER THROWS OUT THE FRAUDULENT RETURNS.—IS REMOVED FROM OFFCE.

There were two very important political movements during the year 1857. One was the projection of the Lecompton constitution, the other was the election of a new territorial legislature. As was said before the pro-slavery people had changed their policy. It had become evident even to them that slavery could not be established in Kansas by force and violence. So there were no more armed invasions from Missouri. But the contest was not ended by any means. It had become a contest of diplomacy instead of arms. The pro-slavery party had the advantage in being in possession of the forms of law. The free-state party had the advantage of preponderating numbers, and probably of skill in management. The pro-slavery men had given up the idea of force, and they had given up the idea of establishing slavery by a fair vote of the people. They had one resource left. The old Shawnee legislature had been elected for two years. Its second session commenced in January, 1857. The plan that they now adopted was that this legislature should provide for a constitutional convention, which should form a constitution, and send it to congress, expecting congress to admit Kansas into the union under it. Thus Kansas would be a slave state in spite of the wishes of three-fourths of its people. The bill for this purpose was very skillfully drawn. Dr. Gihon, Governor Geary's private secretary, says it was drawn up by the southern senators in Washington, and sent to Kansas ready for the legislature to pass. At all events it was so skillfully drawn that the pro-slavery men could easily keep control of the government from beginning to end. Governor Geary opposed the movement, and this brought him into conflict with his former friends. He offered to sign the bill, if a clause were inserted requiring the constitution to be submitted to a vote of the people. But they said, "this would defeat the object of the bill, which was to secure Kansas to the South as a slave state, beyond any possibility of doubt." They said, "the South has reached a crisis, and must have Kansas." They said if the "constitution were submitted to a vote, the free-state fellows would vote it down. If Kansas were a slave state, however, the abolitionists would leave it." The bill, therefore, passed as it had been proposed. Governor Geary vetoed it, but the legislature passed it over his objections.

The election for delegates to this convention was set for June 15th. As the day approached the question arose, shall the free-state men vote at this election, and shall they try to get control of the convention? The question was discussed among the people, and at conventions called to confer on that subject. Governor Walker urged them to vote. But the free-state men saw so many objections, that it was finally decided to let the election go by default. They said it was the product of the old bogus legislature which they had repudiated, and to vote for delegates would be to recognize the acts of that body. Then the bill creating the convention, provided for a census and registration. None could vote who were not in the territory March 15th. The large free-state immigration of the spring was thus excluded. The census was taken by the county officers who were all pro-slavery men. While they were careful to register all pro-slavery voters, hundreds of free-state men were omitted. Worse than this, in nineteen interior counties, which were strongly free-state, no census whatever was taken, and they were practically disfranchised.

The sixteen counties where the census was taken were either on the Missouri border or near that border, and frauds would be easy. The whole thing was framed to give the convention to the pro-slavery party without fail. The free-state men argued that against such odds they had no chance of success, and that it was both more consistent and more wise to ignore the whole thing. When the election took place, therefore, pro-slavery men alone voted, and only about twenty-two hundred votes were cast out of a registration of nearly ten thousand voters. The convention therefore was unanimously pro-slavery, as it was intended to be.

Meanwhile another question began to loom up which obscured that of the convention. In October a new territorial legislature was to be chosen. Should the free-state men participate in this election, and endeavor to get possession of the law-making power of the territory? Governor Walker was very anxious they should do so. Hon. Henry Wilson, of Massachusetts, also urged them to participate in that election. If they could only get control of the legislature, they would have in their own hands the power by which the pro-slavery party had so grievously harrassed them for two years. There were many reasons urged for not participating. The apportionment of members of the legislature was based on the defective census taken in the spring. The census gave the pro-slavery sections all the advantage in the apportionment. Besides this was the fear that fraud would be practiced as it had been before, and the legislature would be stolen from them whatever the real vote might be. Governor Walker promised them, however, that they would have a fair election, and that fraud and violence would not be permitted. After an examination of views and many conferences and conventions, the free-state men decided to go into the election, and they made a thorough canvass of the territory to that end.

The election occurred October 5th. The governor was as

good as his word in preventing violence at the polls, or any invasion of foreign voters. He had troops at all the voting places where there was any fear of trouble, and the election passed off quietly. The next morning the free-state people were made jubilant by the returns. They had won in the contest, and the coming legislature was theirs by a large margin. The people of Lawrence were particularly enthusiastic. They had been harrassed for two years by acts of that bogus legislature which everybody knew was a fraud, but from whose grasp they could not be delivered. Their leading men had been hounded continually by writs and prosecutions which had no valid basis, but which dragged them before a court in which they could get no justice. Many of them had been imprisoned for months on charges which their accusers did not dare to have investigated, and so did not deign to bring them to trial even before their own partisan courts. Others were compelled to keep in hiding, or leave the territory to avoid arrest, and escape persecution. Now the power which had been so effectively used to annoy them, they could use for the furtherance of order and good government. The people of Lawrence had entered into the election with great spirit, and Douglas county had polled a large vote.

Among the means resorted to by the pro-slavery managers to prevent free-state success was that of yoking the free-state counties with pro-slavery counties on the border. Thus Douglas county was yoked with Johnson county, and the combined district was allowed eight members. But the free-state men were able to overcome this. Douglas polled 1638 votes for the free-state ticket and 187 for the pro-slavery ticket, while Johnson county only reported a small majority the other way. The morning after the election showed some 1500 majority for the free-state candidates. But the second day after election put another face on affairs, and the enthusiasm of the people of Lawrence changed to indignation. The little precinct of Oxford, in Johnson, was reported as having cast 1638 votes, overcoming the large vote of Douglas county and giving the election to the pro-slavery candidates. Everybody knew it must be a fraud, and nobody pretended to deny it. But the returns were regular, and sworn to by the judges. On inquiry they found that the polls had been open for two days at Oxford. On the first day 91 votes were cast, the utmost limit of the legal vote. That night they had messengers at all the precincts in Douglas county to watch the count. As soon as the reslt was known they rode during the night to Westport and reported the size of the free-state majority. The polls were opened again at Oxford, therefore, and 1547 additional votes reported. Notwithstanding this large vote, but few people were about the polls that day. The names on the poll list were not known in that community. It was afterward found that the list was written in alphabetical order, and had been copied from the Cincinnati directory.

The people of Lawrence were in what might be called a "state of mind" when they learned these facts. They found the English language a feeble medium through which to express their feelings. Those who had opposed voting said "We told you so." Some were in favor of one thing and some another. But it was finally decided to appeal to the governor. He had promised them an honest election, and it was his assurance that induced them to go into the election. He could do no less than protect them from a fraud so manifest and bold. They drew up a protest, therefore, in which they narrated the facts, and asked him to throw out these fraudulent returns and give certificates of election in accordance with the honest choice of the people. The following are a few of the names attached to this protest: G. W. Smith, A. Newman, C. Hornsby, J. M. Coe, August Wattles, J. F. Griswold, Samuel Walker, George Ford, E. D. Ladd, H. W. Baker, Gaius W. Jenkins, James Christian, and many others.

The pro-slavery people protested against the governor's interfering with the returns. They said he had no right to go back of the returns. It was his duty to give certificates to those elected by the face of the returns. The legislature must be the judge of all the rest. But the governor was as indignant as the people. The case was so plain that there was but one course to pursue. To give certificates to men elected by such unblushing frauds would be an outrage beyond anything yet endured. He refused to recognize the Oxford returns, therefore, and gave certificates to the free-state candidates. It hardly seems credible that an act of such manifest justice should be made the ground for the governor's removal from office. Yet such was the case. Governor Walker went to Washington soon after the election to confer with the administration. He got no satisfaction, and was soon after relieved of office.

The free-state men were very much rejoiced at the governor's decision. But their joy was not without mixture. There was still a fly in the free-state ointment, and a very large fly it was. They now had the territorial legislature, but the pro-slavery people had the constitutional convention. The free-state people had paid little attention to this during the summer, thinking it of very little consequence. But their enemies had not taken all this trouble for nothing. That constitutional convention was created for a purpose, and they did not propose to let it die on their hands. The convention met at Lecompton September 7th, but after organizing and doing some preliminary business they adjourned to October 19th. This would be after the territorial election. They met again October 19th. The election being over and the territorial legislature having passed into free-state hands, it behooved them to make the most of this last remaining instrument for establishing slavery in Kansas. They framed a constitution which declared that "the right of a slave owner to such slave and its increase is the same and inviolable as the right of any property whatever." The constitution was sent to congress without being submitted to a vote of the people of the territory. The free-state people who had thus far looked upon the movement as of little moment, now began to be alarmed. If congress should accept the constitution, all they had done would mean but little. Their success in the territorial election could be of little consequence if this Lecompton constitution was to supplant the territorial government. They bestirred themselves, therefore, to put the real facts before congress, and prevent its adoption if possible. They knew the president would urge it, the senate would accept it, and the house was very close.

A convention, therefore, met at Lawrence December 2nd to confer as to the most effective means for prenventing its adoption. It was one of the largest and most influential free-state conventions that had been held. There were one hundred and thirty delegates, and nearly every district was represented, and by the strongest men they could send. All the trusted leaders of the party were present, and the feeling on all hands was very intense. The debate was one of the ablest ever conducted since the settlement. The delegates felt that they might be on the eve of thrilling events, and might be making history faster than they thought. The debate had something of the spirit which one may suppose animated the continental congress on the eve of the revolution. The burden of every speech was that this bogus constitution should never be forced upon them by any power or under any circumstances. "Appealing to the God of justice and humanity, we do solemnly enter into league and covenant with each other that we will *never*, under any circumstances, permit the said constitution, so framed and not submitted, to be the organic law of the state of Kansas, but do pledge our lives, our fortunes and our sacred honor to ceaseless hostility to the same."

GEO. W. SMITH,
Attorney at Law.

H. M. SIMPSON.
Attorney at Law.

SAMUEL A. RIGGS,
U. S. District Attorney, 1867-69.

JAMES S. EMERY,
U. S. District Attorney, 1863-67.

EARLY MEMBERS OF LAWRENCE BAR.

In addition to all this, Acting Governor Stanton had been petitioned to call together the new legislature in special session to provide for getting the sense of the people in some authentic manner. Stanton at once called the legislature together, and they met five days later, December 7th. They passed a bill providing for a vote on the Lecompton constitution January 4th, the day for electing state officers under that constitution. Over ten thousand votes were recorded against it that day. But the pro-slavery people ignored the election, and there was no negative vote.

At Washington the president urged the adoption of the constitution. The senate passed a bill to that effect, but it failed in the house. The house passed a bill submitting the constitution to a vote of the people of Kansas, and this failed in the senate. Finally a compromise, called the English bill, passed both houses, submitting the constitution indirectly to a vote of the people. This vote was taken August 2nd, 1858, and the proposition was voted down in Kansas by an overwhelming majority, nearly five to one. This ended the Lecompton trouble, and was the last attempt to fasten slavery upon Kansas.

CHAPTER XI.

THE TERRITORIAL LEGISLATURE ADJOURNS TO LAWRENCE.—THE BOGUS LAWS SENT HOME.—THE LAWRENCE CHARTER.—A CITY GOVERNMENT AT LAST.—SAMUEL MEDARY GOVERNOR.

Going back to the legislature we follow its history. After the special session the body adjourned, and met again in regular session at Lecompton January 4th, 1858. The council chose Carmi W. Babcock, of Lawrence, president, and the house of representatives chose George W. Deitzler, of Lawrence, as speaker. After the organization, the body adjourned to Lawrence, where they continued for the balance of the session. They occupied the second and third floors of the new brick building just south of the Eldridge House. The free-state part of the legislature felt very much at home at Lawrence, as they had most of them been their often at free-state conventions, and for purposes of defense. It seemed very fitting, too, that the free-state legislature should sit at the capital of the free-state party, for the free-state party had become the commonwealth. As soon as the forms of law were taken from the pro-slavery party, every body was surprised to find how little there was of it. They never made another important demonstration, but seemed to drop entirely out. The free-state men did not know till now how strong they themselves were. It was very fitting, therefore, that the capital of the free-state party should become the capital of the commonwealth. The Lawrence people, therefore, enjoyed having the legislature with them as the legislature enjoyed being there. The session continued forty days. The amount of business done was not very large. The members were new to the work, and the situation was new. It was not strange that little was done in the way of practical legislation.

A year later the fourth legislature assembled. As before, they met at Lecompton and organized, and adjourned at once to Lawrence. This legislature took hold of their work with more system and vigor. They appointed a codifying commission to arrange the laws of the territory. The first legislature, in 1855, had not taken the trouble to draw up a code of laws. Their own state of Missouri had a very excellent code all prepared, and they adopted that "in bulk," ordering the clerk to make the necessary verbal changes. The only original laws they drew up were those pertaining to slavery, in which the Missouri code was too mild. As the Shawnee legislature adopted the Missouri code "in bulk," this legislature of 1859 repealed it "in bulk." They would not so much as use it as a basis for the new code. It was the old bogus affair, and they would have none of it. They repealed it altogether from preface to conclusion. As soon as this was done the "boys" gathered up all the copies of the bogus laws they could find, and had a glorious bonfire on Massachusetts street. Some wag took a copy, carefully wrapped it, and sent it by express to the Missouri state officials at Jefferson City, with the inscription, "Returned with thanks." The place of meeting in 1859 was the old concrete building on Massachusetts street north of Winthrop. When it was built it was considered quite a magnificent affair, but the march of improvement has left it in the rear. It was a double store and answered very well for the purposes of the legislature.

The session of 1860 repeated the history of its predecessors with variations. The course of true love did not run as smoothly as heretofore. Samuel Medary, of Ohio, was now governor and Hugh S. Walsh was secretary of the territory. Medary was a supporter of the administration at Washington, but he was a broad-minded, large-hearted man, and he and the free-state men got along very harmoniously. But now for some reason there came a change. The legislature met January 7th at Lecompton as usual. As usual also they organized and adjourned to Lawrence. The governor vetoed the resolution for adjournment. The resolution stated that the adjournment to Lawrence was made necessary by the lack of accommodations at Lecompton. The governor replied that while the accommodations at Lecompton were not palatial, they were ample. They were good enough for the territorial officials and he thought they were good enough for the legislature. He doubtless had the best of the argument. But the argument stated in the resolution was not the real reason for the adjournment. The answering of that argument did not change the minds of the members. They adjourned to Lawrence because they did not like Lecompton, and would not stay there if they could help it. In the bitter struggle that had passed Lecompton had become a hated name in freestate circles, and if they had offered palaces instead of hovels, the members would have left just the same. So they passed the resolution over the governor's veto, and went to Lawrence, the "governor's objections to the contrary notwithstanding." The governor and secretary, however, refused to go, and refused to send books and records needed for the transaction of business. One day when Secretary Walsh was in Lawrence it was determined to bring him before the bar of the house to answer for his refusal to honor the request for the needed books. A resolution was passed ordering the sergeant-at-arms to bring the secretary before the house. The sergeant-at-arms was George F. Warren, an officer who, like the poet, was "born and not made." He was born a full-fledged sergeant-at-arms. He delighted in the duties of his office, especially in some mission like this. He sallied forth with all the power of the legislature in his hands, and the dignity of a great commonwealth on his shoulders. While he was gone many of the members felt a little uncomfortable. What if Walsh should refuse to obey their summons? What should they do next to maintain their dignity? There was a wonderful relief felt when the sergeant-at-arms came back, bringing the secretary with him. The secretary was evidently annoyed, and looked pale about the mouth. He looked as if he would like to use some unparliamentary language. But he said nothing. He evidently thought it was not wise to come in conflict with the legislature. He walked up to the speaker's chair, and everybody waited in breathless anxiety. The speaker, in the kindliest and gentlest manner, asked him why he did not furnish the books they asked for containing the proceedings of the previous session. He answered promptly he "did not have the books; the edition was exhaused and there were none." Whether this was strictly true or not, was never known, but it avoided a direct conflict between the executive and the legislature, and relieved the situation. The legislature soon passed a resolution that whereas the secretary of the territory had obstinately refused to coöperate with them, and had refused to supply the necessary books, documents, stationery and printing, making it impossible to conduct the legitimate business, that we adjourn *sine die*. The governor at once issued a proclamation ordering them to meet in extra session the next day, January 19th, *at Lecompton*, "then and *there* to consider and perform such duties as are demanded by the necessities of the people." They met again the next day, therefore, at Lecompton, elected the same officers, and passed the same resolution adjourning to Lawrence. The governor again vetoed the resolution, and the legislature again passed it over his veto. Here it seems as if the struggle ended, for the legislature completed their session at Lawrence without any further interference. In these conflicts there was none of the bitterness of former times, but everything was good-natured, and all parties were on good terms. Governor Medary was universally esteemed, and won the respect of all parties by his urbanity and fairness.

This legislature provided for the Wyandotte convention which framed the constitution under which Kansas, a year later, entered the union as a state.

The sessions of the legislature were a God-send to Lawrence. After the constant excitement of the free-state struggle there was a great calm. There came a quietness, which like the darkness of Egypt, "could be felt." These meetings of the legislature were about the only diversion the people had. Even a session of the legislature, however, was a feeble substitute for one of the free-state conventions. In the exciting issues considered, in the ability of the members, and in the high tone of the debates, a Kansas legislature bore no comparison to a free-state convention.

A writer who came to Lawrence late in 1857, thus gives his impressions of the town. "The town seemed smaller than we expected. There were no streets, and no sidewalks, and the roads ran helter skelter here and there, across lots, between houses, and everywhere as the convenience of drivers might dictate. This gave a scattered look to the town, and the houses seemed to straggle about on the prairie as if they had lost their way on a dark night. There was scarcely a fence or a dooryard, scarcely a garden or tree planted in the whole town. All this gave a lonesome feeling to the new comer."

But the new comer did not have to remain long before the feeling passed away. He soon found that the external appearance did not fairly represent the town. He could not judge the town by the size or number of the houses. Every tenement and shanty, every sod cabin and tent fairly swarmed with people. And they were a lively lot and they made a lively place. There could not have been less than five thousand people in the town, though probably not more than half of them would call it their home, and people were coming and going all the time. They were a remarkably bright and intelligent lot of people who had gathered here, full of vigor and vim. Among the much smaller population of the first winter there were said to be two hundred college graduates. They had been so constantly in plans of self defense that they had no time to show what they could do in the way of developing a community, yet they gave some evidence of their ability in that line. They had maintained a free public school without any power to collect taxes or enforce order. They had maintained a vigorous and effective military organization without any power to enforce military regulations. They had an orderly community of various and diverse elements, and of all conceivable faiths and notions, without any laws or courts to which they could appeal. They had maintained all necessary municipal and sanitary regulations, without any authority to compel obedience to wholesome rules. There were no taxes and all public expenses were met by voluntary subscriptions. The schools were maintained and made free to all children. The voluntary city organization of 1857, for whose suppression Governor Walker ordered out the army of the United States, confined itself to suggestions without any pretense of power to enforce. Its suggestions, however, were quietly acquiesced in, the streets kept clean and the back ways clear. It effected all it was intended for, and yet did it so unobtrusively, that four hundred soldiers sent here for that purpose, could find nothing that indicated the setting up of an independent city government.

When the free-state people gained control of the territorial legislature, one of the first things considered was a charter for Lawrence. February 11th, 1858, a bill was passed by both houses to that effect. February 20th, the charter was accepted. The following city officers were elected: Mayor, C. W. Babcock; councilmen, Robert Morrow, P. R. Brooks, E. S. Lowman, L. C. Tolles, John G. Haskell, M. Hartman,

Henry Shanklin, A. J. Totten, S. W. Eldridge, A. H. Mallory, L. Bullene, F. A. Bailey; city marshal, Joseph Cracklin; treasurer, Wesley H. Duncan, clerk, Caleb S. Pratt; school trustees, J. M. Coe, B. Johnson, T. Dwight Thacher, Albert Newman. Lawrence now had a city government, and regular courts and laws, and could do under legal sanctions and by legal constraints, what she had already been doing by voluntary concession.

EDMUND A. WHITMAN.

FRANKLIN HASKELL.

SAMUEL REYNOLDS.

JOHN ROSS.

EARLY KANSAS SETTLERS.

CHAPTER XII.

LAWRENCE IN 1858.—THE EBB OF THE TIDE.—SPRING IMMIGRATION WHICH FAILED TO COME.—THE UNDERGROUND RAILROAD.—PROGRESS IN BUILDING.—IN CHURCHES.—TEMPERANCE IN LAWRENCE.—THE DROUTH OF 1860.—THE LAST TERRITORIAL LEGISLATURE.—KANSAS ADMITTED INTO THE UNION.—A FREE STATE.

The year 1858 was the reverse of 1857. In the favorite words of Governor Geary, "the benign influences of peace had been restored to the country." But the benign influences of peace had a different effect from what many people expected. For three years Kansas had been the observed of all observers. All eyes were turned towards her, and many feet also turned their steps her way. Notwithstanding the difficulties of travel, and the hindrances thrown in the way, and the disturbances in the territory itself, immigrants came from every quarter and in every conceivable manner. When peace and quiet came and the slavery question was settled, the people expected that this would not only continue, but increase. If people came to Kansas in such crowds when there were so many hindrances and so much peril, they would come in still greater crowds when the hindrances were removed and the perils had ceased. As times were lively in 1857, they expected still more lively times in 1858. But they were mistaken as to the spirit of the north, and as to the causes which gave Kansas her prominence. Her troubles and her perils gave her the prominence she enjoyed, and drew towards her such crowds of immigrants. They came at the call of an idea; at the call of freedom. The greater the obstacles the more they came. But now the conflict was over and the question was settled, immigration instead of increasing, almost ceased. Many who had come were compelled to go back. There was nothing to prevent their returning. For the next three years probably as many left as came. The result therefore which followed the disturbances was a more complete quiet than most of the people cared to see. A general business depression throughout the country increased the depression in Kansas.

It began to be dull in the autumn of 1857, but people said that "Spring immigration would brignten things up." But spring immigration did not come. All things were ready, but the immigrant failed to fulfil his engagement. Land agents sat in their offices as of old, and their maps and diagrams hung around the walls, but no one came to enquire the price of lots, or if any came it was some one who wished to sell and not some one who wished to buy. Merchants stood behind their counters with large stocks of goods about them, but the customer did not appear. The next three years were dull ones, as dull as the preceeding three years had been lively. The people were very slow to understand what had happened. They clung to a hope of a return of the former days, but those days never came back. For a time property was still high, but nobody wanted to buy; money was still held at high rates, but nobody wanted to borrow. Gradually even this found its level, as it always does, and a very low level it proved to be. In real estate and other lines of business the final purchaser had been found, and he was left to hold his purchase. The fortunes gathered in a day dissolved in a night, and men worth vast fortunes in city lots were borrowing money to pay their board. In the spring of 1859, quite a number of the enterprising young men of Lawrence, growing weary of waiting for the tardy immigrant, concluded to turn emigrants themselves. They started over the plains for "Pike's Peak," and were the inaugurators of the movement which brought Colorado in such prominence.

These years, however, were not destitute of exciting incidents. January 20, 1859, John Brown spent a night in Lawrence as he was leading eleven slaves to Canada and freedom. It was John Brown's last appearance in Kansas. In October of that year he made his attack on Harper's Ferry, and December 2, 1860, was hanged by the authorities of the state of Virginia. During the winter of 1859, John Doy and his son, Charles Doy, led a company of slaves through Lawrence northward. The whole party was captured twelve miles from Lawrence and imprisoned at Weston. Doy and his son were afterwards taken to St. Joseph for trial. At a large public meeting in Lawrence funds were raised to assist in their defense at the trial of their case in June. Ex-Governor Shannon was secured as one of the lawyers for the defense. The trial was reported for the eastern and other papers by such correspondents as A. D. Richardson, Henry Villard, and D. W. Wilder. After a tedious trial the son was released, and Doy himself was sentenced to five years imprisonment. Before he was taken from the St. Joseph jail to the state prison, he was liberated one night and came back to Lawrence, where he remained unmolested. Nobody ever exactly knew who did the liberating.

Lawrence had the reputation in Missouri of being one of the stations on the underground railroad. In a certain sense perhaps she deserved that reputation. Most of her people had no sympathy with any attempt to stir up insurrection among the slaves, or to entice them from their masters. But they hated human slavery and believed in every man's right to freedom. They would never consent that any man should be taken back to slavery who came to them in his effort to be free. There is no doubt that a good many slaves, fleeing from bondage, made their way to Lawrence, and there were aided on their journey towards Canada. Not many of the people knew anything about this, but there were a few to whom such fugitives always went and were never betrayed.

But the sympathy of the people was with every one who was struggling for freedom. The town was founded in opposition to slavery, and it could not be otherwise than antagonistic to the right of property in man.

This matter is alluded to here because some have sought to create an opposite impression. A recent writer on Kansas has said that "it is a significant fact, which forcibly illustrates the absence of any general or radical sentiment of abolition in Kansas, that so late as the year 1858 *Missourians hired out slaves at Lawrence, received their wages, and nobody made objection.*" The italics are our own. Anyone who lived in Lawrence in 1858 would know that such a thing as this could not possibly be. Neither at that time nor any other, could a slave be held in Lawrence against his will, by owner or renter. If such a thing was ever done, it was with the mutual consent of all parties—owner, slave and renter. The writer of this knew of a slave who was in Lawrence a large portion of the year 1859. She was employed as a domestic in various families, but her wages were paid to her and not to her master. Late in the autumn her master offered a large reward for her arrest and return. It was decided to make a test case of it, and show that a slave could be taken from Lawrence and returned to slavery in Missouri. The United States marshal, with deputies and detectives, came stealthily to Lawrence, and set themselves to work to locate and capture this woman. They remained two days. There was no resistance offered, but they did not capture the woman, and presumably did not get the reward. So far as known, no slaves were ever taken from Lawrence and carried back to slavery. The Lawrence people were moderate in their views, but they were decided.

In the way of material improvements there had been a good deal of advance. By far the finest building erected was the Eldridge House, which took the place of the Free-State Hotel destroyed by Sheriff Jones, May 21st, 1856. After the destruction of the old hotel nothing was done toward rebuilding for a year. In the spring of 1857 Colonel S. W. Eldridge and his brother began to rebuild the house or rather to build another on the same site. It was of brick, four stories high, extending one hundred feet on the east front and one hundred and seventeen feet on the north front. It was handsomely built and furnished elegantly, and was the finest hotel Lawrence has ever had. It was said to have cost $80,000. It was kept in a style befitting the building. Several other substantial brick buildings were begun on Massachusetts street during the year 1857, and completed in the year following.

There had been considerable progress in the line of church work during this period. The Unitarians appealed to their friends at the east, and by the personal efforts of Rev. Ephraim Nute and Mr. E. B. Whitman they secured $5,700 for a church edifice. They began to build in 1856, but were hindered by various things, and the house was not ready for occupancy until the spring of 1857. The building was of stone of good size, with basement rooms for school purposes. Their eastern friends also gave them a bell and a town clock. The bell was suspended on a temporary frame for many years and was used for a school bell as well as a church bell. The bell was of very fine tone. The clock and bell were afterwards purchased for the city schools, and are now in use on the city high school. About 1858 Mr. Nute resigned and on the breaking out of the war entered the army as a chaplain. Rev. John S. Brown became pastor of the church.

The Congregational Church also erected a house of worship during this period. This church had a varied experience. It was the first church formed in Lawrence; formed before there was a house built. Deacon Franklin Haskell of this church made the first public prayer offered upon the Lawrence town site. Rev. S. Y. Lum, the pastor, preached the first sermon. When the Kansas question began to loom up

Mr. Lum was pastor of a delightful church at Middletown, New York. He was a man of thorough education and good ability. His wife had been tenderly reared, her father being a wealthy merchant of New York city. As soon as interest in Kansas began to take form, Mr. Lum resigned his pastorate at Middletown and asked the American Home Missionary Society to send him to Kansas. In a few weeks he was on his way, with his wife and two little children, and a young lady, a member of the family. They arrived in Lawrence about the same time as the second Boston party, and Mr. Lum began at once the work for which he came. He built the first frame house in Lawrence. It was built of "shakes," and was so open that in winter water froze close by a hot stove, and the snow sifted over them at night as they slept. Mr. Lum had some rough experiences with the border ruffians. They stole a span of horses from him, and at another time assaulted him and threatened to hang him.

The church had as rough a time as the pastor. It was organized in a "hay tent," and worshiped in private rooms, in hotels, in shops or public offices as it could. At one time they met in a little room heated by a stove whose hot pipe ran close by the preacher's head. At another time they met in a small building, boarded up and down and intended for battens. But the battens had been omitted, and chacks supplied their place. During the disturbances of 1855 and 1856 they could have no regular services. They met as they were able. Often the men were called out during service to join in the defense of the town. Often, also, they were away on duty during church hours and only the women and children could meet. The necessity for a house of worship became very urgent. In the summer of 1855, the pastor, and after him, Mr. S. N. Simpson, went east to solicit aid in building a church. They met with a very liberal response, and secured some four thousand dollars. With this aid the church built a substantial stone edifice on the corner of Louisiana and Pinckney streets. The house was forty feet wide by sixty-five feet long. The difficulty of getting material delayed the work, and it was not until the summer of 1857 that the building was enclosed and occupied. In the spring of 1857 Mr. Lum was compelled to resign on account of his health. The American Home Missionary Society appointed him as its first superintendent of missions for Kansas. In the autumn of 1857, the present pastor, having just graduated from the Theological Seminary at Andover, Massachusetts, became pastor of the church. "Having obtained help of God, he continues until this day."

The Methodist Church had also grown. Organized under a tree, they lived in tents and private houses until the fall of 1858, when they erected a frame building on Vermont street. The building was not large, but it was comfortable, and, being near the business center of the town, was very useful in a general way as well as in the work of the church. Under the earnest lead of "Father Dennis" revivals were enjoyed and the church attained a good degree of strength. The church building still stands and is used as a private residence.

The Baptist Church did not attempt to build, but lived more than "two years in their own hired hall." They were an earnest band of Christians and did good work. They continued in rented rooms until they became strong enough to build the elegant house of worship which they now occupy.

The Presbyterian Church was formed in 1858. There was a number of Presbyterian families in the place, and still more in the country near by. In the summer of 1858 Rev. William Wilson, of Lecompton, commenced holding afternoon services in the Congregational Church, coming down after his Sabbath morning service at Lecompton. In a few weeks a Presbyterian Church of twenty-five was organized, and regular services established in Miller's hall. Mr. Wilson having other work, now urged the church to look for a permanent pastor. Soon after its organization, therefore, the church secured as pastor Rev. William Bishop, who now resides at Salina. Dr. Bishop was born in Scotland, but came to America in his ninth year. He is a graduate of Illinois college and Princeton theological seminary. He served as tutor in Greek in his alma mater for two years, and was professor of Greek in Hanover college, Indiana, from 1852 until 1858, when he came to Lawrence. He was strong in logic and scholarly in his tastes, a forcible writer and a fluent speaker. In his ministry of three years the church increased nearly four-fold. In 1860 Mr. Bishop resigned and went with Colonel William A. Phillips to Salina where he assisted in developing the town and forming a church, and where he still resides. The church at Lawrence continued to worship in rented houses until they built their present stone edifice on the corner of Vermont and Warren streets.

The Episcopal Church was also formed in 1858 under the lead of Rev. Charles Reynolds, afterwards a chaplain in the United States army. Mr. Reynolds was born in England and came to this country in his thirteenth year. He graduated at the Protestant Episcopal seminary in New York in 1846, and was settled over a church in Brooklyn. In 1855 he became rector of Trinity Church, Columbus, Ohio, and had for his parishoners such men as Salmon P. Chase. He was a man of fine presence and great executive force, and of high character. He remained in Lawrence five years, and during his ministry here he thoroughly organized the parish and built the main part of the unique and beautiful chapel which still stands upon the grounds of the church. He also secured a rectory for the parish. He resigned about 1863 to enter the army as a chaplain, and continued in that service the remainder of his life.

It has often been noticed that reforms go in groups, and the

MRS. O. E. LEARNARD.

MRS. DR. R. CORDLEY.

MRS. H. M. SIMPSON.

MRS. GOV. CHAS. ROBINSON.

WOMEN WHO HELPED TO MAKE KANSAS FREE.

ardent friends of one reform are usually the friends of all reforms. So it happened that the early settlers of Lawrence were also friends of temperance. Almost without exception they were not only abstainers themselves, but ardent opponents of the liquor traffic. Nearly all the leading men were earnest advocates of temperance. A few days after the first immigrants arrived, the town company adopted unanimously the principles of the Maine law, and it was expressed in all deeds given that liquor should not be sold upon the lots defined therein. In July 1855 a prohibitory liquor law was submitted to a vote of the people and was adopted by a vote of seventy-four to one. In the disturbances that followed the matter was overlooked, and some tippling shops were opened. In the summer of 1856 meetings were held to arouse public interest, and then the women took the matter in hand. They first tried to buy the stock of liquor and thus close up the business. When this was found impossible, they took the hatchet and poured all the liquor they could find into the streets. After this there was no selling for some time. But as the town grew, wild and restless spirits came in, and several saloons were kept in full blast. At last the women undertook the work again, and in January 1857 forty of them visited every saloon in the town and persuaded their owners all to close them. In some cases they used moral suasion, in other cases they used another kind of argument. But in every case they won the battle and closed the saloon. The women had the sympathy of most of the men. The friends of temperance then met and organized a vigilance committee to keep out the sale of liquor from Lawrence. For a long time after this the town had a rest and was free from saloons. There has never been lacking in Lawrence something of the same spirit which manifested itself in those early days.

The part taken by the women of Lawrence in the temperance cause was only characteristic of them in all lines. They came to

Kansas with a full understanding of what they had to meet, and with a full determination to endure their share of the burden and do their share of the work. In all the excitement of those troublous years there is no record of a woman who deserted her post. When the men were on duty the women were providing rations. When the men were in the trenches with their guns, the women were making bullets for them at home. As has been narrated, when ammunition failed, two women boldly rode through the besiegers lines and brought in a new supply. Often and often were they left in lonely cabins on the prairie, while their husbands were on the march or in the camp. If any should think that they were of the kind who take naturally to scenes like these they are very much mistaken. The women of Lawrence were womanly. They had been tenderly reared in cultured homes, and were as modest and retiring as any that could be found. They simply had strong convictions, and devoted their lives to their maintenance. If the pilgrim mothers deserve equal praise with the pilgrim fathers, the women of Lawrence, and of Kansas, deserve equal praise with the men of Lawrence and of Kansas.

In 1860 there came what has ever since been known as "the drouth." There have been other dry seasons, but this was preëminently "the drouth." It needs no descriptive adjectives, and no date, to make any old Kansan know what is meant. He never uses any adjective in speaking of it, any more than he would use an adjective in speaking of the flood. Since then dry spells have destroyed this crop and that, sometimes at one end of the season and sometimes at the other. But this drouth of 1860 swept the calender. It commenced in September 1859, and continued until October 1860, a period of thirteen months. I am not able to say what the rainfall of this period was. The annual rainfall reported at Fort Riley for 1860 was seventeen inches, about one-half of the usual amount. But that report includes the rain that fell in the autumn of that year after the drouth was broken. During the whole period there was not a shower that wet the earth more than two inches deep, and very few that did more than lay the dust. There was a little snow in the winter, but it evaporated as it melted. In April the ground was dry as ashes. Seeds sown in the garden did not even come up in many cases, and in some cases came up the next spring, hale and hearty. On the rich bottom lands below Lawrence, and a few other favored spots, there was a little corn grown in fields that were sown early and well cared for. But over the country generally there were thousands of acres from which not an ear was gathered. The prairie grass, which other years often produces two tons of good hay to the acre, was scarcely two inches high, and it was dried to a crisp. On some low spots near the streams, where the grass often grows ten feet high, a little hay could be gathered. Two brothers, farmers just west of Lawrence, went about the country with team and tools, and gathered up bits of grass here and there as they could find it, and had all the hay they needed. But those less enterprising were as destitute of hay as they were of corn. The streams and wells mostly went dry, and farmers were compelled to haul water for miles for their cattle. The Wakarusa river had pools of water along its course in deep and sheltered places, but there was no stream, whatever, running in the channel. The writer of this drove from Wyandotte to Lawrence in July on the south side of the Kansas river. For twenty-five miles he could not buy or beg a pail of water for his horse. At one farm house after another he was refused. There was no unkindness in it, but the people had not the water to spare for travelers' horses. During this summer the sun poured down its burning rays day after day, and the hot winds seemed like the breath of a hot furnace.

As the autumn came the question pressed "what must the people do?" Most of them were new-comers and had no accumulated stores. A great many left the country. It is said that thirty thousand people, one-third of the population, left the territory. As many more would be compelled to leave unless they could have relief. They would thus have to abandon all they had done and all they had gained. It would throw the country back several years. Under the lead of General S. C. Pomeroy and other far-seeing men, appeal was made to the more fortunate sections, and a very liberal response was given. From Illinois and other prosperous states, large quantities of corn and other provisions were sent, which were distributed among the people. Thus thousands were enabled to remain who would otherwise have been compelled to abandon their farms and their homes and lose all they had gathered. It was feared there would be a great loss in stock as there was no hay and no feed. But the short prairie grass, dried in the rainless air, was cured on the ground like hay. Until the snow came in January, 1861, cattle kept in good condition, running at large on the prairie. They were very lean and weak in the spring, but most of the stock came through the winter alive.

There was less distress about Lawrence than in newer sections. The country was older and the farmers were better fixed. But even here very many farmers would have suffered but for the timely aid rendered them.

The territorial legislature met for the last time January 7th, 1861. The usual order was followed, and they met in Lecompton and adjourned to Lawrence. They did not do much except wait the tardy action of congress in admitting Kansas into the union. The Wyandotte constitution had been framed and ratified more than a year before. It had been presented to congress the preceding April, and had passed the house April 11th, 1860. In the senate it hung fire for months, being opposed by the administration and the entire force of its party. But a great change had come over the country.

Lincoln had been elected president, and the southern states began to secede, one state after another. January 21st, 1861, the senators for Alabama, Mississippi and Florida withdrew from the senate to go with their states which had seceded. William H. Seward at once moved to take up the Kansas bill, and the bill was passed. The house immediately accepted the senate amendments, and the bill went to the president. Mr. Buchanan signed it and Kansas became a state January 29th, 1861. The news was received at Lawrence with unbounded delight. In his speech on the Wyandotte convention at the quarter centennial of the admission of Kansas, Hon. B. F. Simpson describes the scene.

"I well remember the earlier part of the night of January 29th, 1861. I was at the Eldridge House in Lawrence, a member of the last territorial legislature that was holding its session in that dearly beloved free-state city. There was from three to four inches of snow on the ground * * * and the night was windy and cold. It must have been as late as nine o'clock when D. R. Anthony came into the hotel with a sturdy stride and flashing eyes, and told us that the president of the United States had that day signed the bill admitting Kansas into the union. He brought with him and scattered around extras of a newspaper published at Leavenworth called *The Conservative*, announcing the joyful tidings in flaming headlines. * * * There was a sound of revelry that night in Lawrence, for the news spread like wildfire through the town. Houses were lighted, doors were thrown open, and the people gathered in public places. Old Sacramento was taken from his resting place and emphasized with hoarse throat the good tidings."

The rejoicing was universal and sincere. Kansas had good reason to rejoice in the new order. The territorial condition had proved a hard one to her, and admission into the union was her deliverance from oppression. The rejoicings however were moderated by the thought that she came into the union, just as the union seemed to be going to pieces. But she believed in the union, and believed it would be maintained, and was ready to help maintain it whenever her help was called for.

The territorial authorities now gave way to the state authorities. Very appropriately Charles Robinson, who had led the free-state cause with such consummate wisdom, became the first governor of the new commonwealth. As often happens, the political importance of Lawrence was to decline with the success of the cause for which she had stood so long, and for which she had suffered so much. Up to this time she had been the center of all public interest. She might be called the capital of the free-state party, and now the free-state party was co-extensive with Kansas. After the free-state people secured control of the legislature Lawrence was "de facto" the capital of the territory, though legally Lecompton still held that distinction. The new constitution under which Kansas now was to live, provided that the legislature shonld hold its first session at Topeka. This legislature passed a bill submitting the question of the permanent capital to a vote of the people. That vote was taken November 5th, 1861. Lawrence and Topeka were the two competitors. In the election, Lawrence received 5,291 votes and Topeka received 7,996 votes. Thus Topeka became the capital of the state.

CHAPTER XIII.

THE BEGINNING OF THE CIVIL WAR.—EXPOSED CONDITION OF KANSAS.—HER INTEREST IN THE CONFLICT.—THE FIRST ENLISTMENTS.—THE BATTLE OF WILSON'S CREEK.—THE CONTRABANDS.—LAWRENCE IN CLOSE TOUCH WITH THE SOLDIERS.

The old saying is, "If it is not one thing it is another." The drought had passed away and plenty had returned; the territorial struggle had ended in victory and Kansas was a free state. Now new troubles confronted the long disturbed community. The war of the rebellion broke out and the whole nation was in arms. One by one the southern states had seceded after the election of Mr. Lincoln as president, and the confederate states had set up a government of their own. So far no collision had occurred. But on April 12, 1861, the confederate troops opened fire on Fort Sumpter, in Charleston harbor, occupied by a small garrison of United States troops. It was a small affair in itself—an unimportant fort in a southern harbor, occupied by a small garrison of United States troops, fired upon by confederate batteries and compelled to surrender. But it meant that the seceding states had cast off the federal authority, and intended to maintain their separation at any cost. The federal goverment must either abandon all claim over the seceding states or resent the attack. The whole country was ablaze in an instant. It was the overt act for which events had been waiting, and for which both sides had been holding their breath. Everybody had known it was coming in some form or other and were wondering when and where it would be. They knew the explosion could not be long delayed. The southern states had seceded, organized a government and equipped an army, and were everywhere contesting the authority of the United

States. Such a condition of things could not continue long. When a collision came, it would not cease till the question was settled, "By what authority doest thou these things?" The clash of arms occurred in Charleston harbor, but the shock was felt to the remotest limits of the union. A bugle call in a military camp could hardly have brought an army to its feet more promptly than the firing on Sumpter brought the nation to its feet. Three days after, April 15th, President Lincoln issued his call for seventy-five thousand volunteers, and in three days more than seventy-five thousand volunteers were on the march. Of this great uprising at the north, James G. Blaine says, in his "Twenty Years in the United States Senate," "The proclamation was responded to in the loyal states with an unparalleled burst of enthusiasm. On the day of its issue hundreds of public meetings were held from the eastern borders of Maine to the extreme western frontier. Work was suspended on farm and in factory, and the whole people was roused to patriotic ardor, and to a determination to subdue the rebellion." Soon after the call for seventy-five thousand troops, another call was issued for

"Three hundred thousand more."

The whole country, which for forty years had not heard the sound of war, was transformed as by magic into one great martial camp.

The position of Kansas was peculiar and critical. She was a small community, isolated from her sympathizing sister states, so isolated indeed that in 1856 she had been almost entirely cut off from communication with her friends. And if this could be done in a time of peace, what might not be done in a time of war? The rich and powerful state of Missouri lay on her eastern border. Missouri was a doubtful state. She had a large slave population and the most violent pro-slavery sentiment anywhere to be found. Her governor was Claiborne F. Jackson who led the body of Missourians who

R. W. LUDINGTON.

P. D. RIDENOUR.

FRED. W. READ.

COL. S. W. ELDRIDGE.

PIONEER BUSINESS MEN IN LAWRENCE.

invaded Lawrence at the election March 30, 1855, and took possession of the polls and elected "the bogus legislature." The commander of her militia was Sterling Price, who became one of the ablest and most noted of the confederate generals. February 28, 1861, a state convention was called to consider whether Missouri should remain in the union or go with the confederacy. Sterling Price was president of the convention, and he and Governor Jackson used all their influence in favor of secession. The convention, however, decided to remain in the union. In spite of the convention, Governor Jackson and General Price did all in their power to carry the state over to the confederacy, and they would have succeeded but for the prompt action of General Lyon at St. Louis and Jefferson City. The disloyal feeling was especially strong along the western border, or more properly in the western half of the state. It was from this section that the expeditions had been fitted up to invade Kansas during the border conflict. As war became iminent it was a general feeling that Missouri would be hostile ground, as far as Kansas was concerned at least. Kansas would be exposed to all the dangers of a hostile frontier. She would be subjected to all the horrors of a border warfare, unrestrained even by the pretense of law and order.

But there was no flinching. The people of Kansas regarded the war as the inevitable sequence of the events which had preceded it. It was only a continuation and extension of the struggle which had been going on in Kansas for six years. It was simply bringing to a focus conditions which had long existed and which could have but one issue.

Lawrence was in peculiar peril because peculiarly exposed. She was only forty miles from the Missouri border, and was the center of "border ruffian" hate. And the border ruffians lived "just across the border." Three times they had marched upon her with threats of destruction. Twice they had been thwarted by the superior diplomacy of the free-state leaders. And when they entered Lawrence and ransacked the town, May 21, 1856, the affair reacted to their discomfiture and shame worse than defeat. In that turbulent time there were many wrongs done on both sides, and many deep personal animosities created. The rancor of the early struggle had not lost any of its violence by being thwarted in its purpose. All knew that it only wanted an opportunity to accomplish what it had attempted so often and had been so often repulsed. The people felt from the first that they were exposed not only to the fortunes of legitimate warfare, but to the irregular and barbarous inroads of the old foe.

The people of Lawrence had also a peculiar interest in the conflict from another point of view. Some one has said that "When a man fights a bear it is not simply a question which shall whip, but whether the man shall become bear or the bear shall become man; for whichever whips will eat the other." Kansas was much in the same position. She would almost necessarily go with the victors. If the confederacy won she would claim Missouri, and Kansas could hardly stand alone.

The Kansas people, therefore, threw themselves into the conflict with a unanimity that was hardly possible anywhere else. The population of Kansas in 1860 was only 107,206. Out of this population 22,000 men enlisted in the Union army. This would be about equivalent to her entire voting population. Twenty-two regiments entered the service. Lawrence was not behind her sister towns in enthusiasm and enlistments. It is not easy to learn the number of men who went into the army from Lawrence. There were not many of the twenty-two regiments which did not contain Lawrence men. The largest number probably enlisted in the first regiment. In this regiment a number of her most noted men were found. They had been prominent in the early struggle, and were prompt to offer themselves for service in the larger conflict which had grown out of it. The colonel of the first regiment was George W. Deitzler, whose council and courage had so often availed before. In the very beginning of the border ruffian' troubles, when it was necessary to secure arms from the East, he was sent on the secret and delicate mission. He was a member of the committee of safety, and in many relations proved himself a brave and reliable man. He was arrested for high treason, and, with other free-state men, lay for several months in the prison camp near Lecompton. When President Lincoln called for troops he offered himself at once and was placed in command of the first regiment of Kansas volunteers. He led his regiment with great valor at the battle of Wilson's creek a few weeks after their enlistment, and was severely wounded in the fight. He was afterwards promoted to the rank of brigadier general, and served with credit until the close of the war. O. E. Learnard was Lieutenant Colonel of the first regiment and served with distinction in Tennessee and Mississippi. He was much of the time in command of the regiment.

Samuel Walker was also in this first regiment. In fact he raised the first company, and was appointed captain of it. Most of the men of this company were from Lawrence. He had been the most trusted of all the early military leaders in 1855 and 1856. He first organized his neighbors for defense, and soon became a general leader. He led at Fort Saunders and Fort Titus, and many other of the early conflicts. When the war broke out he very naturally entered the larger army for wider service. In the battle of Wilson's creek he was in the thick of the fight, but though his hat and clothes were riddled with bullets, he came through without a scratch. He was promoted afterwards to major, then colonel, and continued in the service till the war closed. Frank B. Swift, who had been captain of the Stubbs, became also a captain in this first regiment. Caleb S. Pratt, the clerk of the city of Lawrence, became a lieutenant, and was killed in the battle of Wilson's creek. Lawrence, perhaps, was more closely concerned in this regiment than any other on account of the number of Lawrence men in the ranks.

When the first regiment was called for almost enough men offered themselves for two regiments. As the first regiment was mustered in, a second regiment was filled up and organized and lay at Lawrence two weeks before they knew that they would be accepted. They were finally mustered in June 20th, 1861, and they marched at once to the front, and in a month or so were engaged in the desperate battle of Wilson's creek. This regiment also contained a large number of Lawrence men. Edward D. Thompson, Shaler W. Eldridge were field officers, while Joseph Cracklin, Thomas J. Sternbergh, Warren Kimball were officers in companies.

To attempt to name all the Lawrence men who entered the United States service from first to last would be almost the same as giving a directory of the city. Even those who served as officers would make a long list. Among the names that would come at once to mind are John G. Haskell and his brother Dudley C. Haskell, Wm. A. Rankin and John K. Rankin, Charles W. Adams, Owen A. Bassett, James Christian, George F. Earl, A. D. Searle, Arthur Gunther, L. S. Shaw, Oliver Barber, Hugh Cameron, H. L. Moore, W. C. Barnes, John Pratt, Charles F. Garrett, and many others, who served as officers of different degrees. James H. Lane was commissioned as brigadier general early in the war, and led a brigade in Missouri at such intervals as he could be absent from his seat in the senate. At least four of the Lawrence pastors served as chaplains: Rev. Ephraim Nute, of the Unitarian Church, in the first regiment; Rev. R. C. Brant, of the Baptist Church, in the second; Rev. Charles Reynolds, of the Episcopal Church, in the second cavalry, and Rev. H. D. Fisher, of the Methodist Church, in the fifth regiment.

Of all the battles of the war Lawrence was perhaps more interested in that at Wilson's creek August 10, 1861. The second regiment had been mustered in only about a month when they were thrown into this terriffic contest, which, considering the number engaged, was one of the most stubbornly contested battles of the whole war. It was also a pivotal event in the progress of the war in the West, and Lawrence, and Kansas, watched the result with very deep concern. It had long been known that a large force of rebels were marching northward to recover the ground they had lost in Missouri. The deposed governor of the state, Claibore F. Jackson, had been driven out of his capital by General Lyon, and was coming with a large army from Arkansas, hoping to recover his office. The fate of Missouri and Kansas might turn on the issue of that battle. There were no regular lines of communication, and it was several days before full particulars could be obtained in Lawrence, and they were days of anxiety, both for the fate of the men engaged, and the tremendous issues at stake. A letter written August 13th by a citizen of Lawrence to a friend in Massachusetts, shows something of the state of mind the people were in:

"We have reports today of a battle near Springfield, Missouri, in which General Lyon is killed, but his army victorious. The rebel account, however, says his army is defeated. It is impossible to get reliable information. We await the result with great anxiety: for if the federal troops are driven from Missouri we shall very likely all be compelled to leave the country. Whether we can stay here or not may turn on the issue of this battle. If the confederacy gets control of Missouri it may carry Kansas with her. In that case the people that are here now will not be able to remain."

The final reports showed that the battle had been so

desperately contested that the rebel advance was checked, and Lyon's forces fell back to their base of supplies at Rolla.

Lawrence felt the throb of the war in many ways. Bodies of troops were almost constantly passing through on their way to battle fields further down. They often stopped on their march and camped for several days. At one time two regiments, fresh from home, lay encamped for several weeks just above the town, waiting to be ordered to the front. They were a noble lot of men, and the citizens became very warmly attached to them, and followed them with deep interest when they went. Sometimes the flow was the other way. Once word was sent that a large number of sick and wounded soldiers from the battle fields of Arkansas and southwest Missouri were coming to us. All the vacant rooms that could be secured were put to use for hospital service, and ladies volunteered to assist in nursing the poor fellows. Everything possible was done to make them comfortable, and to restore them to health and their country. Quite frequently union refugees from the south came to Lawrence and remained till it was safe to return to their homes.

The most unique movement caused by the war was the influx into Lawrence of negroes escaping from slavery. They began to come as soon as the war opened. At first it was only now and then one more energetic and enterprising than the rest. But they kept coming thicker and faster until they were coming by scores. The movement was doubtless accelerated by the measures taken by slaveholders to prevent it. Among other things they began selling their slaves down south where they would have no hope of escape. There was no horror in the negro mind more dreaded than being "sold down south" into the gulf states. It was hopeless bondage there. The news soon spread that the slaves were being sold down south. One man came to Lawrence whose wife had been sold down into Alabama. He was to be sold also and to be sent in another direction. He took a direction of his own without consulting his master.

This same thing was occurring all along the border of the free states. Wherever union soldiers were stationed, slaves would escape from their masters and run into camp. They had the most implicit faith in "Massa Lincoln," and most thoroughly believed that the war was for their liberation. They knew, as everybody did, that it had grown out of slavery. But their coming into the union lines raised a difficult question, and some of the tender-footed generals were at a loss what to do. Slavery had not been abolished, and the fugitive slave law had not been repealed. The owners of these slaves came into camp, claimed to be union men, and demanded the return of their slaves. What must be done? The war had not changed the law. Yet these negroes were enthusiastic for the union and loved the flag. It seemed cruel and absurd to send such men back to the enemy to be beaten and put in chains, perhaps, because they loved their country and wanted to be free. General Ben Butler finally cut the knot. A large number of slaves came into his camp at Fortress Monroe. He put them to work on the intrenchments. The owners soon came with injured tone and look, and asked for the "return of their property" which had escaped into the union lines. Old Ben Butler refused to return them. When asked for the grounds of his refusal he replied that they were "contrabands of war." Whether his answer was sound in a legal point of view has never been determined. But in the words of Shakespeare, "It was enough; it would serve." There were no more attempts to reclaim slaves that had fled to the union lines. For a long time these refugees went by the name of "contrabands."

The slaves escaping from the Missouri border made their way to Lawrence as if by instinct. They had heard of Lawrence in her early struggles. They knew how their masters hated her; consequently they loved her. They all felt that they would be safe if they could only get to Lawrence. Lawrence became to them what the polar star had been to the fugitives of former years. Their "star of hope" had moved up several hundred miles. Whenever one had determined to escape, and was fairly out of the toils of his master, he headed for Lawrence and plodded on by day and by night till he reached the goal.

The people of Lawrence did not need the "contraband" subterfuge to keep these poor fellows from being sent back to their masters. They had met the question before and were fairly well settled in their minds. The "entertaining of strangers" was not altogether a new grace among them. But their "faith" was very severely tried by the numbers that came. They began to feel that virtue was not always its own reward. They almost regretted the reputation their history had given them. Most of those who came were entirely destitute and had no idea or plan beyond getting to Lawrence. Now and then one had "spoiled the Egyptians" and brought some little with him. But the great majority were kept from doing this either by conscience or a vigilant guard. They brought nothing with them but the clothes they had on, and these would have filled the Gibeonites with envy. They were old and torn, tied up with strings and pinned with thorns. The fear was very natural that these unfortunate men would be a serious burden to the people who had about all they could carry already. But in this they were happily disappointed. These people were strong and healthy and ready to work at anything that was offered. They were so glad to be free that they would accept any shelter they could find, and were satisfied with the simplest food. By a little systematic planning work was found for them as fast as they came, and this unique community of freedmen was self-sustaining almost from the start.

GEORGE LEIS.

THADDEUS PRENTICE.

GEO. W. HUTCHINSON.

JOHN H. SHIMMONS.

EARLY BUSINESS MEN IN LAWRENCE.

These people showed a great eagerness to learn. Very few of them could either read or write. They had not been allowed to learn in their condition as slaves. Teaching a slave was a crime punished with severe penalties. As soon as they were free, therefore, they were very eager to learn. To accommodate them a night school was established in Lawrence to which anybody could come who wished. It was taught by volunteer teachers who offered their services freely, some of the most cultivated ladies of the place giving five evenings every week to this work. For greater efficiency it was conducted in the form of a Sabbath school, each teacher having but four or five scholars to care for. A writer in the Lawrence *State Journal* describes a visit to the school in December, 1861. He says there were eighty-three scholars present and twenty-seven teachers. They were of all ages; a class of restless little girls on one bench, and a class of grown men on another. They all began with the alphabet. In five nights some of them were spelling words of two sylables. Some who began when the school opened, were able to read fluently and were ready to commence in figures. After the lesson they sang. One of their songs seemed very appropriate and they sang as if they meant it:

> "Where, oh, where is the Captain Moses,
> Who led Israel out of Egypt?
> Safe now in the promised land."

Most of the early fugitives were among the most energetic and enterprising of the slaves. Most of them remained in Lawrence, and they and their families are among the most prosperous and well to do of our colored population. If the spirit of common sympathy and helpfullness which was so marked at first, could have been kept up it would have been vastly better for both races and for all concerned.

Lawrence was more prosperous during the first three years of the war than she had been the three year's preceding. The war gave employment to many people. Those in the army sent their money back to their families, and farm produce found a ready market at good prices. The country about Lawrence was very rich and many excellent farms were being developed. There was no special growth in the town, and very little building was done, but there were some improvements and a general air of thrift. Business was fairly good, and the frequent passing of troops and travelers made things lively and fresh. People became accustomed to the condition of war and adjusted themselves to it. The frequent alarms which at first disturbed people had come to be regarded as a part of the situation. The progress of the war was watched with closest interest on account of the great issues involved, and also from the fact that Kansas troops were everywhere, and hardly a battle could be fought that did not bring sorrow to some Kansas home. Not only were Kansas troops engaged in the campaigns of the southwest, in Missouri and Arkansas, but also with the army of the Cumberland and the campaigns along the gulf; with Grant at Vicksburg, and with Sherman as he was "marching through Georgia." A battle could hardly occur in which Kansas was not concerned and Lawrence with the rest. While her men were more numerous in the first and second regiments, they were found in nearly all the regiments, and her people scanned the death roll after nearly every battle looking for names that were familiar and dear. No matter where it might be in the great field of the war, the lines reached into Lawrence, and the names of the dead was a matter of personal solicitude.

CHAPTER XIV.

THE LAWRENCE RAID.—ITS ANTECEDENTS AND CAUSES.— WILLIAM C. QUANTRILL.— ITS UNIQUE CHARACTER.— OTHER RAIDS.—ITS UNPARALLELED BRUTALITY.

In 1863 there occurred the most important event of the war as far as Lawrence was concerned; that was what has ever since been spoken of as the "Raid." The possibility of such a thing was recognized from the first. An incursion of maurauders from Missouri was considered likely to occur from the breaking out of the war. Lawrence had been the center of the free-state struggle, and had been the center of pro-slavery hate. That struggle had left a good deal of bitter feeling on both sides. It was especially bitter on the Missouri side because they had been defeated in the end they sought. They had three times undertaken to destroy Lawrence and three times had been foiled. It would not be strange, the people thought, if the men of the border should not forget their disappointment, and should take advantage of the war to accomplish what they had so often failed in. And there were signs from across the border which confirmed these fears. There were threats and intimations of what might be, enough to show at least that they had not been forgotten. The negroes who ran away from bondage and came to Lawrence, had one story of the state of feeling on the other side of the border. They all said that the "border ruffians" had lost nothing of their hate for Lawrence, and they predicted with great positiveness that Lawrence would feel that hate before the war was over. The writer of this had in his family for several years a very intelligent mulatto who had been a slave in one of the border towns across the river. She had been a house servant, and had gained a good deal of culture from coming in contact with the family, and with friends of her master. It was quite noticeable that house servants were much more intelligent than field hands. This woman belonged to a prominent citizen who stood high in pro-slavery circles. He was a man of means and a man of good political standing. He was in secret sympathy with the rebellion, but did not avow his sympathy. This woman said that her master's house was the common resort of all the rebels of that region. They met at night usually, to discuss plans and talk over the situation. Many a time she had cooked all day and filled the cellar with meat and bread and other provisions, and in the night they would be all taken away and the cellar left empty. She never asked any questions, but she knew that the provisions were carried off to supply the guerrilla bands which were prowling about the country. When the guerrilla chiefs were at her master's house, as they often were, it was her work to serve them. So she passed in and out with perfect freedom. The slaves had a remarkable faculty of seeming to be utterly ignorant of the conversation going on, and seeming utterly blank, while they heard and understood every word that was said. So this woman could pass in and out of the room, and they would not think it necessary to stop their conversation or even guard their expressions. But she knew why they were together and caught every word that dropped. She said that oftener than anything else they were talking of Lawrence, and planning for its destruction. This was early in the war, and she used to speak of it in Lawrence months before the raid took place. She used to say with great earnestness "that the bushwhackers were surely coming, and the people were very foolish not to be prepared for them." This was the common testimony of the ex-slaves who came up from Missouri at the opening of the war. They knew the sentiment of their masters, and the common purpose of the rebels on the border, to repay Lawrence and Kansas for the defeat they had suffered in the former conflict.

Rumors and alarms were common also. In the early days of the war an alarming report was one day brought to Lawrence that a large body of men, fifteen hundred the story went, were marching up from the border. Whence the story came no one knew, and no one cared to scrutinize it very closely. The whole country was aroused. The writer of this was calling around that day among the farmers at one of his out stations ten miles from Lawrence. He only found one farm house where the men were not either gone or preparing to go. They were going one by one, with their rifles and shot guns, after the manner of the heroes of Lexington. They came back next day and reported no enemy in sight. As the war continued and rumors and alarms thickened, people became accustomed to them, and took little notice of them. Now and then, however, there would come a report that seemed to have a foundation, and the whole community was in a quiver. A very common feeling at first was that some of the troops furnished by Kansas should be retained for the defense of the state. Some thought it very cruel that Kansas towns should be left exposed while so large a proportion of her men were fighting the battles of the country in distant parts. But the wiser people contended that Kansas would be best protected in the long run by vigorously prosecuting the war to a successful issue. The fate of Kansas was wrapped up in the fate of the union.

It has often been a matter of wonder that after all these warnings Lawrence was not on her guard when the blow was finally struck. But this is readily explained by the situation itself. These frequent alarms had produced a state of indifference. It was the "cry of the wolf" with the usual effect. The danger had been threatening for all these years and had not come, and people began to feel that it would never come.

They smiled at the wild reports that kept flying in and began to analyze each report as it came and show how absurd it was. They knew there was danger, but it grew more and more indefinite and far away.

There were also frequent efforts at preparation. In the earlier months of the war the citizens maintained a guard about the town, taking their regular turns like soldiers. This was kept up until the spring of 1863 with more or less steadiness. Not being under military orders it was not a very reliable service, but most of the citizens faithfully fulfilled their part. In the spring of 1863 Gen. George W. Collamore was elected mayor of the city. He had been quartermaster general of the state under Governor Robinson for two years. He was a man of means and well connected in the East. He was a very active man with a good deal of executive ability, and had an air of self-sufficiency which made him want to do everything his own way and made other people disposed to stand aloof from him. He realized as few others did the danger in which Lawrence stood, and he endeavored earnestly and constantly to arouse the people to a sense of the situation. In this he was partially successful. He organized an effective military company and secured arms for them from the state. He also organized and armed companies in the country about Lawrence. A peculiar notion of his was that the guns should be kept in the armory and not be carried home by the men. The result was that when the attack was made the men were scattered about the city at their homes and their guns were inaccessible. The Wakarusa company, six miles south, assembled the morning of the raid near Blanton's bridge, but had no arms. It is easy to see, however, that there are points of advantage in General Collamore's policy, though this time it proved a mistake. General Collamore worked in another line for the defense of the town. He saw, as everyone did, that the citizens' guard was very unreliable. While most citizens did their duty when appointed for picket service, others failed, and it was never known whether there was a guard out or not. Besides he insisted that it was unfair to ask men who worked all day to do picket duty all night. It was enough if they held themselves in readiness to rally when danger threatened. He appealed to the military authorities to station at Lawrence a body of soldiers sufficient to do picket duty. This would insure a reliable guard, and relieve the citizens of this double service. He insisted that Lawrence could defend herself if she could only be warned in time of the approach of danger. After many efforts he gained his point and some time in May a small squad of soldiers was stationed at Lawrence, and the citizen soldiery was relieved of patrol duty. About August 1st the military authorities withdrew this guard for service elsewhere. They affirmed very positively that the guard was not needed. Lawrence was in no possible danger. The line between Missouri and Kansas was patrolled along its whole length, and no body of guerrillas could pass into Kansas without the fact being reported. General Collamore protested against the removal of the troops, but without avail. The people were disposed to accept the assurance of the military authorities, and nothing was done to revive the old plan of citizen patrol. The result was that Lawrence had never been so thoroughly off her guard, and so thoroughly at her ease, as at this time of her greatest peril. There could hardly have been a time in the three preceding years when she was feeling entirely secure. Mayor Collamore himself had struggled persistently against a good deal of indifference and some ridicule, and when the troops he had worked so hard to secure were taken away, he was himself half discouraged, and had not undertaken any new lines of defense. The whole town was just resting from the long strain.

The guerrilla method of warfare was adopted early by

the rebel element in Missouri. As soon as Fort Sumpter was fired upon the whole state was in confusion. There were disturbances here and there; railway tracks were torn up, bridges burned, and travel generally became dangerous. When the war became thoroughly organized order was restored in the country, railways were protected, and the guerrillas compelled to go into hiding, and apply their vocation more secretly. Of these guerrilla bands, Quantrill soon became the most noted leader. His gang of outlaws, varying from two or three score to two or three hundred, found a hiding place among what was called the "Sni Hills." This was a general name for a rough region lying south of the Missouri river and below Kansas City and Westport, through which the Sni river and the Blue river and some other small streams flowed. It was a country of high bluffs, deep ravines and rocky ledges, all covered with a growth of young timber so dense that a bird could hardly fly through it. It was an ideal hiding for a band like Quantrill's, superior for that purpose to Sherwood forest, the famous hiding place of Robin Hood. Here they could make their preparations unobserved and sally forth unheralded. When the work of robbery and arson was done they could dash back, and once among these wild fastnesses and thickets they were practically beyond pursuit. They could not have lived here but for the sympathy of the surrounding population, and a large portion of the population of this region were secretly in sympathy with the South, while professing loyalty to the union. From the granaries and the herds of those rich farmers the guerrilla bands were secretly maintained, and many a man who claimed to be a friend of the union was secretly feeding the enemies of the union, and making possible their inhuman warfare. Before the end of the war the union cavalry learned the methods of the bushwhackers, and could follow them to their hiding places. When this was done guerrilla warfare

WM. CRUTCHFIELD. JOHN L. CRANE.

O. A. HANSCOM. GEORGE FORD.

EARLY KANSAS SETTLERS.

became less a one-sided affair, and the bushwhackers were pretty much driven from the country. But the method was learned too late to be of much avail in protecting the country. It availed for retaliation but not for safety.

William Clark Quantrill was born at Dover, Ohio, in 1837. His father, Thomas Quantrill, was a school teacher of good family and good character. His father and mother were both honest, plain people, respected by all. His mother's maiden name was Caroline Clark. William received a fairly good education and was intended for his father's profession. From some of his early letters it appeared that he had in his youth some high ambitions of an entirely different type from those which afterwards possessed him. In 1857, at the age of twenty, he went to Kansas. He and some friends took up claims in Miami county near Stanton. In the winter of 1857 and 1858 he taught school in Stanton and did quite well. The next spring he went to Salt Lake and remained two years. In 1860 he returned to Kansas and made his headquarters at Lawrence. He went by the name of Charlie Hart and boarded at the Whitney house on the bank of the river. At the time of the raid he spared the Whitney house on this account. He said they had treated him well there. Whether he went by this assumed name on account of crimes already committed, or whether he was now engaged in doubtful transactions which he did not wish to attach to his real name, is not known. At all events he associated with a bad lot of men, and they were engaged in doubtful and shady operations, which soon drew upon them the attention of the police. He escaped them and went over into Missouri, just across the line, not far from where he formerly lived in Miami county. He persuaded four reckless young men to join him in robbing the home of a rich slaveholder in Missouri. He then betrayed his associates to the intended victim, and three of the four were shot dead, he himself shooting one of them. He was arrested and lodged in the Paola jail. Some of his friends secured his release on a writ of habeas corpus, and when he was out of jail some friends placed a fleet horse in a convenient place, and this horse soon took him "beyond the jurisdiction of the court." He had heretofore been in sympathy with the free-state people, but from this on he identified himself with his Missouri friends. He became the leader of their marauding bands, and in a short time was the most distinguished of the guerrilla chieftans. All the most successful raids were under his guidance, and there were no marked successes after he withdrew to another part of the country. He began to be noted in 1862 when he made numerous raids into Kansas. In October 1862 he made a raid on Olathe with about one hundred and forty men. He kept the citizens under guard in the public square while his men carried off whatever they wished in the way of horses or goods. One man was killed. A little later he made a raid on Shawneetown, burned a good portion of the place and killed several men. At other times the same process was repeated at Spring Hill, Aubrey and other points. The next season, the summer of 1863, his movements were more numerous and bold. The whole region along the border was kept in a continual state of commotion and fear. Every night lights against the sky showed that some poor fellows house was going up in flames. Men on the farms did not dare stay in their houses over night, but slept in the cornfields and in the woods. This state of things continued during the summer of 1863. These depredations did not extend more than ten or fifteen miles from the Missouri border into Kansas. The people of Lawrence used to argue that guerrilla bands could not get further than that into the country without being reported. They therefore reasoned that Lawrence was safe because she was forty miles from the border. It would take all night to make the march, and the news would certainly travel faster than a troop could travel. It is surprising now how clear they made this argument appear to themselves. Every day's delay confirmed their conclusion. The military authorities who "undersood such matters," were even more positive. So their sense of security grew strong as the enemy drew near, and they were never more at their ease than when the peril was at their very door.

The Lawrence raid was unique. It differed from any other raid in history. Other raids were made for plunder or for military purposes. The earlier raids of Quantrill and his men were made for plunder largely. They dashed into Olathe at night, ordered all the men to the public square and kept them under guard till they were done. Only one man was killed and he was killed in a fray. Often raids were made for the purpose of putting out of the way some persons who were obnoxious to them. Houses were burned, horses were taken, and other things stolen such as took their fancy. But in no case was there a general slaughter. At Lawrence it was butchery from the first charge to the last shot. The butchering and burning began with their approach and hardly ended with their departure. It was not the picking out of a few obnoxious persons as was the case elsewhere. The killing was indiscriminate and mostly in cold blood. There was no provocation and no resistance. There was nothing to irritate or provoke. The few who resisted fared better than those who did not resist. There were men in Lawrence whom they very naturally would look for. But very few of these were found. Governor Robinson was in town that morning. On account of his position and his prominence in the early difficulties they would have counted him a valuable prize. But he was permitted quietly to survey the whole transaction from his stone barn on the hillside. They sought for him elsewhere, but did not look in the barn. General Lane was in town that morning, and perhaps no man in Kansas would have been dispatched with more relish. But when they called at his house in the early morning, he was "not at home." General Deitzler was in town, having just come from a victorious campaign through the very region from which they hailed. But he was not found. The two Rankins were home on a furlough. They were soldiers and expected no quarters. When they were pounced upon in the street therefore they drew their revolvers and blazed away, and were given a wide berth. They are both living today to tell the story. The men the raiders did kill were quiet, peaceable citizens. Few of them had taken any part in the early disturbances or in the border troubles since the war began. There was Judge Carpenter, a very conservative man, never extreme in any line, and having no sympathy with extreme men on either side. There was Edward P. Fitch, one of the quietest of men, a lover of home and of peace, as brave as a lion, and gentle as a woman. There was S. M. Thorpe of whom no one could cherish a hard thought. Only a few months before he had been elected to the state senate on the issue of opposition to all irresponsible warfare. He had the utmost abhorrence of all parties on either side who were disposed to take advantage of the condition of war for plunder or prey. This suggests the further point that Lawrence herself was a conservative town. The depredations complained of found as little sympathy in Lawrence as in any town in the state. If retaliation was the motive, Lawrence was one of the last towns that should have suffered, and the men killed were among the last that should have been selected. As a matter of fact the victims were not selected at all. The raiders killed whom they found never asking who they were or what they were. It was enough that they were found in Lawrence. Other raids was for plunder, the Lawrence raid was for slaughter. That some of the raiders should assign retaliation as the motive was to be expected. It was the nearest motive at hand and made a plausible excuse. That some of the raiders had suffered personal wrongs and were inspired with feelings of revenge, we can well believe. But this could not have been the inspiration of the attack, nor the cause of its excessive brutality. These things show that it had roots deeper than this. Its roots ran back into the old pro-slavery hate of six years before. Individual members of the band no doubt had their individual motives. But the thing itself had a deeper ground. Its inspiration and its venom flowed from the same source and sentiment whence the earlier invasions came. It sprang from the same sentiment which had three times before assailed Lawrence and been foiled. Individuals of the band may have had a variety of motives, but as a whole the movement sprang from the same soil which produced the Wakarusa war and the troubles of 1856. It was the same conflict on a larger scale. The same principles were at stake, and the same parties confronted each other. The same feelings inspired either side. The same hate sought to gratify itself under the new conditions. The border ruffians of 1856, became the bushwhackers of 1863.

CHAPTER XV.

THE LAWRENCE RAID.—THE APPROACH.—THE CHARGE AND THE SURPRISE.—THE SURRENDER OF THE HOTEL.—THE BURNING AND KILLING BEGIN.—FOUR HOURS OF SLAUGHTER.—MARVELOUS ESCAPES.—THE HEROISM OF THE WOMEN.

It is not easy to get any inside view of Quantrill's movements. When not in motion his men were in hiding. He laid his plans in secret and executed them in the night, and neither plan nor execution was open to inspection. Since the war closed what remained of the raiders were scattered all over the country, and most of them are very shy of saying anything of the part they played. A gentleman of Kansas City, who was a citizen of Lawrence at the time of the raid, has recently interviewed one of Quantrill's men who has lived a quiet life since the war and become a respected citizen. From him a more full account of Quantrill's approach has been gathered. Quantrill assembled his men at Columbus, Johnson county, Missouri, August 19th, and moved over to Lone Jack in Jackson county. Here the organization was completed and the final orders given. The roll was called and two hundred and ninety-four responded to their names. They were organized in four companies under four captains. Two of these captains were the notorious Bill Todd and Bill Anderson, the most desperate and bloodthirsty of the border chieftains. The writer of this sketch once came up the Missouri river on the same steamboat with Bill Anderson. It was before the war, and Anderson had not yet developed into a bushwhacker. But his capacity in that line was easily seen. He was playing the part of a gentleman just then, and seemed to be the favorite companion of some southern ladies who were coming up the river at the same time. He was easy, affable, well

informed and entertaining, and was evidently in good humor
with himself. He was somewhat tall with rather long dangling
arms. He was well dressed, and when he walked on deck
he always wore one of those circular broadcloth cloaks
which were then common. He had long, black, flowing hair,
sharp features, a hooked nose, and an eye such as one will
see but once in a life time. The writer did not know anything
of him then, and judged simply from his appearance. But his
eyes impressed him as being a sort of a cross between an
eagle and a snake, the most vicious looking eye he ever saw.
Over his features continually there played a look of infinite
conceit and a sneering smile of ineffable contempt. This
pictures him in his character of a gentleman. A picture of him
later, in his character of bushwhacker, was drawn by another
hand. It gives the same general form, the same hooked nose,
the same flowing locks, the same sinister eye and the same
diabolical sneer. But now he is dressed in homespun butter-
nuts; he is coatless and hatless and sits upon a horse which is
almost a counterpart of himself. The horse goes without
guidance, and the man rides without support. The horse is
dashing after men as they run, just as a hunter would follow
a fox. His rider sits erect with a revolver in each hand, and
fires with either with unerring accuracy at any poor fellow
that comes in sight. Such are two pictures of the most cold-
blooded and brutal of all the guerrilla leaders. Before the war
closed he was killed as he dashed along in the manner indicated in the second picture above. Besides these four
captains, there were with Quantrill all the noted guerrillas of
the border, Dick Yeager, the James boys and others. Jesse
James was but a boy of sixteen, but he boasted of having
killed thirteen men in Lawrence. But all stories with "thir-
teens" can safely be discounted. Thirteen seems to have
been a favorite number with them, and enough of them
boasted of having killed thirteen each to have exterminated

the entire population of Lawrence. But his killing was probably limited only by his opportunities.

After all arrangements were completed the band moved from Lone Jack and marched towards the Kansas border. They crossed over into Kansas about five o'clock in the afternoon. They passed in plain sight of a camp of United States troops some miles away at Aubrey. The troops made no attempt to intercept them. It would have been madness to do so, as the raiders outnumbered them four or five to one. This camp was in command of Captain J. A. Pike. He sent word at once to Kansas City, but why he did not also send word to Lawrence has never been explained. The raiders proceeded a short distance when they halted to rest their horses and to eat supper. The horses refreshed themselves on prairie grass, and the men on such as they had. Some of them even went to the farm houses near by and procured milk and other things they wanted, and some of them ordered supper. After a good rest they mounted and rode on. They struck directly across the prairie toward Lawrence. About eleven o'clock they passed Gardner on the old Santa Fe trail. Here they burned a house or two and killed a man. But even from here no word was sent in to warn those in danger. The citizens were probably too much occupied with their own perils to think much of the dangers of others. The troop passed through Hesper about three o'clock in the morning. The moon had now gone down and the night was dark and the way quite doubtful. Quantrill took a boy from a house near Captain's creek and compelled him to lead them to Lawrence. They kept this boy during their work in Lawrence, then Quantrill dressed him in a new suit of clothes and gave him a horse and sent him home.

Somewhere along here a man whose name ought to have been preserved attempted to give warning to the doomed town. As soon as the troop had passed his house he

FOREST SAVAGE.

JOSEPH E. RIGGS.

SAMUEL KIMBALL.

JOSEPH SAVAGE.

EARLY KANSAS SETTLERS.

mounted a horse and started for Lawrence by a circuitous route. He had proceeded but a few miles, however, when his horse stumbled in the darkness and fell forward and killed himself. The man could do no other than abandon his heroic purpose and return home on foot.

It is a very singular thing that during all these hours no word should come to Lawrence of the danger which was approaching her. As Hovey E. Lowman says in his account of the affair, the bushwhackers "passed leisurely from their hiding place in Missouri through the federal lines, and almost within shooting distance of a federal camp in the day time, then just as leisurely made their way over forty miles of traveled road through Kansas settlements at night, and halted, called the roll in early dawn within pistol shot of the houses of the residents of Lawrence, and yet no warning voice rang through her quiet streets, 'Quantrill is coming!'" All the while he was coming the people slept as peacefully as if there had been no foe within a thousand miles. One of the strangest of the many strange things of this strange affair was that every thought of help or warning was frustrated, and the foe that had been coming all night pounced upon an unsuspecting people in the morning.

Quantrill and his men entered Franklin, four miles east of Lawrence, at the first glimmer of day. They passed quietly through the village, leaning over upon their horses so as to attract as little attention as possible. A few persons saw them, but in the dimness could not make out who they were. The command was distinctly heard however: "Rush on, boys, rush on! It will be daylight before we are there. We ought to have been there an hour ago."

It was growing lighter now and they traveled faster. As they drew near to the town they grew eager for blood. About two miles east of Lawrence they passed the farm of Rev. S. S. Snyder, a minister of the United Brethren church. Here a couple of them left the main body and rode through his gate, found him in his barnyard and shot him. He was a very quiet man and very highly respected. He had been commissioned as a lieutenant of colored troops and this was doubtless the reason they singled him out.

About a mile from town they met young Hoffman Collamore, the son of Mayor Collamore. He was riding out early to his father's farm to spend the day shooting game. He was riding a pony and carried a shot gun. He was a young lad of about sixteen. When he met them in the dim dawn he supposed that they were a body of United States troops, and he turned aside to pass them. They halted him and asked him where he was going. Suspecting nothing, he made an indifferent reply and kept on. At that they began firing at him. He put spurs to his pony and dashed out into a field. They continued firing and soon one bullet hit the boy and another the pony, and they both fell headlong. The boy lay as if dead until they had passed and then crept away. He was severely wounded in the thigh, but recovered.

Just outside of the town two of them turned aside and rode into the yard of Mr. Joseph Savage, who then lived at the Hanscom place. They went up to his front door and knocked. Mr. Savage had the good fortune to be suffering with weak eyes at the time. He had just risen and was in the rear part of the house bathing his eyes. He heard the knock but could not go to the door till he had washed his eyes. He had seen the troop going by the house, but supposing them to be Union soldiers, he gave the matter no thought. As soon as he was able he went to the door and opened it just in time to see two horsemen riding out of his gate. His weak eyes undoubtedly saved his life.

As they drew near to the town they seemed to hesitate and waver. Coming from the east the town appeared in its full proportions as the first light of the morning shone on it. It is said some of them were disposed to turn back. But Quantrill said "he was going in, and they might follow who would." Two horsemen were sent in advance of the troop to see that all was quiet. They rode through the main street without attracting attention. They were seen by several persons but excited no suspicion. They returned to the main body and reported the way clear. They now moved on quite rapidly, but quietly and cautiously. When they came to the high ground facing Massachusetts street, not far from where the park now is, the command was given in clear tones, "Rush on to the town." Instantly the whole body bounded forward with the yell of demons. They came first upon a camp of unarmed recruits for the Kansas Fourteenth regiment. They had just taken in their guards and were rising from their beds. On these the raiders fired as they passed, killing seventeen of the twenty-two. This diversion did not check the speed of the general advance. A few turned aside to run down and shoot the fleeing soldiers, but the main body swept on down Rhode Island street. When the head of the column came about to Henry street the command was heard all over that section, "On to the hotel! On to the hotel!" At this they wheeled obliquely to the left, and in a few moments were dashing down Massachusetts street toward the Eldridge house. In all the bloody scenes which followed nothing surpassed for wildness and terror that which now presented itself. The horsemanship of the guerrillas was perfect. They rode with the ease and abandon of men who had spent their lives in the saddle amid rough and desperate scenes. They were dressed in the traditional butternut, and belted about with revolvers. Their horses seemed to be in the secret of the hour, and their feet scarcely seemed to touch the ground. Their riders sat upon them with bodies erect, and arms free, some with a revolver in each hand, shooting at each house or person they passed, and yelling at every bound. On each side of this stream of fire were men falling dead and wounded, and women and children, half dressed, running and screaming, some trying to escape from danger, and others rushing to the side of their murdered friends.

They dashed along Massachusetts street, shooting at every person on the sidewalk, and into almost every window, until they came in front of the Eldridge house. The firing now ceased and there was a silence for a few moments. They eviedently expected resistance at this point, and sat gazing up at the long rows of windows as if doubtful of what might come. In a few moments Captain A. R. Banks, provost marshal of the state, opened a window and displayed a white sheet and called for Quantrill. Quantrill rode forward and Captain Banks surrendered the house, stipulating for the safety of the inmates, mostly strangers. At this moment the big gong of the hotel began to sound through the halls to arouse the sleeping guests. The whole column fell back at the sound, evidently thinking it to be the signal for attack. But as nothing came of it they soon pressed forward again, and began the work of plunder and destruction. They ransacked the hotel, taking what they found in the rooms and robbing the guests of their valuables as they came out. The guests were not long in assembling at the head of the stairs, and thence they went down to the sidewalk. They were marched to the corner of Winthrop street when Quantrill appeared and ordered them to go to the City hotel, and they would be safe. He had boarded there some years ago and had been well treated, and should spare the hotel on that account. He ordered them to go into the house and stay there and they would not be harmed. The prisoners were as obedient as Quantrill's own men, and lost no time in seeking their house of refuge. In marked contrast with what followed, Quantrill kept his word with the Eldridge house prisoners, and they were not molested so long as Quantrill remained in town. He evidently regarded the Eldridge house as the citadel of the place, and considered its surrender equivalent to the surrender of the town. He was looking for resistance, and was relieved when the white flag appeared. He therefore felt inclined to abide by the terms of capitulation. Among the guests at the Eldridge house were James C. Horton and Carmi W. Babcock. They came down as soon as the alarm was given, and met the raiders in the hall. They persuaded them to delay the pillage till the guests could get out. As soon as they reached the City hotel they discovered that a brother of Colonel Eldridge, the proprietor of the Eldridge house, was not with them. They feared he had not been awakened, and would perish with the building. Mr. Horton and Mr. Babcock asked for a guard to go back and get him. A horseman returned with them, but the building was already in flames and they could not enter it. Their guard then escorted them safely back to the City hotel. Mr. Eldridge was afterwards found safe.

The other hotels and the other houses had no such experience of clemency or honor as was accorded to the Eldridge house. The treatment of the Eldridge house guests was in marked contrast with all the dreadful scenes that followed.

As soon as the Eldridge house had surrendered, the raiders scattered all over the town. They went in bands of six or eight, taking street by street and house by house. The events of the next three hours find no parallel outside the annals of savage warfare. History furnishes no other instance where so large a number of such desperate men, so heavily armed, were let perfectly loose upon an unsuspecting and helpless community. They were not restrained even by the common rules of war, and went about their work of death with the abandon of men with whom murder was a pastime and pity a stranger. Instead of wearying of their bloody work, they grew more brutal as the work proceeded, for they secured liquor at some of the stores, and added the recklessness of drunkenness to the barbarous purpose for which they came. The carnage was all the worse for the fact that the people were not expecting an indiscriminate slaughter. The general feeling was that they would do what they had done elsewhere—rob and burn the town, shoot a few marked men if they could find them, and then leave. No one dreamed of such wholesale butchery as followed. Hence many who could have escaped remained in their homes and were killed. They naturally thought that there would be more danger in running through the streets filled with armed men than in quietly waiting in their homes and taking their chances. For this reason the men who were specially marked for slaughter fared the best, for they knew what to expect and took themselves out of the way. There was a large number of military men in town, but scarcely one of them was killed, except the unarmed recruits who were shot in their camp, almost in their beds, at first onset. Soldiers knew they could expect no quarter, and so took care of themselves. The same was true of the colored people. They knew what kind of men slavery had made, and they ran to the brush at the first alarm, and comparatively few of them were killed. But the raiders made no discrimination. They came to kill, and it was a butchery from the first. Those who were naturally marked for slaughter mostly escaped, while those killed were mostly quiet, unoffending citizens. They killed whom they met without knowing who they were or caring what they were. They said their orders were "to kill every man and burn every house." They did not quite do this, but they went to work as if this was their intent. They were not all alike of course. Some reveled in the work they were doing, some recoiled from it, and some were touched with pity. But even their pity did not often effect much. For if one gang was touched with pity, the next would be pittiless, and the result was often the same. A gentleman who was concealed where he could see the whole, said it was the most vivid realization of the slang phrase "Hell let loose" that could be well imagined. They were a desperate looking lot of men, rough in dress, and coarse in speech and brutal in conduct. They carried from two to six revolvers apiece while many also carried carbines.

The attack had been perfectly planned. Every man seemed to know his place and what he was to do. Detachments scattered to every part of the town, and it was done with such promptness that before the people could gather the meaning of the first yell every part of the town was full of them. They flowed into every street and lane like water poured upon a rock. Eleven rushed up to Mount Oread to keep watch of the country round about. From here they could see over the whole country for several miles, and note any gathering among the people to come to the rescue. Another and larger band struck for the western part of the town, where they had more reason to fear the organization of the citizens for defense. So quickly were they dispersed to every section that any concentration for resistance was out of the question. The surprise was so complete that no organized resistance was possible. Before the people could comprehend the real meaning of the affair, every part of the town was occupied by the raiders. The attack could scarcely have been made at a more unfortunate hour. People were just awaking from their sleep, and could hardly comprehend what had come upon them. The men of Lawrence were organized in a militia company, but the mayor had insisted that the arms should be kept in the armory instead of being carried home by the members. From the very first attack, therefore, these guns were inaccessible. Even if the company could have got together they had no arms, and there could be no resistance from the houses themselves. It is not likely, however, that any other arrangement would have changed things much. The attack was so sudden and the occupation of the town was so complete, that no general rally was possible. There was neither time nor opportunity for consultation or concert of action. Everyone had to do the best he could for himself.

There were a few individual attempts at resistance, but most of them resulted disastrously. Mr. Levi Gates lived in the country about a mile away, and in the opposite direction from which the rebels came in. As soon as he heard the firing he siezed his rifle and started for town. He supposed a stand would be made somewhere by the citizens, and he could join them. When he reached the town he saw at once it was in possession of the rebels. Being an excellent marksman he could not leave without trying his rifle. His first shot made a rebel jump in his saddle but did not kill him. He loaded again and fired one more shot, but by this time the rebels were all around him, and he soon fell a victim to their bullets. After he was dead they brutally beat his head to pieces. Captain George W. Bell was county clerk. He lived on the hill overlooking the town. He saw the raiders before they made their first charge. He siezed his gun and started out with the hope of reaching the main street before them, and joining the citizens in defending the town. His family tried to dissuade him, but he only replied, "If they take Lawrence they must do it over my dead body." With a prayer for courage and help he started on the run. But he was too late. Before he could reach the main street the raiders had possession. He endeavored to get round by a back way and came to the ravine west of the street. Here he met other citizens and asked them: "Where shall we meet?" They assured him it was too late to meet anywhere, and urged him to save himself while he could. He turned back as if intending to go home again. But the raiders had now scattered all over and he was in the midst of them. Finding escape im-

MRS. SARAH MACK-PINKSTON.

MRS. COL. SAML. WALKER.

MRS. DR. S. B. PRENTISS.

MRS. O. A. HANSCOM.

SOME OF THE PIONEER WOMEN

possible, he went into an unfinished brick house and climbed up on the joists together with another man. A raider came in and began shooting at them. He interceded for his friend, and soon found that this assailant was an old friend of his who had often eaten at his table. He appealed to him in such a way that he promised to spare their lives if they would come down. They came down, and the man took them outside where about twenty of his companions were waiting. "Shoot him, shoot him!" was their cry. He asked for a moment to pray, which they granted him, when they shot him through with four bullets. Mr. Bell was a man of excellent character, widely known and everywhere respected. He left a wife and six children to miss and mourn him.

The two Rankins, Lieutenant John K. Rankin and Captain William A. Rankin, cousins, were military officers at home on a short furlough. Being out for an early walk when the attack was made, they started for home. Turning a corner they came upon two raiders attempting to shoot a man lying in a yard. They drew their revolvers and rushed toward the two horsemen. Just then four others came up behind them, and they all began shooting. John K. Rankin feels sure he wounded one man severely for he saw him jump up in his saddle and then ride off in a hurry. How many shots were exchanged it is not known, but the Rankins had emptied their revolvers, and the six raiders had kept up a constant racket. One shot was deliberately aimed at William Rankin and would doubtless have ended his part in the affair, had not the bullet hit the muzzle of his own revolver which he fired at the same time. Just as their ammunition gave out the raiders somehow got parted from them, and the Rankins escaped unhurt.

With but few exceptions, however, the raiders had their own way, and made the most of their opportunity. For some four hours the town was at their mercy, and it received no mercy at their hands. Along the business street they did the most thorough work. The first fire that broke out was from the Lawrence Republican building, where the opera house and post office now stand. They then proceeded southward down the street firing the buildings as they went. They robbed the buildings before they burned them, usually shooting the occupants they found in them. Many of these were left to be consumed in the flames. The air was so still that the smoke from each building shot up straight into the sky, and stood like great black columns all along the street. One at a little distance could follow their work by the fires they kindled. Every now and then an explosion told that powder had been reached in some of the stores. After a little the smoke hung like a cloud over the town. Bits of charred paper and burnt cloth floated off on the air. Everybody was so isolated that few knew much that was going on except what he himself could see.

It is only possible to give a few of the incidents of the massacre. These must be taken as specimens of the whole. To gain any idea of the horrors of that morning these few incidents must be multiplied by the number of the killed and wounded. Even this would not give the entire picture. For many of those who escaped could tell as thrilling a tale as any that could be told by the dead. Every house had its story of incredible brutality or marvelous escape. The story of that morning would of itself fill a volume.

In marked contrast with the experience of the Eldridge house was that of the Johnson house, the next largest hotel in the place. The raiders came here after they knew they were in possession of the town. They had no further need of making terms. As soon as they entered the house they ordered all the men to surrender, "If they would do this they would not be hurt, but the house must be burned." Trusting this the men gave themselves up, and were marched across the street to the alley back of where the G. A. R. hall now stands, there they were shot. They were all killed except Mr. Hampson, who fell as if dead, and lay quietly until he could escape. Mr. Ralph C. Dix lived next door to the Johnson house. His own house being of wood, he thought it would be safer in the hotel. When the hotel was taken he was taken prisoner and shot with the rest. A brother of his, Stephen H. Dix, was killed while trying to escape from the rear of the hotel. Another brother was shot three times and fell almost helpless. The building he was in was on fire and burning rapidly over him. With great difficulty he managed to drag himself out and kept concealed until they were gone.

George W. Collamore was mayor of the city. He lived in the western part of the town, but his house was attacked almost at the first onset. The raiders evidently knew who he was and knew he would be likely to organize resistance if possible. They planned, therefore, to forestall any action of this kind. He was awakened by their shouts, and looking out of the window he saw the house was entirely surrounded. There was no possibility of escape and there was but one hiding place. In the rear of the house there was a well quite close to the back door. He and Pat Keefe had just time to slip down into the well as the raiders came in at the front. They searched the house from top to bottom, swearing and threatening all the while. Failing to find him they set fire to the house, and waited about until it was burned to the ground. Mrs. Collamore went to the back door while the house was burning, and spoke to her husband and he responded. She knew he was alive and safe when she left the house which she was soon compelled to do. After the flames had subsided and the ground was clear, she went again to the well and spoke but there was no response. As soon as the raiders were gone, Captain J. G. Lowe, a warm friend of General

Collamore, went down into the well to seek him. He also lost his life and the three bodies were drawn out together. The cause of their death could only be a matter of conjecture. The common supposition was that the heat of the burning house exhausted the air from the well and suffocated Mayor Collamore and Mr. Keefe, and that Capt. Lowe, in his eagerness to rescue his friend, lost his footing and fell.

A block south of Mayor Collamore lived Dr. J. F. Griswold. There were four families living in the house, Dr. Griswold and his wife, and three couples who were boarding with them. These were Hon. S. M. Thorpe, state senator; Mr. Josiah C. Trask, editor of the *State Journal*, and Mr. Harlow W. Baker, grocer; and their wives. The house was attacked about the same time as Mayor Collamore's. They called for the men to come out. As the men were armed, and were vigorous young men, they were disposed to remain in the house and defend themselves. But the raiders were very plausible. They assured them they would not be harmed. "We have come to burn Lawrence, but we do not want to hurt anybody, and we do not want to get hurt. If the citizens will make us no trouble, we will do them no harm. We want you to go with us over to town where we can keep you under guard till we are through, then you can go. It will be better for everybody if you quietly go with us." Mr. Trask said to his companions, "If it is going to help the town we had better go with them." Then they came down stairs and went out. The raiders ordered them into line, and marched them towards the town, they themselves following on their horses. They had scarcely gone a dozen yards before they were shot. All four fell as if dead. The four wives were on the balcony looking on, but were not permitted to come out and minister to their husbands or even to know whether they were dead or alive. After the shooting the ruffians went in and robbed the house. They demanded even the personal jewelry of the ladies. Mrs. Trask begged to be allowed to retain her wedding ring. "You have killed my husband; let me keep his ring." But the ruffian snatched it from her hand with a brutal oath. The men lay in the hot sun outside, and no one could go to them. About half an hour after the shooting, some horsemen rode up to them, and shot them again. Mr. Baker received his only dangerous wound at the second shooting. It was not till after the raiders had left the town that the friends could know who was dead and who was alive. Dr. Griswold and Mr. Trask were found to be dead. Mr. Thorpe was mortally wounded and lingered in great agony till the next day. Mr. Baker was shot the first time through the neck. At the second shooting a ball passed through the lungs. He received besides one or two other slight wounds. For many days his case was in doubt, but having a strong constitution, he finally recovered, and is still a member of the firm of Ridenour & Baker, leading wholesale grocers at Kansas City.

One of the most shocking murders was that of Judge Louis Carpenter. Judge Carpenter was a young man of marked ability, and had already won some distinction. He had been judge of probate for Douglas county, and the year before had been a candidate for attorney general of the state. He had been married less than a year and had a delightful home in the eastern part of the town. Several gangs came to his house, robbed him of his valuables and took what they pleased from the house. But his coolness and self possession, his genial manner and tact every time diverted them, and they left him unharmed and his house unburned. Towards the last another gang came who were harder to divert than the others had been. He accosted them in his usual pleasant way, hoping to engage them in conversation. One of them asked "where he was from." "New York," he replied. "Oh its you New York fellows who are doing all the mischief." The fellow drew his revolver and Carpenter ran into the house. The man dismounted and followed. Mr. Carpenter ran first one way and then another, and finally escaped into the cellar. He was already badly wounded and the blood lay in a pool where he stood. His hiding place was soon discovered, and he ran out into the yard. The man followed and shot him again. He fell mortally wounded. His wife ran to him and threw herself over him to protect him from further violence. The brute deliberately walked around her to find a place to shoot once more. He finally raised her arm, thrust his revolver under it, and fired so that she saw the charge enter her hnsband's head. They then set fire to the house, but Mrs. Carpenter's sister extinguished the flames and saved the house. There was nothing in Judge Carpenter's character or life which could give any reason for the venom with which he was pursued. He was moderate and conservative in his views and had taken no special part in the early conflict. There is no evidence that they even knew who he was, or anything about him beyond the fact that he lived in Lawrence.

Another case of singular brutality was the murder of Edward P. Fitch who lived a couple of blocks from Judge Carpenter. He was up-stairs when they came to the door. They called to him to come down and as soon he appeared they shot him, and he fell in his own doorway. Although he was evidently dead, they continued to shoot until they had lodged six or eight bullets in his body. They then came in and set fire to the house. Mrs. Fitch endeavored to drag her husband out from the house but they forbade her. She then tried to take his picture from the wall, but she was forbidden to do even this. Stupefied by the horrors of the scene and the strange brutality exhibited towards her she stood in a half dazed condition looking at what was going on about her. As the fire progressed one of the ruffians came up and drove her out of the house. Otherwise she might have perished with the rest. She then took her three little ones a short distance away, and sat down on the grass and watched the flames consume her husband who still lay in the doorway of his home. While she sat looking on, one of the ruffians went up to the door, and drew the boots off Mr. Fitch's feet, and put them on himself, and walked away. Mr. Fitch was a young man of excellent character and highly esteemed by everybody. He was one of the first settlers and taught the first school ever taught in Lawrence or in Kansas. He was an earnest Christian and was secretary of the Congregational Sunday school. He was quiet in his habits, mild and gentle in his spirit. He was not at all partizan in his views, and was always a friend of order and justice and peace. The occasion of the peculiar ferocity exhibited towards him is one of the many mysteries of this very mysterious affair. His wife could think of but one explanation. The children had a little toy flag stuck up on the shed in the back yard. She was of the opinion that this little flag, a few inches square, angered them and drew out the singular hate they manifested.

James Perine and James Eldridge were clerks in what was called the "Country Store," kept by George Ford, who lived two blocks away. They were young men of about seventeen years of age. They slept in the store and had no opportunity to escape. A squad of the raiders came in and ordered them to open the safe. "They said the key was at the house." Some of the ruffians went with one of them to get the key, while the rest kept guard over the other. They promised to spare them both if they would open the safe for them. As soon as the key was brought and the safe thrown open, they shot them both and left them dead upon the floor. Mr. Burt was standing in front of his house when a squad rode up and demanded his money. He handed him his pocket book, and as the fellow took the pocket book with one hand, he shot Mr. Burt with the other. Mr. Murphy, a short distance up the same street, was asked for a drink of water. He brought out the water, and as the ruffian took the cup with his left hand, he shot his benefactor with his right hand. Mr. Ellis, a German blacksmith, ran into some corn near his house, and took his little child with him. For a time he remained concealed, but after a while the child grew weary and began to cry. The ruffians outside hearing the cry, ran into the corn and killed the father, leaving the child in the dead father's arms. Mr. Albach, also a German, was sick in his bed. The ruffians came into the house and ordered it cleared at once that they might burn it. The family carried him out on the mattress and laid him in the yard. In a few moments some of them came out of the house and killed him in his bed.

But even these atrocities were surpassed. Mr. D. W. Palmer kept a gun shop on Massachusetts street south of the business portion. It was a small wooden building and stood alone. He was so surrounded by them that it was not possible to escape and he was compelled to remain in his shop while they were doing their work. For quite a while he was not disturbed. Towards the last a gang of ruffians who had become drunk on the liquor they had found in the saloons of the town, came to the shop on their way out. Mr Palmer and another man were standing in the door of the shop, and they fired upon them wounding them both. They then set fire to the shop, and the shop being all of wood, without plastering, burned rapidly. While the shop was burning, the brutes took up the wounded men, bound their hands together and flung them into the flames. They rose to their feet and tried to come out from the fire, but their assailants pushed them back with their guns. After the bandages were burned from their wrists they threw up their hands and begged for mercy, but were answered only by shouts of derision from their merciless tormentors. As soon as the poor fellows were dead the brutes passed on with a shout of triumph, and joined their comrades who were now leaving the town.

JOHN G. HASKELL.

DUDLEY C. HASKELL.

FRANK A. BAILEY.

CHAS. W. SMITH.

EARLY MERCHANTS IN LAWRENCE.

Mr. J. W. Thornton, a laboring man, was awakened by the shooting all around him. He remained up stairs till his house was on fire, and then came down and ran out and tried to escape. The ruffians fired at him and inflicted three ugly wounds in his hips. He still went on, however, but as he was trying to get over some bars into a yard, another ball struck him just back of the shoulder, and passed down the whole length of his back and came out at the hip. His wife ran to him and tried to protect him from further violence. One of the men sat on his horse over them, and finally got his pistol between the two and fired again, the ball grazing his eye and passing through his cheek. The fellow then cried "I can kill you," and began beating him over the head with the butt of his revolver until the poor man fell senseless to the ground from sheer exhaustion. The brute not yet satisfied, leveled his revolver to shoot again, but the wife flew at the man and pushed the revolver aside. The fellow soon left, supposing his victim to be dead. But strange to say the poor fellow, after being shot with six bullets, two of which always remained among the joints of the hips, and pounded over the head with a revolver, still lived for many years, a cripple and a great sufferer, yet able to get about and to do some sorts of work.

Age was no protection, and many old people were brutally killed. Mr. Otis Lonley lived about a mile from town to the southwest. He was a quiet, peaceable christian man, about sixty years of age. He had never taken any special part in public affairs and certainly never could have given any offense by extreme views. He and his wife were a kindly couple living alone in a cottage on a little farm. Two of the pickets stationed on the hill to watch the country, came down to their house. The wife, a charming old lady, begged them to be merciful. "We are old people" she said, "and cannot live long at the best." They paid no heed to her entreaties, but shot the old gentleman in the yard. The first shot not doing its work, they shot him again and again, until he was dead. They then attempted to burn the house, but by the energy of the old lady the house was saved.

While the entreaties of women sometimes availed for the saving of property, they very seldom availed for the saving of life. In many cases men were shot with their wives clinging to them. Mr. George H. Sargent lived in a house on New Hampshire street. He came out in front and they at once assailed him. His wife clung to him and begged for his life. She tried to keep between them and him. But one of them at last shot by her so close that the passing ball burned her neck. The bullet struck him in the face and he fell mortally wounded.

All the persons thus far named were private citizens, quiet and peaceable and moderate in their views and speech and action. None of them had been connected with the army, and none of them had been active in the early trouble. There could not possibly be any personal reason why any of them were attacked. In most cases the murderers could have known nothing whatever of them, as to who they were or what they were. They killed them simply because they found them in Lawrence, and they came to kill.

The colored people were pursued with peculiar malignity, but they knew what they might expect from their old masters, and they all ran who could at the first alarm. As a result they fared better than the white people. One active young colored man ran at the first charge, and made for the Wakarusa river four miles south. In describing his flight, he said "the prairie just came to me." Reaching the Wakarusa he climbed into a tree to watch operations. After a while he was startled to see the whole troop coming away from town on the road which passed right under his tree. There was no getting away, so he concealed himself among the leaves and brances and luckily was not seen. He said "they were a mighty long while passing under him." Most of the colored people who were killed were old and decrepid. "Old Uncle Frank" as he was called was about ninety years old. He was born in "Old Virginny." He said he was the first slave to come to Lawrence after the war opened the way. "When I was a slave I pray de Lord to let me go somewhere, so I could tend meetin all I wanted to. And now de good Lord has answered my prayer." He was a short heavy set man, crippled with "rheumatiz," and compelled to hobble about on a cane. In spite of all this he would work, getting a job of chopping at one place and a job of hoeing at another. In this way he earned what little his simple habits required. He always worked faithfully and did his work well. When the raiders came he was too lame to get out of their way. He was seen hobbling away and they shot him. He fell and they left him for dead. After a little when he thought himself unobserved, he got up and began to hobble off again. But some of them saw him and dashed upon him and killed him.

"Uncle Henry" was another decrepid old negro. He crawled into a barn and hid himself. He was discovered and killed and burned with the building. Old man Stonestreet was a Baptist preacher among the colored people. He was about sixty years of age. He and another old negro were together and were both killed. Anthony Oldham was another colored preacher. He was a man of fine character and was very highly regarded. He was shot in the doorway of his own house in the presence of his daughter.

As a rule the raiders took good care of themselves. While full of bluster and brutality they were shy of danger. They came to kill and not to be killed. While tearing about like tigers among helpless people, they took good care to keep away from all places where resistance might be developed. They were especially shy of brick and stone houses, and seldom entered one until they knew it was unguarded.

Mr. A. K. Allen, an old gentleman, lived in a solid looking brick house. A gang of them came to his door and ordered him to come out. He replied, "No, but you come in if you want to see me. I am good for five of you." For some reason they did not accept his invitation and he and his house were not molested any more.

Ex-Governor Charles Robinson was an object of special search among them. He was one of the men they particularly wanted. During the whole time they were in town he was in his large stone barn on the hillside. He had just gone to the barn to get his team to drive out into the country, when he saw them come in and saw them make their first charge. He concluded to remain where he was. The barn overlooked the whole town, and he saw the affair from beginning to end. Gangs of raiders came by several times and looked at the barn and went round it, but it looked so much like a fort, that they kept out of range.

On the opposite bank of the river there were twelve soldiers stationed for some sort of police duty on the Indian reservation. When the raiders first came in they filled Massachusetts street right up to the river bank. But these boys in blue on the opposite side the river made free use of their minnie rifles and shot at every butternut that came in sight. Their minnie balls went screaming up the street and soon cleared the whole region along the river side. Two or three tiers of houses all around the "bend of the river" were thus saved, as well as those who were fortunate enough to take refuge in them.

There was a deep wooded ravine running almost through the center of the town, to which scores of men escaped. The raiders often chased men to the edge of this ravine, but never followed them into it. To their wholesome fear of some hidden foe, many a man owed his life. A large cornfield just west of the town was also full of refugees. The raiders came to the edge of the field a number of times and looked in but did not venture among the corn. They asked a lady who lived just outside, "What there was in that cornfield." "Go and see, and you will find it the hottest place you were ever in." Having been in several times to carry water to the men, she could speak from experience as to its being a "hot place" on a warm summer morning. They put another meaning on her words, however, and did not care to make any personal examination. Whenever they had occasion to pass by the wooded ravine or the cornfield, they were careful to keep at a safe distance. In like manner every little ravine and thicket about the outskirts of the town became a refuge to those who could reach them, for the raiders shunned them as if an ambush lay in each one of them. Had they been as brave as they were brutal, and dashed into these hiding places, the number of victims would probably have been doubled. But men who are brutal are seldom brave, and brave men are never brutes.

There were many remarkable escapes. Anything served for a hiding place in the stress, and often the least promising proved the most effective. Some fled to the cornfields near town, others to the "friendly brush" by the river bank. The cornfield to the west and the woods to the east were all alive with refugees. Many hid in what has since become "the park," but which was then a field of corn. Some who could get no further, laid among the plants and weeds of their own garden. Mr. Troy Strode, a colored blacksmith, had a little patch of tomato vines not more than ten feet square. He took his money and buried himself among the vines. The raiders came and burned his shop not more than ten feet from him, but did not discover him. Old Mr. Miner ran into the park and hid among the corn. Hearing a great racket near by, his curiosity got the better of his judgment, and he came to the edge of the corn to see what was going on. They saw him and began shooting, and he ran back into the corn.

He heard them breaking down the fence and knew they were coming after him. He ran through the corn therefore and hid himself in a little patch of weeds beyond. They dashed through the corn after him, but not finding him where they expected they turned back, never thinking to look into the bunch of weeds at their feet where their horses must almost have stepped on him.

Near the center of the town was a sort of out-door cellar with an obscure entrance. A woman whose name has not been preserved, but who ought to be put on record as one of the heroines of the day, stationed herself at a convenient distance from the entrance to this cave. Every poor fugitive that came near she directed to this hiding place. Thus eight or ten had escaped their pursuers and disappeared they knew not how nor where. Finding at last they always disappeared after passing this woman, they began to suspect that she had something to do with it. They came upon her in a blustering way and demanded to know the place of their hiding. She calmly refused to tell them. One of them drew his revolver and aiming at her said with an oath: "Tell me or I will shoot you." Looking him in the eye she said softly but firmly: "You may shoot me if you will, but you will not find out where the men are." Finding they could not intimidate her they turned away and the men remained safe to the end.

John Bergen was wounded and taken off with six or eight other prisoners. After taking them a short distance their captors shot all of them dead except Mr. Bergen. He had fallen and was lying down exhausted from loss of blood, and they probably supposed him dead already. He now lay among the dead feigning death. After a little a ruffian came up and seeing he was yet alive aimed at his head and fired. He felt the ball pass and instantly dropped his head. The man thought from this he had finished his work and rode off. His head was now brought under the body of a young man who had been killed with the rest. The mother came soon after to wash the blood from her dead boy's face. As she began to lift him, Mr. Bergen begged her to let him remain there as his only hope of life was in lying under the dead body. The mother laid her boy gently back where he was, and left them there together, the dead protecting the living from death.

Hon. Samuel A Riggs, district attorney, was set upon by one of the most pitiless wretches in the whole troop. He encountered him in the street in front of his house. His wife ran out and stood by his side. A few words passed between them, when the man drew his revolver and took aim. Mr. Riggs knocked the revolver aside and ran. The man whirled his horse and started after him. Mrs. Riggs instantly seized the bridle rein and clung to it till she was dragged around the house, over a wood pile, through the back yard and round to the street again. Mr. Riggs was not yet out of sight and the man took aim again. Mrs. Riggs seized the other rein and whirled the horse about and clung to him till Mr. Riggs was out of reach. All this time the man was swearing at her in the vilest fashion, beating her over the head and arms with his revolver, and threatening to shoot her.

Perhaps the most remarkable escape was that of Rev. H. D. Fisher. Mr. Fisher had been pastor of the Methodist church in Lawrence, and for some months had been chaplain of a Kansas regiment doing service in Missouri. For this and other reasons he was one of the men the raiders particularly wanted. He was at this time at home for a few days and the raiders knew of this fact. As soon as he heard their charge on the town, he started out for a place of safety. He soon saw he had little chance of escaping by flight, and returned to the house and hid himself in the cellar. It was not many minutes before his house was surrounded, and they came in and demanded that his wife tell them where he was. Of course she would not tell. They then said they knew he was in the house and they would find him. They insisted that he was in the cellar. She lit a lamp for them, and told them to go down and see for themselves. The cellar was unfinished, being only partly excavated. He had climbed upon a bank and was lying in a drain by the farther wall. They searched the cellar, held the lamp up to the bank so that it shone in his face, but it did not reveal him to them. They went up and still insisted that he was certainly in the house, and they would smoke him out. They began to kindle fires about the house, and Mrs. Fisher put them out as they lit them. But the fires grew too many for her, and it was evident the house must be burned. They then went out and stood round the fence waiting for him to come out as they knew he soon must. Mrs. Fisher kept pouring water over the spot where Mr. Fisher was lying to keep the fire from him as long as possible. At last she whispered to him that she could do no more, and he must get out in some way. The cellar had a small window right by the kitchen door, so Mr. Fisher crawled out at this window, his wife threw a carpet over him, and rolled him up in it and dragged the whole bundle into the yard, and threw it under a peach tree. Then she brought out other pieces of furniture and piled around it, and there they were all left. The raiders meanwhile were yelling and screaming all around the place, watching for him to appear. They did not leave till the house was consumed.

Some saved themselves by their ready wit. An officer in the camp of recruits which was fired upon at the first charge, ran for his life. Several horsemen gave chase, firing at him as they followed. Finding escape impossible he dashed into the shanty of a colored family, seizing a dress that was hanging on the wall, he threw it over him and putting on the woman's sunbonnet, he went out at the back door and deliberately walked away. His pursuers burst in at the front door as he went out, and searched the house. They did not

GURDON GROVENOR.

JAMES C. HORTON.

find him of course, but never thought of questioning the old woman who walked out as they came in.

A son of John Speer hid himself under a sidewalk. The fire soon drove him from his hiding place into the street which was full of raiders. He went boldly up to some of them and offered his services in holding their horses. They asked him his name, and thinking the name of John Speer might be too familiar, he answered "John Smith." Under that name he remained among them till they left and was not harmed.

One man was shot at as he was running away, and fell headlong into a gutter. His wife thinking him dead began to scream and wring her hands. From her grief the raiders thought her husband was dead and rode off. As soon as they were gone the man said: "Don't take on so, wife, I don't know that I am hit at all." And so it proved to be. The cashier of the Lawrence bank crawled under a sidewalk. Nearby was an old colored man who had sought the same refuge. Being a pious old man, he called mightily upon God to save him. His cries could be heard half a block away. The cashier suggested to him that "the Lord would hear him just as well if he did not pray quite so loud, and the raiders couldn't." He hushed for a minute, but soon began to "cry aloud" again. The cashier thought it prudent to find a quieter, if less pious hiding place.

Mr. Winchell, being hard pressed, ran into the house of Dr. Charles Reynolds, formerly rector of the Episcopal church. The doctor was away from home, a chaplain in the army. Mrs. Reynolds and two other ladies were in the house. They at once set their wits at work to devise a plan for saving Mr. Winchell in case the raiders came to the house. They finally hit upon a plan which proved successful. Getting a razor they shaved off the man's whiskers, put a lady's wrapper over him, and tied an old woman's cap on his head. They then placed him in an invalid chair with a stand beside it, covered with cups and spoons and medicine bottles. One of the ladies sat by his side fanning him. This was to be their "Aunt Betsie," very ill. It was not long before a band of the raiders came in. The ladies bade them take anything they could find, but begged them to be as quiet as possible, so as not to disturb "Poor Aunt Betsie." They helped themselves to what they wanted, looked suspiciously several times at the invalid chair, but finally went away without disturbing the poor invalid.

The women of Lawrence always proved themselves heroes when the occasion presented itself. Their brave deeds and shrewd devices did very much to lessen the calamity of the raid. Their courage and vigilance were a marked feature of that terrible day. It was said that Quantrill made the remark "that the women of Lawrence were a brave lot, but the men were a set of 'blank' cowards." The fact that the women had nothing worse to fear than brutal oaths and vile threats, while the men knew they would be shot at sight, possibly had something to do with the difference, but the conduct of the women was worthy of all praise. Some of them by their tact and ingenious conversation diverted the ruffians till their husbands had made good their escape. Often they met the raiders at the gate and entertained them with bright and witty talk. Others boldly faced them and extinguished the fires as they were kindled. But for this the number of houses burned would have been doubled. In fact there would have been very few houses left. One woman hid her husband in a safe place in the house. The raiders set fire to the house and remained near by to see it burn. She did not dare extinguish the fire for fear they would come in again and make sure work of it. So she kept it smouldering and smoking until they moved away. Then she extinguished it.

The house of Mr. F. W. Read was visited some seven times, and fire kindled three or four times. Each time Mrs. Read extinguished the flames. The last gang swore the house should be burned. One of the ruffians seized Mrs. Reid by the wrists, and held her fast while the rest kindled the fire. They piled up broken chairs and other things by the window, and set fire to them. They waited till the whole window and window frame were in flames. They then released her and told her with an oath "to put that out if she could." The moment they were gone she seized an armful of blankets and holding them before her, threw herself with all her force against the burning window, and knocked the burning sash and frame clear out into the street. She then easily extinguished the rest. She was badly burned but she saved the house.

Just north of Mr. Read's on New Hampshire street lived Mr. L. Bullene. He was in New York buying goods, and Mrs. Bullene and her children were at home. A sister of Mr. Bullene, afterwards Mrs. Major Warner, of Kansas City, was with them. New Hampshire street being next east of Massachusetts street, was full of raiders continually. They made the Bullene house a sort of rendezvous. Captain Bill Todd came in with a lot of men and ordered breakfast. Captain Todd promised that the house should not be burned. Other bands came and wanted breakfast and Mrs. Bullene cooked for them as long as anything was left in the house. The two ladies displayed consummate skill in getting them into conversation and diverting them. One raider called for a drink of milk. When they brought it he compelled them to drink of it first. Then a band came in and said they must burn the house. Mrs. Bullene said "you must help me carry out my invalid mother." As soon as they looked into the room where the old lady was, they were touched by her pale and feeble look, and went away. Another band insisted on burning the house, and Mrs. Bullene assured them that Captain Todd had ordered it spared. "In that case we will not burn it, we obey orders." Though constantly overrun by them it escaped the torch, and was the only house left standing in that neighborhood. William L. Bullene the son, was a lad old enough to take it all in, but too young to think of being in danger himself. He was out among them all the time in front of the house. He saw the whole thing in the very center of it. He saw nine men killed. Young John Speer was killed not far from him. The man who first shot him had an American flag tied to the tail of his horse, dragging in the dirt. Young Speer fell and lay as if dead, but was not seriously hurt. Soon another came along and shot the boy through the head. One of them a little later drew a revolver on young Bullene, but his mother seized the fellow's arm and pushed him back. The raiders dropped two guns in the yard, which young Bullene picked up and kept as mementoes of the day. One was a musket, the other a shot gun.

Young Bullene witnessed one very remarkable escape. There was a recruiting office on Massachusetts street just across from their house. The officer in charge found himself shut in when the raiders came. He could not stay in his office and to show himself in his uniform was to invite death. The building which his office was in ran back to the alley just in front of Mr. Bullene's house. It was a cheap wooden extension standing on blocks. The officer went to the rear end, and slipping out, crawled under the building. But the building was soon on fire and he must leave. New Hampshire street was full of horsemen and there was no place to conceal himself. There was nothing to be done but to dash through them and take his chances. He dared not attempt that in his uniform. So he threw off all but his shirt and drawers, then ran for his life across the street. Every man that saw him running shot at him, and the bullets rattled about him like hail. But he dashed through it all to the rear of the Bullene house, where young Bullene disguised him in woman's clothes and he remained safe to the end.

Another singular event occured right here, showing the power of imagination and fright. A young printer was staying in the same house with Mr. Sargent. He came out of the house and a number of the raiders fired at him. He fell headlong and they supposed him dead. He himself supposed he was mortally wounded, and made no attempt to rise. He lay so close to the burning house that he was nearly roasted. Yet he did not stir and those who saw him left him never thinking he was alive. After it was all over some friends came to remove him, and found him still living. They asked him where he was hurt, but he could not tell them. He did not know, but thought he was badly wounded. They looked him over carefully, and found he had not received a scratch. He was so badly burned, however, that he had to be carried away in a sheet, and was several weeks before he recovered. The strange thing is that he all the while supposed he was dangerously wounded.

Many men escaped by a very narrow margin. Mr. Gurdon Grovenor lived at the corner of Berkley and New Hampshire streets. He was standing on his porch when one of them rode up within ten feet of him and snapped his revolver in his face. He aimed it again and a second time it missed fire. Just then some more of them came up and the leader compelled the ruffian to desist. He advised Mr. Grovenor to keep out of sight. That was not an easy thing to do as the house was on fire. But he hid in the back cellar as long as he could, and then kept in background as much as possible.

General Lane was naturally in demand among them. They seemed to know he was in town, and were determined to get him. General Lane also knew they were in town and were looking for him. Before they reached his house he slipped out and went into the cornfield just back of his house. Lest they should suspect this, he passed through the field and went on

"Over the hills and far away."

They were soon at his door and were met by Mrs. Lane. "They wanted to see the general." She told them "he was not in." They broke up his furniture, smashed the piano, and then set the house on fire. On leaving Quantrill tipped his hat to Mrs. Lane, and "wished her to give his compliments to General Lane and tell him he would have been very glad to meet him." Mrs. Lane assured him that "Mr. Lane would be no less glad to meet him under different circumstances, but it was not convenient that morning."

The number left wounded was very small. In battle the wounded outnumber the killed some three to one. In this slaughter the killed outnumbered the wounded five to one. Only about thirty were left wounded, while one hundred and fifty were left dead. They came to kill, not to cripple. Most of those wounded were left for dead, and lived either by feigning death, or recovering from wounds which are usually fatal. They intended to finish their work every time. If the first shot did not do its work a second was fired, and sometimes a dozen. Sometimes they returned and fired into a heap of dead bodies, lest some of them might still be living. Whenever they passed a body they thought showed signs of life, they would pour into it some more lead. One of the most brutal features of the whole affair was their treatment of the wounded. They would fire charge after charge into a man, and return again and again till they felt sure the work was completed. In spite of all this a few of the wounded survived and recovered. The few slightly wounded were those shot on the run, or able to run before the fatal shot.

How long this went on is only a matter of conjecture. If any man noted the time of Quantrill's coming or going, he has kept the matter a profound secret as far as the writer of this has ever heard. A very close estimate can be made, however. When they came in the flash of the pistols could be plainly seen, yet their dress and carriage could be readily noted.

At the season of the year this condition would indicate that it was not far from five o'clock. From many circumstances it is evident that they left about nine o'clock. This scene of slaughter and burning, therefore, went on for four hours. They took their time to it and did thorough work. During these four hours the work of destruction and death went on unchecked. The business street was burned first, and then the destruction was carried to the furtherest limits. Very few houses were omitted except those along the river bank, which were omitted because of the squad of soldiers across the river who kept firing at everyone who came in sight. About nine o'clock they began to leave all parts of the town at once and to come together at the center. It is supposed they got knowledge of the coming of Major Plumb, who was on his way from Kansas City with a body of mounted troops. By some concerted signal they were all notified, and they left their murdering and their burning and came together, and began to move off in a body. It was not all over yet, however. As they were receding in the south part of town, one of their number not satisfied with his share in the bloody work, galloped back to the City hotel where the Eldridge house prisoners had been kept. Thinking themselves now safe they were out in front of the house. The brute galloped up and fired several shots into the crowd, killing the landlord, Mr. Stone, and wounding two others. He then whirled his horse and galloped back. He had miscalculated his chances, however. A son of John Speer, two of whose brothers were dead, had just picked up a loaded rifle which one of the raiders had dropped. Seeing the fellow hurrying off he leveled the gun and fired and brought him to the ground. This was said to be "Elder Scraggs," the hard-shell preacher, who was the hardest of all that hard company. It was said that his motive in going back was to fill out his number. "He had killed twelve and he wanted to kill thirteen." But so many claimed the thirteen limit that the whole idea was probably an after invention. Another motive assigned is more probable. This was that he was dissatisfied with Quantrill for keeping faith with the Eldridge House prisoners and protecting them.

DR. J. F. GRISWOLD.

H. W. BAKER.

JOSIAH C. TRASK.

S. M. THORPE.

QUANTRILL RAID VICTIMS SHOT DOWN TOGETHER.

CHAPTER XVI.

THE LAWRENCE RAID.—THE DEPARTURE AND THE PURSUIT.—THE SCENE LEFT BEHIND.—THE BURIAL OF THE DEAD.—THE RUIN AND THE LOSS.—SYMPATHY AND HELP.—REBUILDING THE TOWN.

Quantrill did not go out by the way he came in. He came in from the east passing through Franklin. After four hours of slaughter and burning they seemed to leave the work in all parts at once, and come together as by some common signal. They had become aware that Major Plumb was approaching from the east with a body of troops. They could not return the way they came without meeting him. To avoid this they struck out directly south, crossing the Wakarusa at Blanton's bridge. They kept up their work of destruction as they went away, burning most of the farm houses which they passed. The farmers themselves had had warning and kept out of their way. The last murder was one of the most shocking of the whole list. About ten miles from Lawrence they came to the house of Mr. Rothrock, a Dunkard preacher. A gang of them turned aside at his house, went in and demanded breakfast. The women folks cooked them a good breakfast which they eat with relish. Mr. Rothrock was an old gentleman, quiet and peaceable, and very highly respected by his neighbors. He was about the house when they came in, and having no suspicion of personal harm, he remained around while they staid. After a while they began to inquire of the women serving them, who that old gentleman was? They told them his name, and said he was a preacher among them. "Oh! we intend to kill all the ——— preachers." With that the fellow shot the old gentleman and left him for dead. They then went out and galloped on to overtake the main body. This was the last of their depredations, for their pursuers soon after overtook them, and they had all they could do to take care of themselves.

As soon as Quantrill began to move off, the men in town began to come in from their hiding places, and country people began to come in from outside. Many of these last were mounted and had guns of one kind or another. As they began to gather on the street corners wondering what to do, Senator Lane, or as the boys called him, "Jim Lane," came dashing down Henry street, shouting, "Let us follow them boys, let us follow them." A small company of these mounted farmers soon gathered about him, and they proceeded by the road Quantrill had taken.

They were enabled to follow the trail of Quantrill's men by the burning houses along their line of march. From the Wakarusa to where they were overtaken, a line of smoking ruins marked their track. The pursuers followed rapidly and overtook the rear guard of Quantrill's force at Brooklyn on the old Santa Fe road, about twelve miles south of Lawrence. As they came up a gang of the enemy were on the point of burning the house of Thadeus Prentiss. On seeing the pursuers they desisted and hurried on. The main body was in plain sight going along the Ft. Scott road. After this there was no more burning. The raiders were compelled to keep in a compact body, and to hurry on as fast as they could. The pursuing force was not sufficient to attack, but it was sufficient to prevent further mischief.

It is now necessary to go back and trace up another line of events connected with the pursuit. When Quantrill crossed the state line the night before, he was seen by the federal pickets who reported his movements at once to Captain J. A. Pike who was in command of a small force at Aubrey, some eight or ten miles north. Quantrill crossed the state line about five o'clock, and Captain Pike received the word about half past six. As quickly as horses could be saddled, messengers were dispatched to headquarters at Kansas City, about thirty miles distant. The messengers reached Kansas City a little after nine o'clock in the evening. General Thomas E. Ewing, the commander of the post, was at Leavenworth and the command devolved on Major P. B. Plumb. He got together four companies of mounted men and started for Lawrence about midnight. At nine o'clock the next morning they were twelve or fifteen miles from Lawrence. Quantrill seems to have become aware of their approach, and started off in another direction towards the south by a route which would take him some ten miles from Plumb's line of approach. Major Plumb, however, soon learned of Quantrill's change of direction probably from the smoke of burning houses which marked his line of departure. Instead of keeping on to Lawrence, therefore, struck across the prairie towards the south to intercept the guerrillas on their way.

The Lawrence pursuers meanwhile were at Brooklyn, with the main body of Quantrill's men in full view on the prairie. Here Lane halted, lined up his men and counted off. He had thirty-five men. He sent a messenger back to Lawrence to say that "they had overtaken them, and for all citizens to come forward as fast as possible." He then placed Lieutenant John K. Rankin. who had joined them about a mile south of Lawrence, in command of the company. He said it would be madness for this handful of farmers to attack the main body of Quantrill's men on the open prairie. He said: "We will march on their left flank towards Prairie City, and try and join the militia there." After proceeding a mile or two, they were met by Mr. George Wood, of Black Jack, who came dashing up on horseback. After saluting, he said to Senator Lane: "Major Plumb is over there with two hundred and fifty men." On looking in the direction Wood pointed Plumb's men were in plain sight about half a mile to the east. Senator Lane replied: "Tell Major Plumb, Quantrill is just on the other side of this cornfield. We will attack him at once. Tell him to come forward as quickly as possible." As soon as the messenger had wheeled about and was returning to Major Plumb, Senator Lane ordered Lieutenant Rankin to charge upon the enemy who were on the opposite side of the cornfield on the Ft. Scott road, moving at a brisk pace. Lieutenant Rankin ordered a charge and they all dashed forward. Rankin's company had other weak points besides its small numbers. They were mounted on all sorts of steeds, and armed with all sorts of weapons. There were saddle horses of fair speed, dray horses, mules and colts. Lieutenant Rankin rode a fiery steed who dashed ahead at a breakneck pace. The rest followed each in his own gait. Before he had gone half a mile Lieutenant Rankin looked about and found he was all alone. The rest were straggling along behind him for half the distance he had come. As soon as he could bring his own fierce charger to a halt, he turned about. He concluded that no very effective charge could be made with the force at his disposal. While he was awaiting the coming up of his men, two companies of Major Plumb's force passed him on the gallop, and disappeared down a lane leading to the road on which Quantrill was marching. He saw it would be impossible to bring his straggling band into the impending fight. He ordered one of those who came up to him to remain, and have the men come forward as fast as their promiscous mounts would permit. He then galloped after the two companies who had just passed him. As he passed out of the lane he came upon side-saddles, bolts of calico and other goods which Quantrill's men had dropped of their plunder, in their hasty flight. It seems Plumb had divided his force into two parts, one to join Lane and attack the enemy in the rear, while he led the other part to the left by the way of Prairie City to protect that town, and head off Quantrill in that direction. Lieutenant Rankin came up with the first body just as the officer in command of the advance company had ordered a charge. This company was deployed as skirmishers while the other moved in column. They charged rapidly down the road, and were soon on Quantrill's rear guard, which they pressed closely till they reached the farm of Josiah Fletcher. Here a cornfield stood across the old prairie road, and a new road had been broken around the field to the right. Quantrill's men went round the field by this new road, followed closely by the skirmishers. Lieutenant Rankin knew that the road bore to the east beyond the field, and he suggested to the officer in command of the company in column, that if they would go up through Fletcher's cornfield, they would come upon the enemy's flank as they were passing along south of the field. The suggestion was adopted, and the company dashed through the corn. When they came to the fence on the other side of the field, they saw Quantrill's men draw up in line, a little distance in advance, at the mouth of a lane. Senator Lane now came up and he and Lieutenant Rankin shouted to the men: "Throw the fence and charge; throw the fence and charge." They themselves leaped from their horses and began throwing the fence. Just then the officer in command of the company shouted: "Dismount boys, and give them a round or two with your Burnsides at three hundred yards." The order was promptly obeyed. As soon as the men began to dismount and prepare to fire, Quantrill's men answered with a shout and came swooping down upon them, yelling and shooting as they came. The horses of the union men stampeded, the line gave way, and the company fell back to the other side of the field. Lane and Rankin urged the officer to remount his men, and attack them again. By the time the men were remounted, Major Plumb came up with the other two companies, and the whole body moved forward together. When they again reached the other side of the field, they found that Quantrill had taken advantage of the delay and was rapidly moving on, his heavily laden horses in the advance, while his fighting men were in the rear ready to charge back whenever the pursuit became too close. In this skirmish the troops fired a round or two, and Quantrill's men fired a large number of shots, but no one seems to have been hurt. The Lawrence part of the pursuit ceased here, and the military took full charge. This was about one o'clock in the afternoon. They followed all the rest of the day, till night overtook them not far from Paola. Both parties halted with the darkness. But Quantrill's men disappeared in the night and escaped to their hiding places, leaving their pursuers in full possession of the open prairie.

If it seem incredible that three hundred armed desperadoes should be able to pass over forty miles of Kansas territory by night, and pounce upon a town like Lawrence without warning at day-break, it seems even more incredible that the same men, having accomplished their purpose, destroyed the town and murdered its people, should be able to march leisurely back over fifty miles of the same territory, with two hundred and fifty mounted troops following closely on their heels. Nothing seemed lacking to make the calamity as great and the humiliation as complete as it could be. Lawrence was struck down without being able to strike a blow, and her destroyers escaped almost without the loss of a man.

The scene the raiders left behind them was sad and sickening. The buildings on Massachusetts street were all burned except one, and that had been ransacked and robbed, and two boys lay dead upon the floor. The fires were still glowing in the cellars. The brick and stone walls were still standing bare and blackened. The cellars between looked like great caverns with furnaces glowing in the depths. The dead lay all along the street, some of them so charred that they could not be recognized, and could scarcely be taken up. Here and there among the embers could be seen the bones of those who had perished in the buildings and been consumed where they fell. About the ruins of the *Republican* printing office might be seen the editor, John Speer, raking among the embers in the cellar searching for the bones of his boy. One of his boys was dead, another could not be found. He had slept, as his father supposed, in the printing office up-stairs in the northeast corner. The father thought he must have perished where he lay, and searched for him under where he knew his bed had been. But he could find no signs of the body, and no signs of the boy were ever found. As one passed along the street, the sickening odor of burning flesh was oppressive. Sights of horror met him at every turn. Around one corner lay seventeen bodies. Back of a livery stable on Henry street lay five bodies piled in a heap. Going over the town one saw the dead everywhere, on the sidewalks, in the streets, among the weeds in the gardens, and in the few remaining homes. The women were going about carrying water to the wounded, and covering the dead with sheets. To protect the wounded from the burning sun, they sometimes spread an umbrella over them, and sometimes made a canopy with a sheet or a shawl. The men were hurrying about gathering up the dead, and bearing them to the old Methodist church on Vermont street, which was taken as a sort of morgue. Now and then one came across a group, a mother and her children watching their dead beside the ashes of their home. A little later there could be seen a woman sitting among the ashes of a building, holding in her hands a blackened skull, fondling it and kissing it, and crying piteously over it. It was the skull of her husband, who was burned with the building. But there was not much weeping and not much wailing. It was beyond all that. It was too deep and serious for tears or lamentations. All addressed themselves to the sad work that had to be done.

No one realized the extent of the disaster until it was over.

Every man was so isolated by the presence of the raiders in every part of the town, that each knew only what he saw. The magnitude of the disaster was beyond the wildest thought of even those who were in the midst of it. Almost everyone was startled when the extent of the affair began to reveal itself. Besides the buildings on the business street, about one hundred houses had been burned, and probably as many more had been set on fire and saved by the heroic exertions of the women. Most of the houses not burned were robbed. Every house had its tale of horror or of a marvelous escape. So many were dead that the first salutation on meeting an old friend was, "Why, are you alive?" Every living man seemed to have come up from the dead.

The burial of the dead began at once and continued till all were laid away. There were no coffins to be had. There was lumber in some of the yards, and among the ruins of the hardware stores was found an abundance of burnt nails which were made to serve. Many carpenters had been killed, and most of those who remained had lost their tools. But they managed to get tools enough to cut up the boards that remained in the lumber yards, and they fastened the boards together into boxes with the burnt nails they gathered out of the fires in the cellars. Many had to be buried without the formality of even a box. Fifty-three were laid side by side in one long trench. A record was kept and the bodies could be identified by their numbers, whenever the name was known. Most of the dead were buried in the cemetery on the hill west of town. But many were buried in private yards with the thought of removing them later on. The work of burying occupied several days, and it was at least a week before it was all done. Not much else was done or thought of until this first work was over. It was at least a week before all the dead were found. The remains of Mr. E. P. Fitch, for example, who was consumed with his home, were not found for several

R. C. DIX,
First Blacksmith and Carriage Mfg.

E. A. SMITH,
Cashier First Bank of Issue in State.

REV. JOHN S. BROWN,
Early Pastor Unitarian Church.

C. S. DUNCAN,
General Merchant.

EARLY KANSAS SETTLERS

days, though diligent search was made. At last a young lady who was living with the family discovered them. She had been going to the ruins every day to search for them. The family did not know what she went for. They only noticed that she came in weeping every time she returned. One day she found the charred bones among the hot ashes. She got down into the cellar and took them out with her hands one by one, and tenderly laid them together. They were so hot that her hands were all burned and blistered when her sad work was done. Thus they kept finding the dead for several days. Some that were missing were never found, and possibly some were killed of whom no one knew.

Religious services were held for the dead whenever this was possible. Sometimes it was in the homes, sometimes on the street corner, and sometimes beside the grave in the cemetery. When the fifty-three were laid in one long trench, the minister stood at the head of the trench and offered a prayer. It was a week of almost uninterrupted funeral services. The whole population were engaged in burying the dead. Little else could be done and little else could be thought of.

The Sabbath after the raid a service was held in the old stone Congregational church. There was a large congregation, mostly women and children. They were most of them dressed in the clothes they hastily put on the morning of the raid. Not many saved anything else. The men were in their working clothes. Some of them were in their shirt sleeves, not having saved even a coat. The women came, some in sunbonnets, some in hoods, some with handkerchiefs or shawls over their heads. It deepened the impressiveness of the scene to remember that a large portion of the women and children, were newly made widows and orphans. Rev. G. C. Morse, of Emporia, brother-in-law of Judge Carpenter, who was killed, assisted the pastor in the service. There were no remarks made, for no one felt like talking. There was simply a Psalm read and a prayer offered, and the congregation dismissed. The Psalm read was the seventy-ninth, which seemed to have been written for the occasion: "O God, the heathen are come into thine inheritance. They have laid Jerusalem in heaps. The dead bodies of thy servants have they given to be meat unto the fowls of the heaven, and the flesh of thy saints unto the beasts of the earth. Their blood have shed they like water round about Jerusalem, and there was none to bury them."

No complete list of the dead has ever been made out. Many bodies had to be buried among the "unknown dead." Some who were known were not reported. In the shock and confusion of the hour, no systematic record was kept even of names that could then have been obtained. A little later when an attempt was made to do this, there had been so many changes and so many of the broken families had moved away, that it was only possible to make out a partial list of names.

The first list below contains the names of the seventeen recruits for the Kansas Fourteenth who were shot at the first charge. They were under the command of Second Lieutenant L. J. Beam, who had gone to Leavenworth on business the day before. They had been recruited but a short time. They had drawn clothing, camp equipage and tents, but had not been mustered in nor armed. They were dressed in United States clothing the morning of the raid. But for this distinctive mark they probably would have fared better. They were just rising as the charge was made, and only five of the twenty-two made their escape. Lieutenant Beam always regretted that he was not with them, as he thought he might have done something towards organizing them for defense. After the raid Lieutenant Beam rapidly recruited another lot of men, and went into the Kansas Fifteenth with the same rank, second lieutenant, but was promoted until he became major of the regiment.

The second list contains the names of citizens killed, as far as now known.

Names of seventeen recruits killed from a total of twenty-two:

Anderson, C.	Parker, Asbury
Allen, Charles R.	Parker, Isaac
Cooper, James F.	Riggs, Charles F.
Green, John R.	Speer, Robert
Griswold, Walter B. S.	Watson, John
Halderman, Aaron	Waugh, William A.
Markle, David	Wilson, James
Markle, Lewis	Woods, Andrew
Markle, Samuel	

NAMES OF CITIZENS KILLED:

Albach, George	Coleman, L. D.
Allen, E.	Cornell, —
Alwes, —	Dix, Ralph C.
Anderson, John	Dix, Stephen H.
Allison, D. C.	Dyre, Uncle Frank
Argel, —	Dulinsky, Sylvester
Allen, Clay (col.)	Ehles, August
Bell, Capt. Geo. W.	Eldridge, James
Bowers, Samuel	Ellis, — (col.)
Brechtlesbauer, James	Evans, John
Brant, —	Engler, Carl
Burt, George	Englesman, —
Burns, Dennis,	Fitch, Edward P.
Burns, Michael,	Fillmore, Lemuel
Carpenter, Judge Louis	Frawley, John
Coates, George	Frank, Joseph
Collamore, Gen. George W.	Fritch. S. H.
Crane, John L.	Giebal, Anthony
Cloud, Charles	Gentry, —
Cooper, James,	Green, John

Gates, Levi
Gill, John
Griswold, Dr. J. F.
Griswold, Abner
Griswold, Watt
Gregg, —
Hendrix, —
Hay, Chester
H———, Cal
Holmes, Nathan
Johnson. M.
Johnson, Ben
Jones, Samuel
Kimball, Fred
Keefe, Pat.
Klaus, William
Klaus, Fred
Kleffer, W. M. R.
Lawrie, John
Lawrie, William
Leonard, Christopher
Lambert, —
Little, John
Limboch, Henry
Laner, Christian
Longley, Otis
Loomis, Rich.
Lowe, Joseph
McClellan, ——
McFadden, J.
Martin, R.
Murphy, Dennis
Makin, Michael
Martha, ——
Meeky, M.

McFarland, —
Nathan, W.
Oldham, Anthony (col.)
Oehrle, —
O'Neil, James
Palmer, Charles
Palmer, Daniel W.
Perine, James
Pope, George
Pollock, J.
Purington, David H.
Roach, —
Reedmiller, A.
Reynolds, Samuel
Range, George
Range, Samuel
Speer, John M.
Snyder, Rev. S. S.
Stewart, Henry
Smith, Charles
Schwab, John
Sanger, George H.
Sargeant, G. H.
Stonestreet, Benj.
Stone, Nathan
Swan, L. L.
Thorpe, S. M.
Trask, Josiah C.
Turk, —
Wise, Louis
Williamson, W. T.
Zimmerman, John
Wood, James
Waugh, Addison

The number of men with Quantrill has been variously estimated. Some have placed it as high as six hundred, and some as low as one hundred and seventy-five. The first number is altogether too high, and the second is altogether too low. There is no reason to question the substantial accuracy of the statement at the beginning of this account, that two hundred and ninety-four answered to the roll call at Lone Jack before starting. While in Lawrence some of the raiders were free to talk of themselves. These said they had something over three hundred men. When they charged into town they passed within three hundred yards of the writer of this sketch, and he saw the whole body pass from his window. They seemed a long time passing, and there could not have been less than three hundred. They were counted two or three times on the way by persons who saw them pass along the road. All these testimonies concur in making the number of the raiders about three hundred.

As may well be supposed, the raiders differed very much in their spirit. Some were like fiends incarnate. No tales of savage warfare could surpass their barbarity. Others again were as humane as men well could be who came on such an errand. They would allow the women to get out the furniture before they burned the houses, in some cases even helping them to lift heavy articles. They sometimes expressed regret at the necessity of burning the houses; they were under orders. Some even advised men to keep out of the way. A young man who talked with Mrs. Gurdon Grovenor said he had never intended to take part in such a scene as this had proved to be. "They told me they were only coming up to recover some stolen horses. I have not killed a man nor burnt a house yet, and I do not mean to." But the more humane sentiment of the few did not change the general result very much. In all mobs the worst men give tone to the whole affair. If a more moderate set spared a house, a more violent set would come next and burn it. But in judging of the raiders we must not assume that they were all fiends alike, or that they all assented to what the worst men did.

The number killed can never be exactly known. As nearly as could be ascertained there were one hundred and forty-two. This included the missing who never returned, two or three. A few of the wounded died later, and possibly some were killed who were never heard of. One hundred and fifty would not be far out of the way for the whole number. Then there were about thirty wounded. It was estimated that the raid made eighty widows and two hundred and fifty orphans.

The amount of property destroyed is still more difficult to estimate. There were about seventy-five buildings burned on the business street, and all their contents destroyed or stolen. There were about one hundred dwelling houses burned, and most of those not burned were ransacked and robbed, and many of them partially burned. Then most of the women had their money, jewelry, watches, etc., taken from them. Mrs. F. W. Read who so heroically saved her house had to give them the bracelets of her little girl who was dead. She begged to be allowed to keep them, but they said "her dead baby would not need them anymore." There was not much left in Lawrence when their work was done. There was one double store standing, but the goods were gone, and two clerks lay dead on the floor; a few houses remained unburned, but bare; the women and children were alive, but robbed of all their money and valuables; possibly half the men were still living, but in hiding, and glad to escape with their lives. This was about the condition of things. As careful an estimate as could be made placed the loss at about one million and a half of dollars. Two-thirds of the people had no homes, not many of the men had a complete suit of clothes, few had any money. There were no clothes in town to be bought and there were only four sacks of flour for sale.

But what did the people do? The spirit of humanity which always asserts itself at such a time, had full play. Those who had houses shared them with those who were homeless, and those who had bread shared it with those who had none. But this would not have sufficed. There were probably not provisions enough in the whole town to supply the people forty-eight hours. But before the first day was over, the kind-hearted farmers from all around drove in with wagon loads of vegetables, and such things as they had, and dealt them out freely to all who needed. The neighboring towns, Leavenworth, Wyandotte, Topeka and other places, hurried off wagon loads of provisions and clothing and all things needed by their stricken neighbors. As the news spread the circle of sympathy extended, and help poured in from distant parts, and all who needed were supplied. In the more distant places, this sympathy expressed itself in more substantial help, giving assistance in re-building. The friends in St. Louis, for example, raised a fund of some ten thousand dollars, and put into the hands of the city to be loaned without interest to parties desiring to build. When the money was repaid the city was to hold it for an educational fund, and it was afterwards turned over to the State University.

For some days after the raid not much thought was given to the future. The terrible present occupied all hearts and hands. The dead must be buried, the wounded cared for, and the immediate necessities of life secured. Fully half the remaining population were homeless, and many who saved their homes lost everything else. There was a general spirit of accommodation, and it came very near to the condition of "having all thing common." Those who had shared with those who had not. Every house that remained did its utmost to meet the pressing need for shelter. Many families were reduced to narrow quarters and short rations, but none suffered from want. Many who had lived in comfortable homes were glad to secure one or two small rooms in which to begin again their home life. Small rooms, however, were usually ample for all the household effects, and small as they were they often seemed bare with their very scanty furniture. If people had to move, as was often the case, it was a small matter. A man with a wheelbarrow could transfer them from one house to another in an hour or so. The houses were sometimes very full, and the supplies sometimes rather scant, but no one was left unsheltered, and no one was allowed to go hungry. Many had lost most of their clothing, and those who had two coats divided with those who had none, and all were comfortably, if not fashionably clad.

But the future was coming right along, and must be faced. "What shall we do," was a question that must be met. "The birds of ill omen" were in "high feather," and their croaking filled the air. "Lawrence had received its death blow," "the rebels had burned it once and they would do it again." "It was folly to attempt to rebuild the town." In addition to this there was a constant sense of exposure and peril. That three hundred men could come fifty miles in the night, and pounce upon them without a whisper of warning, was a revelation to the people. They had assured themselves so many times that such a thing could not be done. There was no guessing what might come next. Frequent alarm kept them in a quiver. They had had alarms before and had treated them as idle tales. They could not do so any more. The wildest alarm occurred on Sunday evening the second day after the raid. A farmer two or three miles below the town had been burning some straw. Some one on the hills some distance away seeing the flame, mounted his horse and galloped into town, screaming at the top of his voice: "They are coming again, they are coming again; run for your lives, run for your lives." He that heard ran and hollowed. The report spread like wild-fire, and in a few minutes men, women and children were wildly running down

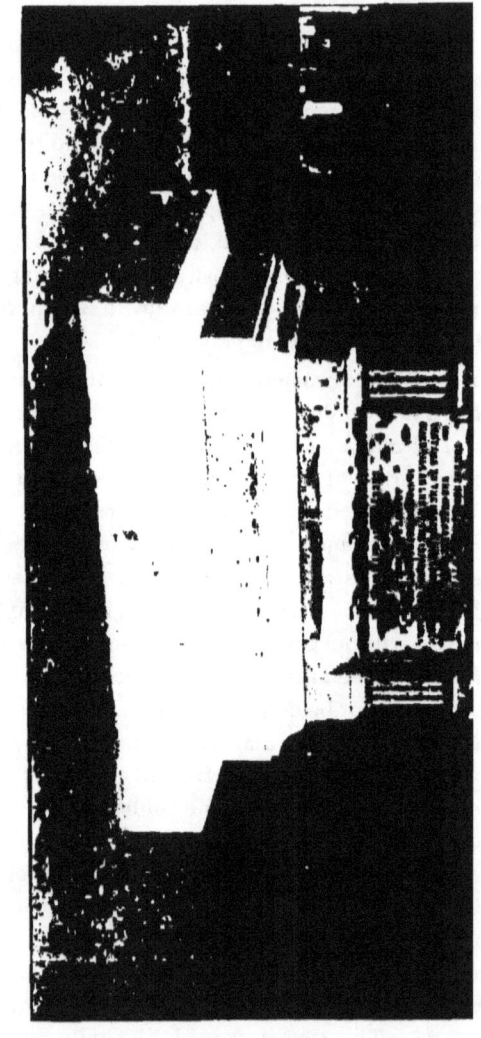

CITIZENS' MEMORIAL MONUMENT.

The monument measures 8 feet by 4 feet at the base, and stands 8 feet and 7 inches high; weight, 45,000 lbs.; cost, $1300. It is carved from Barre, Vt., granite. The front bears the inscription: " Dedicated to the memory of the one hundred and fifty citizens who, defenceless, fell victims to the inhuman ferocity of border guerrillas, led by the infamous Quantrill, in his raid upon Lawrence, August 21st, 1863. Erected May 30th, 1895." On the reverse side is this notice: "The roll of their names can be found in the City Clerk's office, Lawrence, and in the State Historical Society, Topeka."

the different streets towards the river, uttering the most piercing screams as they ran. The impression was that the enemy was right upon them. Some recovered themselves from the panic in a few minutes, and a hundred or more men were soon assembled in the center of the town, and the guns from the armory were given out to them. They sent out scouts to learn the origin of the alarm, and they very soon ascertained the state of affairs. But most of those who ran did not turn back to learn the contradiction of the report. They kept on till they found a hiding place. Some crossed the river, and some hid themselves in the cornfields outside the town. A cold drizzly rain set in during the night, and many of the fugitives remained out till midnight. Some few women as well as men remained out all night in the cold rain, fancying the town was being sacked again. The horror of that Sunday night was in some respects worse than the raid itself. At the raid there was no panic and no outcry. Everybody was calm and quiet. There had been no warning and there was no escape. But this night alarm gave room for the wildest imaginations and the most exaggerated fears. It unnerved the bravest with its undefined dread. In some respects; panic is worse than peril. People who passed through the raid without flinching, were utterly unstrung and demoralized by this Sunday night panic.

But in spite of fears and perils and pains, the courageous spirit continually gained ground. The better sentiment of the people never settled upon but one conclusion. Lawrence must be rebuilt at all hazzards, and rebuilt at once. More and more the people began to insist that every house must be replaced, and every business block renewed. This became the dominant thought, and in an incredibly short time it began to take form. They had not been able to save Lawrence from destruction, but they must put her back as she was. Before the fires were out they began to lay plans for rebuilding. One of the first to begin to build was the grocery firm of Ridenour & Baker. They had lost their building and a heavy stock of goods. Mr. Ridenour's home was burned and all in it. Mr. Baker was so severely wounded that he lay lingering between life and death. In spite of all this, work was commenced on a new building, and business resumed in a small way, before a week had passed. In clearing away the ruins, the barrows blazed with the live embers as the workmen wheeled them out from the old cellar. In the line of unconquerable pluck the equal of this would be hard to find. Simpson brothers, bankers, lost everything except their safe. This the raiders were not able to open or demolish, and it stood the fire without damage. With what remained in the safe the firm resumed business at once, and began rebuilding. Inside the old walls they built a cheap structure of wood, which could be thrown together in a couple of days. Then they put in the foundation and reared the building of brick around and over their temporary shelter. W. E. Sutliff had built up a very extensive clothing business. He had a large stock of goods, he lost everything but his home, and had to begin again as he began six years before. But he at once erected a better building, filled it with a better stock of goods, and prepared to do a larger business. B. W. Woodward lost building and goods. But he at once selected a better site, erected a handsomer building, and put in a larger stock of drugs. J. G. Sands had a large harness establishment. It was all consumed. He at once replaced his wooden store with one of brick and stone, and filled it better than before. For years his advertisement told his history in a sentence: "Established in 1855; stood the drought in 1860; totally destroyed in 1863; defies all competition in 1864." This surely was making one's misfortunes serve as aid to success. Loring Guild & Son lost store and home. The father was away. When the raiders entered the son, E. B. Guild, who was a member of the guard, seized his musket and started out, but saw the town was in their hands, and he could do no more than save himself. Mrs. Guild remained at home and saw the house burned, but saved most of the furniture. They rebuilt and restocked their store and resumed business at once.

These are but samples of the whole community. The sentiment for rebuilding was universal. Everybody said: "We must put Lawrence right back better than she was." The restoring of Lawrence became a sort of religious obligation. It was a matter of conscience with them that they should all stand by the town. There were business reasons, too, for immediate restoration. They who rebuilt and resumed at once would retain their trade, and in many cases that was a fortune, and in all cases a promise. In a few week the work of rebuilding was going on all along the business street, and all over town. Before winter came Lawrence began to look like a town again. A number of buildings were completed that autumn, and a still larger number were well under way. In almost every instance the new buildings were better than the old, and the stocks of goods larger than before.

But all the while they were rebuilding the town they were compelled to defend it. Every man took his turn on guard, and stood ready at a moment's notice to rally to the defense of the place. Rumors of danger were constantly coming, and no rumor was so idle that the people could afford to ignore it. Thus like the Jews of old did these men work, "every one with one of his hands wrought in the work, and with the other he held a weapon." In a few weeks however, they were partially relieved. The military authorities sent two companies of United States troops to protect the town, and they remained until the close of the war. They threw up earthworks and built a stockade on the point of the hill southeast of the university, and planted two or three cannon there. This overlooked the whole Wakarusa valley, and would be an effective defense against any force coming in that direction. These troops were under the command of Major E. G. Ross, afterwards United States senator, and still later governor of New Mexico. The soldiers were received with great delight, and nothing was too good for them. Major Ross, who was a very genial gentleman, soon became the most popular man in town. The people now felt comfortably secure. They knew there would always be a reliable picket guard out every night, and that it would be impossible to surprise them again. As winter came on the sense of security became still stronger, as guerrilla operations had to be suspended as soon as the leaves fell from the trees and exposed the hiding places. By spring the usual tone had been restored, and affairs went on as before. Building continued, new men and new capital came in, and Lawrence bid fair to out-do her former self.

CHAPTER XVII.

ANOTHER SUMMER.—LAWRENCE RESTORED.—IMPROVEMENTS.—THE NEW BRIDGE.—ENLARGEMENT.—NEW ALARMS.—PRICE IS COMING.—PREPARATIONS FOR DEFENSE.—MARTIAL LAW.—MILITIA ORDERED OUT.—THE BATTLES OF THE BLUE.—A NIGHT OF ANXIETY.—"JOY COMETH IN THE MORNING."—THE WAR IS OVER.—PEACE AT LAST.

The winter of 1863 and '4 was a severe one. In spite of all that had been done, many of the people of Lawrence were as illy prepared to meet its severity as were the early settlers of 1855. In families accustomed to every comfort, the supply of clothing and bedding was very scant, and people accustomed to spacious and comfortable homes, were compelled to live in very contracted quarters. They were glad to find shelter in single rooms, in garrets and basements, or unfurnished houses wherever they could find cover. The writer of this was perhaps a fair example of the more fortunate of those who lost everything. He secured one small room and little half story garret, and thought himself very fortunate. About Christmas he was compelled to leave these quarters and take a single room. He made the change while the thermometer registered ten degrees below zero. But fortunately his household effects were so few that a single man with a wheelbarrow made the transfer in a couple of hours, and he was established in his new quarters in a single afternoon. This room was so cold that they were compelled to hang quilts around the stove in the coldest weather to shut in a little space where they could be comfortable. Even this shelter they had to leave early in the spring, and find other accommodations. When spring came building was resumed and everybody was busy repairing losses and restoring what had been destroyed.

With the spring, however, there came a renewal of the alarms of the year before. The people was kept constantly on the alert. The bushwhackers returned with the returning leaves, and rumors of their coming were frequent. It was not as easy to enter Kansas as it had been. The union soldiers had learned the bushwhackers' tactics, and could follow wherever they could flee. They knew their hiding places, and they could dash around among the rocks and through the thickets, as well as those who had been born and bred in the jungle. Besides this, General Ewing's famous "Order No. II" had stripped the border counties of Missouri of supplies, so that the bushwhackers were compelled to find their hiding places and their maintainance thirty miles farther back from the Kansas border. As a result of all this, Kansas was not much disturbed during the summer of 1864. The bushwhackers continued their depredations, however, on union men in Missouri, and on isolated bodies of union troops. Some of the most tragic scenes of the war were enacted in Missouri during this summer. Quantrill disappeared from the scene early in the season, but his successor, Bill Anderson, though not fully equal to Quantrill in skill or courage, far surpassed him in cold-blooded brutality. What was known as the "Centralia massacre," where twenty-four sick and wounded soldiers were taken from a railway train which was bearing them to their homes, and were all shot in cold blood, is only a fair sample of his work. But he never came into Kansas after the raid at Lawrence.

But these operations in Missouri were too near to leave the people of Lawrence entirely at their ease. Rumors were thick and the people were peculiarly sensitive to them. Their experience had made them sensitive. All the guerrilla movements in Missouri had their effect in Lawrence, for no one knew how soon they might turn their attention that way. Reports of the coming of some foe were frequent, and it was no uncommon thing for all the people to be called out at midnight by some alarming story. The report that alarmed them at night was always found to be false in the morning, but so had all reports that preceded the raid. They reasoned from this. A score of rumors might prove false but the next might be true. Rumors meant more to them than before, and they were not disposed to treat lightly even the more unlikely reports. The slightest alarm would bring all the people to their windows. The firing of a gun at night, or the galloping of a horseman through the streets, would bring all the men to their places of rendezvous in a very few minutes. Any unusual noise at night would startle the whole town. One night for example, the whistle of one of the mills kept sounding an unaccountably long time. It was about one o'clock at night, but it awakened the whole town, and in a few minutes, men with their rifles were running from all directions towards the mill. It was found that the machinery was out of order and the whistle could not be stopped. They all laughed at each other as they turned homeward, but they were just as ready to rally at the next alarm.

The men were organized into military companies, and had regular times for drill. There were five companies, one of which was composed of men beyond the age of military service. They were called the "Silver Grays." The state furnished the arms, but one rifle company armed themselves with the best repeating rifles. This company was composed mostly of business and professional men. The city built five block houses at the different points of approach, and each company was given charge of one of these block houses. Each company was divided into sections, and one of these sections slept in the block house every night. There were, therefore, always fifty men or more ready for immediate service. These were intended as a nucleus around which the rest could rally as they came. The rifle company occupied the block house at the crossing of Massachusetts and Berkley streets, and was on the line of Quantrill's approach.

In the midst of all these alarms and all this military demonstrations, building went steadily on. The business street was built up again almost solid, and many of the houses were restored, and new houses were erected. Many improvements were made. The Lawrence Bridge company had been incorporated in 1859. It was organized with Carmi W. Babcock as president; Josiah Miller, treasurer; and E. D. Thompson, as secretary. They began to build the bridge in 1863, and had the work well under way when Quantrill came. In the raid one sub-contractor, and seven workmen were killed, and a large amount of material destroyed. The company, however, resumed work very soon, and the bridge was opened for travel at the beginning of 1864. The structure cost about $40,000. For many years it was the only bridge across the Kansas river except at its mouth, and it drew to itself an immense amount of travel. It proved to be a very profitable investment for the company.

The first railroad, too, was built to Lawrence this year. The Union Pacific railroad began work on its Kansas line at Kansas City in 1864, and by September of that year the rails were laid as far as Lawrence, though regular trains did not run till several months later.

The school board also had plans to build a school house. The site was selected, money arranged for, and plans agreed upon. On account of the troubles in the autumn the matter lay over another year. It seems a little singular that a people as much interested in education as those of Lawrence should be ten years without a school house. The delay is easily understood by those familiar with the disturbed condition of affairs. This delay in building did not indicate any lack of interest in schools. Whittier knew his men when he sang:

"We go to plant the common school
On distant prairie swells."

W. A. RANKIN,
Major and Quartermaster General, Wilson's Staff

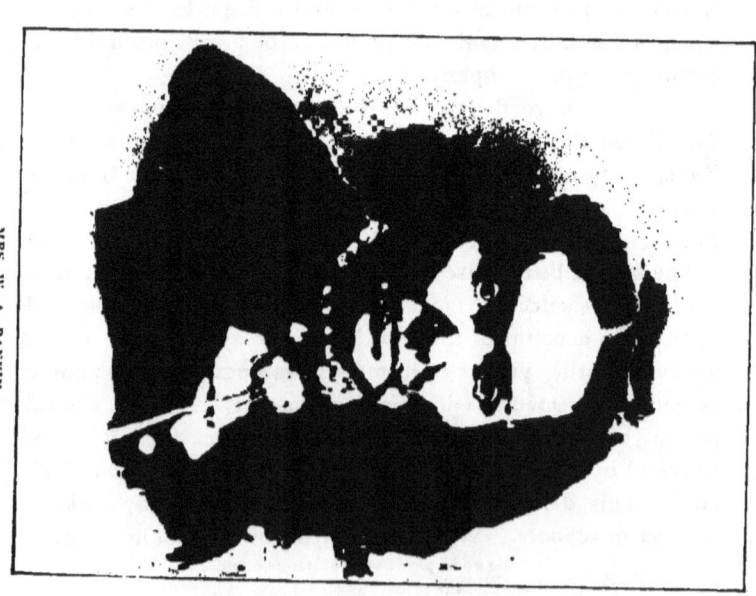

MRS. W. A. RANKIN.

The first settlers of Lawrence opened a free school before many of them had a roof over their heads. At first the school was supported by private subscriptions, and made free to all who would come. As the place grew, citizens met and appointed a committee on schools. Dr. S. B. Prentiss was chairman of this committee. He was a "southern man with northern principles." He came from Georgia but was an ardent free-state man. He held several positions and did valuable service for the free-state cause. He was a very calm, soft-spoken man, but full of purpose and persistence. In the matter of schools he was simply chairman of a voluntary committee, but he went to work as zealously as if he had been a public officer with a good salary. In 1857 the Quincy high school was opened in the basement rooms of the Unitarian church, which had been arranged with that in view. Mr. Charles L. Edwards was principal. He was assisted by Miss Lucy M. Wilder, Miss Sarah A. Brown, Miss Lizzie P. Haskell and Miss Isabella G. Oakley. This school acquired quite a reputation, and there went out from it many students who have made their mark in Kansas history. The next year the city government was organized and the schools came under the control of a board of school trustees of which Dr. Albert Newman was secretary. The next year Mr. Edwards became county superintendent and Mr. C. W. Adams succeeded as principal of the high school. A year later Mr. Adams entered the army and served as a colonel to the close of the war. Then came S. M. Thorpe, a graduate of Union college, New York, a fine scholar, a poet and a wit. He was a man of chivalrous spirit, with a large intellect and a large heart. He was cultured, bright and breezy, and filled all his scholars with his own enthusiastic spirit. After two years of teaching he was chosen to the state senate, and was a candidate for state superintendent of instructions at the time of his death. Right at the beginning of his career he was treacherously murdered by Quantrill's ruffians. As soon as could be after the raid, the schools were reorganized. Mrs. Mary Carpenter, the wife of Judge Carpenter who was so brutally murdered by Quantrill, was principal of the high school for a number of years. She was a woman of remarkably strong character and a very highly accomplished teacher. The other teachers also were no less efficient in the work assigned them. The need of better accommodations was everywhere felt. The schools were kept in rented rooms wherever these could be found, the high school being in the basement of the Unitarian church. The school board, therefore, pressed the matter of building. They wanted to build three buildings in different sections of the town. But for economy's sake the city council decided to erect one central building first. The plans for this were matured when the disturbances of the autumn put an end to all plans except those pertaining to the public safety.

In the midst of all this progress, and just as the people were becoming accustomed to the new order of things, and were feeling fairly comfortable in their security, a new peril loomed up in the distance. This was the approach of General Sterling Price, with an army of some twenty thousand men. Rumors of his coming were heard as early as August. Price was in Arkansas gathering supplies and evidently intending some forward movement. Just what he was intending to do nobody knew. It might be to "redeem Missouri," or it might be to "chastise Kansas." In either case Kansas would be involved. General Price was a citizen of Missouri, and had been held in high esteem. He had served as a general of volunteers in the Mexican war, and had won some distinction. He had been governor of Missouri, and when the rebellion broke out he was in the confidence of Governor Claiborne F. Jackson. He was an advocate of secession, and he and Governor Jackson did all in their power to swing Missouri into the confederate column. They were defeated by the prompt action of Captain Lyon, who was in command of the union forces at St. Louis. The governor and his major general were both compelled to flee the state. General Price had tried several times to return and "redeem Missouri," as he called it, from the grasp of the union forces. He now had an army of some twenty thousand veteran troops, and was evidently coming into Missouri, or into Kansas, or both.

These undefined rumors had more effect in Lawrence than anywhere else. The people of Lawrence had had an object lesson, and knew what a rebel invasion meant. It was not supposed that General Price would repeat the barbarities of Quantrill. He was a general in the regular confederate service, and an honorable soldier. But his coming would be a signal for all the guerrillas in Missouri to pour over into Kansas. While Price himself would be governed by the usual rules of war, he would have with him several thousand bushwhackers over whom he would have no control, and could exercise no restraint. As Price lingered and hovered, therefore, the Lawrence people watched his movements with nervous anxiety.

The latter part of September Price began to move northward, but deflected towards the east. He captured Pilot Knob, the garrison escaping, and then moved towards St. Louis. After threatening St. Louis a while, he turned westward and besieged Jefferson City, the capital of the state. Without any serious attempt to capture the place, however, he raised the siege on the eighth day of October and marched still westward with his whole force. There was no longer any doubt as to his intention. He was coming to Kansas to chastise her for the part she had taken in the struggle. Lawrence was in his direct line of march, and must be included in his plan. There was no time to lose, for a very few days would bring Price to their doors. The governor issued a proclamation the very day Price left Jefferson City, calling out the entire militia of the state, and putting the whole state under martial law. The proclamation was sent by special messengers to all parts of the state, and in four days sixteen thousand men had responded, and over ten thousand militia were on the border ready to meet Price. General Curtis had some three thousand regular troops at Kansas City, and nineteen or twenty pieces of artillery. This was not a very strong force to withstand the onset of twenty thousand veterans well supplied with cannon.

The news of the governor's proclamation reached Lawrence Sunday noon, October 9th. It met the people at the close of morning service in the churches. All further services for the day were suspended, and one thought occupied all minds. Monday morning the military companies were ordered to assemble on the open space just west of town. Every man was ordered to come with arms and ammunition and whatever was needed for the march and the camp. The five Lawrence companies responded promptly, and were mustered into the service of the United States.

The governor's proclamation made no exceptions. "Every man from sixteen to sixty" was ordered out. And there no shrinking. It was not a mere matter of patriotism or state pride, but every man had a personal interest in the issue. Price must be beaten or Kansas desolated. The ranks of the militia companies were full. Everybody came, and came promptly. There were merchants and ministers, lawyers and doctors, laboring men and men of leisure, all shouldering their muskets and taking their places in the ranks. No one asked to be excused no matter what his emergency might be. For the public emergency overtowered all private considerations. One young man, a banker, had his wedding day set for the second day after the general rally. But even the old Jewish exemption did not avail, and he was mustered in with his company and marched to the front leaving his expectant bride to wait

"Till the cruel war was o'er."

Price, however, very kindly delayed his coming, and on Wednesday the young man secured a furlough, came home and was married at the appointed time, and returned to camp. There was no distinction or class or condition. Solon O. Thacher had been judge of the district court, and was at this time a candidate for governor of the state, to be voted on in a few days. But he went with the militia to the front, and took his place in the ranks with the rest.

And they rallied from all quarters. Not only from Lawrence, but from the country round about they came. Some of the companies from the country joined with those from town, and others marched from more convenient points. What was true about Lawrence was true all over the state. So general was the response that a man coming seventy-five miles through the country a few days later, saw only two men in the whole distance, and they were too old to be of service. Had all the Lawrence companies been marched away, there would hardly been a score of men left in the town.

After the formalities of the muster, and an inspection of arms by the officers, the men were ordered to fall in line, and prepare to march. The Lawrence companies contained about four hundred men. About ten o'clock everything was ready, and they were ordered to march. They went first to town, then down Massachusetts street, and then eastward towards Kansas City. There had been no hint thus far that any would be left in Lawrence, and all alike prepared for the march and camp and were expecting to go to the front. But as they were marching down Massachusetts street, the rifle company and one other, were cut off from the column, and taken to their block houses. These were to remain for the defense of the town. The other three companies went on to Kansas City, and remained in camp till the end of the campaign. The Lawrence brass band, which dated back to the earliest settlement, went with the Kansas City contingent, and enlivened the camp with their music.

In the meantime nothing could be heard of Price or his army. He had left Jefferson City on the eighth, and moved westward. Since then he had given no sound or sign. His army lay somewhere in the great bend of the Missouri river near Boonville, but just where he was, or what he was doing, or what he intended to do, were mysteries nobody could solve. For nearly two weeks his movements were involved thus in mystery, and all inquiry seemed to be baffled. Some few began to look upon the whole thing as a gigantic hoax, practiced on them for some political purpose. But a more common feeling was that Price and his army were quietly slipping away, and that nothing would come of the Price invasion. It was a common remark that we should hear no more about Price. The militia at Kansas City became restless, wanted "to go home and attend to their fall plowing." Some even went so far as to complain that the governor had been hasty in calling out the militia, that there really had never been any danger of Price coming into Kansas. Most of them, however, took it all good-naturedly, and got what they could out of the experience. It gave them a little taste of real military life, and some little experience in military drill. They were sworn into the United States service and subject to all the rules of military discipline, and a good many of the discomforts of camp life.

Lawrence was forty miles from what was called the "seat of war," but felt as intensely as if she had been in the focus of it. All business was suspended, and all work laid aside, and just one thing occupied everyone's thought. The companies remaining at Lawrence were required to be "in camp" just as much as if they had been at the front, only their block houses served for camps. They drew rations like regular soldiers, and became familiar with government bacon and split peas. Old government Java was kept boiling in the camp kettle, and if it was not always clear, it was always strong and hot.

Guard duty was exacted as regularly as of veterans, and every belated traveler coming into town was compelled to "dismount, advance three paces and give the countersign," or in default, to be presented to the "officer of the guard." They had frequent drills, and were put through all the ordinary military evolutions, and were acquiring something of a soldierly step. Frequent target shootings developed their proficiency as marksmen. To most of them the handling of arms was no new experience. They were somewhat of an awkward squad in the manual, but when it came to shooting they were at home. "An October freeze" added to the variety of their life, if not to its comfort. One night two or three inches of snow fell, and these soldiers "pro tem," found themselves covered with an extra blanket in the morning, not provided for in the regulations. The block houses were built to keep out bullets. They were not proof against snow flakes. "The cold snap" continued two or three days, and part of the time it was quite severe. But this only added the spice of variety to their monotonous life as they were "waiting for Price."

The "boys" as usual managed to get some fun out of the affair, grim and wearisome as it was. The most important practical joke was the "trial of Dr. Leiby." Dr. Leiby was an eccentric old gentlemen quite independent in his ways. He was placed on guard one day, and was to be releived at five o'clock. It was arranged that the relief should be a trifle late. When the hour came the doctor considered his time up, and went home. "The relief" coming up a moment later found the post deserted. The matter was reported and a detail sent to Dr. Leiby's house to arrest him for deserting his post. Under martial law this was a serious charge, and the doctor at first was very much alarmed. A court martial was organized and he was put on trial. But the doctor was shrewd and soon saw by the way things went on, that it was a "put up job." He entered into the joke as heartily as any of them, and rather spoiled the fun for "the boys."

In spite of all these diversions and variations, the time dragged heavily. Shut in as they were they knew little of what was going on below. They had nothing to do but to drill and to shoot, and eat and stand guard. Much as they dreaded Price's coming they almost began to dread longer delay as much. They began to think anything would be a relief from the monotony. It had almost ceased to be a suspense, for the feeling became common that Price would disappear and the whole thing would end and their soldier life be recalled as a huge joke. The prevalent hope was, that whatever Price was going to do, he would do it quickly and let it be over.

About October 20th, Price was "found." The advance guard of the union army met him near Lexington marching rapidly westward in full force. The next day, Friday, he came up to the line of the Blue river, the union advance retiring as he came, but contesting stubbornly every inch of ground. Saturday, October 22nd, he made an advance along the whole line of the Blue, forcing the union troops back at every point. In the afternoon he was practically master of the field. The union troops were being forced in upon Kansas City, and it seemed as if they could do little more than concentrate and defend that post. Two regiments of militia were ordered to march to Lawrence that night, to aid in its defence. It seemed as if there was nothing which could hinder Price's army from sweeping over Kansas. About five o'clock there came a turn in affairs which meant as much to Kansas as the coming of Blucher meant to the English at Waterloo. In a speech before the old soldiers a few months ago, Judge Solon O. Thacher described this scene in very vivid colors: "About five o'clock Saturday afternoon, October 22nd, 1864, I was standing with some of the officers of the union army on a high knoll near Kansas City, looking over the field. Our boys were everywhere fighting bravely, but along the whole line they were being slowly pressed back by Price's men. He would soon be in position to detach a body of his troops to over run Kansas. We all knew what that meant, home and all we held dear would soon be at the mercy of this conquering army. Looking eastward at this moment we saw a great cloud of dust rising a few miles below Kansas City. We could only see it was moving our way, and we were sure it was a body of troops. Who could it be? Was it reinforcements for Price to complete his victory and our desolation, or was it Pleasanton's cavalry coming to our relief? We watched the cloud of dust anxiously as it moved rapidly up the river. After a little they came up to the rear of the rebel army. Then as we watched anxiously we saw them charge upon the rebel lines. We now knew it was Pleasanton with his five thousand veteran cavalry, and the fortunes of battle were changed." It proved to be General Pleasanton with five thousand fresh troops who had been following from below ever since Price had left Jefferson City. They soon broke through the rebel lines and joined the union forces in front.

Before night the rebel advance was checked. The next morning the union forces renewed the battle at the earliest dawn, and Price was driven towards Arkansas.

At Lawrence the people were in a state of anxious suspense all this time. There were in the town two companies of regulars and two companies of militia, probably about three hundred men. These would make but a feeble stand against any such force as Price would be likely to send. Defeat at Kansas City meant the destruction of Lawrence the second time. On Saturday, as the news kept coming of the rebel advance and of rebel successes, the people began to prepare for the worst. A large train of empty government wagons happened just then to pass through the town, and the merchants persuaded those in charge to load them with goods. Clothing and dry goods and other merchandise were packed into these wagons, and the officers requested to keep them out of Price's hands. Families also filled trunks and boxes with clothing and sent them out into the country. Many people buried their valuables in the yard. They thus hoped to save something if the town were burned again. The men were mostly relieved from duty Saturday afternoon, that they might look after their goods and their homes, and put things in as good a shape as possible in case an attack should be made. It seemed quite probable the town would be attacked before morning. There was no panic and no excitement. The women as well as the men went cooly to work to prepare for the worst. At sundown the men came together again at the block houses ready for the duties of the night. Orders were given that the men should sleep on their arms, that the fires and lights should all be put out at nine o'clock, and that there should be no loud talking. The coming of General Pleasanton and the turning of the tide of battle at Kansas City were not known in Lawrence till the next morning. They had simply heard that the union troops had been forced back and flanked, and that no obstruction lay between Price's army and Lawrence. A few hours would suffice to bring the enemy upon them. There was not much sleep in the block houses that night, and presumably not much in the homes where the situation was fully understood. All night long stragglers were coming up from the battle field below. They each told a doleful tale inspired by their fears more than by the facts. According to these reports the union forces had been completely flanked, and Price was at liberty to go where he pleased. At three o'clock the whole force was ordered out and marched around for an hour or two, in consequence of some reports received at headquarters, that the enemy was within a few hours march of the town. As there was no confirmation of the report, the men were permitted to lie down again and rest till morning. It was a night long to be remembered, a night of undefined fears, and of gloomy reports. It was all the more gloomy from the fact that no reliable information could be obtained. Rumors were thick, but they could be neither confirmed nor refuted. It was a glorious night for the croakers. They had things pretty much their own way. They exaggerated every rumor and expatiated on every fear. The utter uncertainty of the situation added to the gloom. They might be attacked in an hour, or they might not be attacked at all. They might be attacked by five hundred men against whom there would be some hope of success, or they might be attacked by five thousand men against whom resistance would be madness. Everybody, however, kept his place, and there was a general determination to await the event, and to do the best they could in whatever situation the future might reveal.

In the morning the prospect very much brightened. There was no news, but there was no foe in sight and none to be heard of. Daylight dissipated the uncertainties of the night. The predictions and fears of the night had not been fulfilled. Price had not come as predicted, and that was so much toward the conclusion that he would not come. About ten o'clock there was further news from the battle field. The coming of Pleasanton, the turning of the tide of battle the night before, and the prospect of complete victory, changed the gloom into gladness. It was Sunday and it became a day of general thanksgiving. There were no public services held, no gathering of the people. Every man was required to be in his place, but every man felt thankful. The Sabbath that began in fears, ended in peace and rejoicing. The sense of relief was general and profound.

The next morning, Monday, more full reports came in. The details of the battle were reported, the marvelous deliverance in the very nick of time, the completeness of the victory. Price's army was not simply checked, it was routed, and was

flying southward to escape capture and destruction. The union cavalry were in hot pursuit. The militia companies from below were coming home that morning. They were coming upon the new railroad, and they were to cross the new bridge. Never were returning heroes welcomed home with more general rejoicing than were these veteran militia-men of three weeks' service. The whole population turned out to meet them at the bridge. The two companies in town forgot they were soldiers, and rushed down to the bridge helter-skelter like a lot of school boys let loose. The troops came over the bridge in military order, preceded by the dear old Lawrence band playing:
"When Johnny came marching home again."
They were dusty and bronzed, and had evidently had a rougher time than those who had been left behind. As they came up Massachusetts street, all the people did shout, and the whole town was one scene of gladness. The returning companies soon broke ranks and hastened to their homes. In a few days the order came and the militia-men were mustered out, and resumed their voluntary service as before.

"Price's invasion" was the last of the war for Kansas. She was not disturbed any more. The season was too advanced for guerrilla operations, and in a few weeks the falling of the leaves and the coming of winter, gave a sense of absolute security. Everybody was now comfortably housed, and the winter passed quietly and without any marked incident. In the spring came Appomatox and the surrender of Lee's army, and the end of the war. No people in the land were in a condition to appreciate the blessedness of peace as were those of Lawrence. From the first settlement until now they had never known quiet. It had been wars and rumors of war for ten years. The town had been besieged and sacked, burned and butchered again and again. When one trouble ended another began, and when one difficulty was settled another appeared. And the people of Lawrence were not lovers of strife. Her people were lovers of order and peace. They only stood in the gap for conscience sake and not from preference. Now peace had come after all these years of strife. And it was peace that would stay. The roots of the conflict were gone. Not only was Kansas a free state, but slavery itself was abolished. Kansas had won her case, not for herself alone but for the nation. She had not stood in the focus of the fight for naught. When Lawrence realized that peace was really assured, it seemed as if a new sun had arisen in the heavens, and a new atmosphere had given vigor to life.

And peace found Lawrence prosperous as she had never been before. The ravages of Quantrill had been more than restored. Nearly all the business houses and dwellings destroyed had been replaced by better, and nearly every business broken up had been resumed and enlarged. The population had increased, and the town had spread beyond the former limits. Now under the "benign influences of peace" she could look forward to years of progress and prosperity. She could appreciate, for all there was in it, the motto of the state seal,

"Ad astra per aspera."

www.ingramcontent.com/pod-product-compliance
Lightning Source LLC
Chambersburg PA
CBHW032048220426
43664CB00008B/906